Demystifying TCP/IP
3rd Edition

Michael Busby

Wordware Publishing, Inc.

Library of Congress Cataloging-in-Publication Data

Busby, Michael.
Demystifying TCP/IP / by Michael Busby. —3rd ed.
   p. cm.
Includes index.
ISBN 1-55622-665-9 (pbk.)
1. TCP/IP (Computer network protocol). I. Title.
TK5105.585.B98   1999   99-12085
004.6'2--dc21   CIP

ISBN 1-55622-665-9
10 9 8 7 6 5 4 3 2 1
9903

All inquiries for volume purchases of this book should be addressed to Wordware Publishing, Inc., at the
above address. Telephone inquiries may be made by calling:

(972) 423-0090

Dedication

For my loving wife, Alethea, my best friends, Marty, Shane, Drew, and Stuart, and my long-time, "best good friend," Danny. I wish each of you all the best.

For a special family who is always in my warmest thoughts:
J.D., Gail, Johnny, Jimmy, and Caroline Carlson.
You really give meaning to "Semper Fi."

Contents

Introduction

This book is intended to give the reader an understanding of the basic principles and methods of TCP/IP and the technology's role in the global internetworking environment. Due to the limitations imposed by such mundane concerns as page count, the material presented is of an introductory nature. Who should buy this book? Professionals, business people, investors, technicians, educators, students, and any other individual with a need or desire to understand local area networks, metropolitan area networks, wide area networks, and global area networks and their place in today's complex business environment. For without TCP/IP and networking, global economies could only be regional or national economies.

The book is organized by TCP/IP topic. Topics include TCP/IP history, TCP fundamentals, IP fundamentals, TCP and IP advanced topics, networks and networking, TCP/IP related issues, and network administration. A chapter synopsis follows:

Chapter 1 introduces TCP/IP and the world in which TCP/IP works its magic. Issues such as TCP/IP and what it is, why TCP/IP is important, where TCP/IP comes from, and the components of the TCP/IP suite of protocols are explored.

Chapter 2 introduces networks and TCP/IP's place in networking technology. The issues explored in this chapter are networks, network topologies, intranets, and internets.

Chapter 3 covers various network protocols and where TCP/IP fits into the OSI networking model.

Chapter 4 digs deep into the fundamentals of Transmission Control Protocol. Topics such as ports, sockets, TCP segment formatting, TCP header fields, and managing a reliable connection are discussed.

Chapter 5 covers Internet Protocol. Topics include IP datagram format, IP header fields, data encapsulation, datagram transmission, and data reception.

Chapter 6 discusses the TCP user process commands. The main topics are the commands, their format, and functionality.

Chapter 7 details how a TCP/IP connection is established and closed, including the connection handshake, TCP data transmission, and TCP data reception.

Chapter 8 introduces FTP. Topics are the relationship between TCP/IP and FTP, FTP working details, and the FTP user commands.

Chapter 9 introduces Telnet. Topics include the relationship between TCP/IP and Telnet, Telnet charisteristics, and the Telnet commands.

Chapter 10 introduces SMTP. Topics are the relationship between TCP/IP and SMTP, SMTP working details, and SMTP user commands.

Chapter 11 introduces ICMP. Topics are the relationship between TCP/IP and ICMP, ICMP working details, and ICMP messages.

Chapter 11 introduces SNMP. Topics are the relationship between TCP/IP and SNMP, SNMP working details, and PDU processing.

Chapter 13 covers several issues that are encountered in the TCP/IP world. X Windows, the World Wide Web, and the role of Ethernet and TCP/IP are discussed.

Chapter 14 introduces TCP/IP network administration. Network reports and host files are discussed.

Acknowledgments

I wish to thank Jim Hill for his guidance, encouragement, and patience; Beth Kohler for her manuscript suggestions and very professional editing job; and Pam Alba for her very courteous and professional assistance.

Chapter 1

Introduction to TCP/IP

Questions answered in this chapter:

What is TCP/IP?

Why is TCP/IP important?

Where does TCP/IP come from?

What are the components of the TCP/IP suite of protocols?

Introduction

TCP/IP is perhaps the most important suite of computer software existing anywhere in the world today. TCP/IP can be thought of as a two-part adhesive, one part TCP and the other IP, with both parts required to form a very strong and reliable glue. But a glue for what purpose? TCP/IP is the glue that binds the diverse parts of a global network of computing resources into the Internet, the World Wide Web, and a multitude of intranets and internets, including LANs, WANs, and GANs. Without TCP/IP, or some similar type of software, global economies would only be regional, national, or continental economies. Even global unification, a much-talked-about topic and perceived necessity among some, would probably not be anything more than a pipe dream. For without something to bind the pieces together, the pieces remain just that, pieces. But TCP/IP binds the diverse computing pieces of companies and organizations, governments and universities, consumers and homeowners into interconnected global networks. The ability to interconnect the diverse computing pieces is what makes TCP/IP the most important suite of software existing in the world.

TCP/IP is actually two separate software protocols defined by a variety of Request for Comments (RFCs) documents. TCP is the acronym for Transmission Control Protocol and IP is the acronym for Internet Protocol. TCP/IP comes to us originally from the U.S. Department of Defense via a special government office called the Advanced Research Projects Agency (ARPA), now known as DARPA. The Department of Defense was eager to interconnect defense and university computers in the late 1960s to expedite the exchange of defense related information. Just how to accomplish the task was not immediately clear, as various proprietary computer systems were deployed, both in the military and at the research facilities of leading universities supporting defense research.

Attempts to connect these diverse computing environments were awkward and even impossible in some instances, due to the unwillingness of computer manufacturers to reveal proprietary aspects of their equipment and operating systems. Some degree of networking success was achieved when manufacturers interconnected their own equipment. A step in the right networking direction was the adoption of a standards-based operating system called UNIX that was placed in the public domain and made available to equipment manufacturers and end users. The Department of Defense funded the development of UNIX and required contractors to adopt the operating system in equipment sold to the Department of Defense. With a standards-based common operating system now in widespread use, it remained but a short time before someone was able to connect all these computers together in a much more coherent manner. Thus was born the idea for a networking standard, giving us the TCP/IP networking glue. Let's take a brief look at the two parts of the glue.

TCP is one part of the software glue that binds the computing hosts in packet-switched, computer-based communications networks and in interconnected systems of these types of networks. A packet-switched network is a collection of interconnected computing devices that exchange data in groups of bits called packets. The TCP/IP is designed to transmit the host data stream in small groups of bits by breaking the data stream into smaller segments. Besides the group of data bits, packets include all the information required to get the packet from its source to its destination. RFC 793 fully describes in great depth the TCP protocol. RFC 793 is the tenth version of TCP and certainly will not be the last. TCP is a highly reliable host-to-host (computing device to computing device; a computing device is also known as a computer) communications protocol.

The requirements for the IP are detailed in great depth in RFC 791. IP specifies a class-based internet protocol used to connect distinct and separate networks regardless of their physical location into a mesh of interconnected networks, now called local area networks (LANs), metropolitan area networks (MANs), wide area networks (WANs), and global area networks (GANs). The specification governs data communications via the familiar World Wide Web (WWW) and its associated Internet. There are six earlier versions of RFC 791.

TCP/IP was designed to be machine independent, capable of operating on any computing platform desired. TCP/IP works equally well on a UNIX-based machine or a DOS-based machine. TCP/IP works equally well on a personal computer or a mainframe computer. And TCP/IP can interconnect each of these diverse computing environments together into networks, allowing users to easily transmit data back and forth, seemingly without effort.

The intent of TCP/IP is to interconnect diverse computing environments using a standard communications protocol that can provide a platform for a broad range of application processes. Application processes are as diverse as human ingenuity can define. Application processes range from simple to complex and include simple file transfer and more complex e-mail and Web pages. TCP/IP must provide a means for computing resources to exchange information without regard for the overlying application processes. In actuality, TCP/IP performs its intended function admirably, for the moment. Who knows what lies ahead?

An Historical Overview of TCP/IP

TCP/IP's origins are in a Department of Defense organization called the Advanced Research Projects Agency (ARPA) dating back to 1966 when ARPA began an active search for a project head to lead a team in the development of standards to interconnect diverse computing resources. The goal was the development of the first wide area packet-switched network.

ARPA conducted research and experiments in search of a solution to provide interoperability between different computer equipment. ARPANET was the result and was operational with one node in September 1969 by interconnecting Xerox Data Systems Sigma-7 and the ILLIAC IV. By January 1970, four nodes were connected and by January 1971, 13 nodes were connected. By April 1972, 23 sites were interconnected. The diversity of those interconnected computing devices included General Electric's 645 Multics System, Burroughs' 6500s, Digital Equipment Corporation's PDP-10s and PDP-11s, IBM 360s, Xerox Data Systems Sigma-7, and the ILLIAC IV.

An interesting footnote in the history of the turbulent 1960s and early 1970s is the proliferation of nodes connecting sunny California sites to the DOD site of greatest activity and import, Washington, D.C. While California hippies were demonstrating against the defense complex in the front yard of society with the tacit approval of university management, California technocrats on the same university campuses were enriching the university bank account at the public trough of government contracts while getting paid to develop one of the most useful tools known to humanity.

ARPANET eventually expanded across the country and formed the main network of what began to be called the Internet. The Defense Advanced Research Projects Agency (DARPA) succeeded ARPA in 1971, and thus ARPANET was under its domain. DARPA focused on research and experiments using packet-switching technology emphasizing satellite and radio technology for transport mechanisms rather than public switched network (Ma Bell) transmission technology. Focusing on broadcast technology was a natural progression in the evolution of communication networks for the Department of Defense.

In 1975 the Defense Communications Agency (DCA) took responsibility for ARPANET's operation. About this time a new set of networking protocols was proposed. These protocols laid the foundation for TCP/IP, and by 1978 TCP/IP had become stable enough for a demonstration. TCP/IP contributed to the growth in the number of networks located around the country and consequently an increase in the number of networks connected to ARPANET.

In 1982 DOD created the Defense Data Network (DDN) and designated it as the focal point for distributed networks comprising the Internet. Shortly after this (in 1983), DOD stated acceptance of TCP/IP as the protocol that nodes should use to connect to the Internet. This statement of acceptance of TCP/IP ignited explosive growth of TCP/IP networks because now a recommended network protocol existed with the sole intent to permit interoperability between different vendor computers. TCP/IP continued to grow in universities, government organizations, and other places, providing many people with exposure to TCP/IP.

Networked computers were originally intended to speed the development of weapons systems, but were now seen by large companies with defense contracting subsidiaries as a tool to streamline operations and enhance their competitive posture. These larger defense contracting companies, with the economic resources and technological know-how, began to network their in-house computers into campus-based networks called local area networks (LANs). Local area network growth in the '80s contributed to additional TCP/IP growth. LANs were easily installed and could be expanded as needed. TCP/IP growth profited from mergers and acquisitions that swept the business community in the late 1980s. To a certain degree TCP/IP seemed to be the natural "link" that could bring together different companies' computer systems, and by the end of the '80s TCP/IP had become a dominant networking force throughout the world.

What Does a Network Protocol Do?

TCP and IP are two networking protocols of a group of networking protocols that include other protocols such as Telnet, SNMP, PPP, and FTP. But what is a protocol? A network protocol defines all operations within a network. Protocols even define how entities outside the network must interact with the network. For example, some network protocols define how data gets from point A to point B. Other network protocols define how a computer or device communicates over a particular transmission medium, like a telephone line or other type of connection. Simply put, protocols define how things are to be done if a device is going to operate in a network.

Network Protocols Formalized

An international standards-making body called the International Organization for Standardization (ISO) has formally defined a networking model called the Open Systems Interconnection (OSI) model. The OSI model defines the layered (software) elements that should exist in any network, and is a reference point to explain basic aspects about network protocols. The OSI model consists of seven layers. Each layer is actually a software program or programs that perform some intended function. All seven layers may, and usually do, operate on the same computing platform. Each layer passes data/information/parameters to/from the layer immediately above it and immediately below it. The formalized channel for protocol communications is very much like the military. There is a "chain of command" with each layer confined to communicating with its immediate subordinate and immediate superior only. Jumping ranks, as in the military, is forbidden in a layered approach to networking.

Sometimes, there is not a one-to-one correspondence when attempting to explain different network types by layers. Some protocols, like TCP/IP, predate the OSI model. In other cases, vendors developing protocols have found that there are advantages, in terms of speed, memory, or some other efficiency, resulting in some economic incentive to deviate from the OSI model. Some network protocols do not appear at all like the OSI model. However, the OSI model works well as a reference point to discuss and understand TCP/IP.

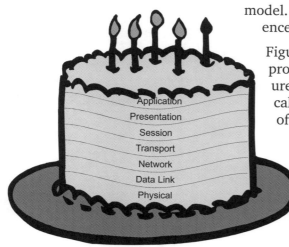

Figure 1.1 represents the layered levels of the OSI protocol. While a birthday cake is used in the figure to visualize the individual layers, a wedding cake is more appropriate for TCP/IP. The marriage of TCP and IP is the (computing) social event of the century, and the very legitimate offspring of their union is the World Wide Web and the Internet. To give the reader a clearer image of the OSI protocol model, and hence a better understanding of the TCP/IP relationships to their computing environment, a short discussion of the individual layers follows. A more in-depth treatment of the topic is presented in Chapter 3.

Figure 1.1 The layered approach to network communications

Once, it was thought that all equipment suppliers and users would switch to the OSI network protocol model. Various parts of the federal government issued mandates for future compliance. State governments mandated state agencies to plan for a conversion to OSI. However, very few organizations actually built an OSI network. Sensing a lack of a sizable market, equipment suppliers developed hardware and software to build the kind of networks that their customers would purchase today. The OSI protocol, while very useful in explaining how network elements interrelate, may actually be the protocol of the future that ends up as a historical footnote.

TCP/IP Protocol Suite Overview

In the beginning of networking time, the original network designers wished to accomplish specific networking objectives for which TCP/IP would provide the basic connectivity. Among those objectives were the ability to easily transfer files among the various computing environments, the ability to exchange electronic mail (e-mail) among network users, and the ability to connect to other computing devices by using telephone lines and "dialing into" the

remote computer. To accomplish all the desired networking objectives, various software modules, or programs, were required. All of these software modules have become known as the suite of TCP/IP protocols. Strictly speaking, they are not a part of the TCP/IP but form their own (more or less) stand-alone software programs. But to leave them out of any TCP/IP discussion seems like leaving some useful ingredients out of the wedding cake. So, we (yes, I do have a mouse in my pocket) endeavor to introduce the suite of TCP/IP protocols in the following paragraphs with respect to their relationship to the OSI protocol model.

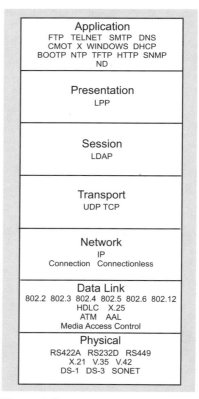

Application Layer Protocols

TCP/IP was designed to be a client-server technology at the application layer. A client starts an application, and servers serve the requests of clients. Because of TCP/IP's design, Telnet (the application for remote "dial-up" logons) has a client and a server application, as well as the FTP system used for file transfers, the World Wide Web system

Figure 1.2
The TCP/IP protocol suite

of clients (typically called browsers) and servers, and SMTP (the protocol used for e-mail). Notice Figure 1.2 which depicts the TCP/IP application services (FTP, TELNET, etc.) residing at the application level.

File Transfer Protocol (FTP) is used to copy files from one host to another. FTP uses the TCP for the reliable data transfer TCP provides. FTP provides the ability for remote users to perform all the file management functions of a local user. If the proper permissions are granted, the remote user can rename directories and files, delete files and directories, move files and directories and directory contents, and usually perform other file management functions that are allowed locally. FTP perceives files as a group of bytes, to be transferred as a data stream without regard for file structure. FTP does not care if the native file format is binary, ASCII, or record. All are the same in the eyes of FTP. FTP commands are not defined by RFCs. Rather, the commands are defined in the operating system software and vary somewhat from operating system to operating system. Chapter 8 includes the generic FTP commands found in typical UNIX operating systems.

Telnet is a virtual terminal application in the TCP/IP protocol suite. What is a virtual terminal? Back in the Dark Ages, long before the Age of Gates, circa 1960s, computers were expensive. I am talking about real expensive. The economics for computers on every desktop was prohibitive. However, "dumb" keyboards and monitors were priced within reason. These "dumb" keyboards contained enough computing muscle to communicate with hosts/servers and display the resultant information on the monitor. However, all actual computing was performed by the remote host/server. The "dumb" keyboard was useful only for sending and receiving information to and from the host/server. To put it another way, the virtual terminal was nothing more than a remote access keyboard and monitor.

So, to provide greater access to expensive computing resources, DOD and universities placed monitors and "dumb" keyboards on desktops. Telnet provided the software basis for communicating and displaying information to and from the remote host/server. Telnet is a text-based protocol. In the richness of today's graphical user interfaces (GUIs), Telnet seems awfully antiquated with the text-based user screens it provides. However, it still finds a welcome home in the world of UNIX computing. Of course, no one would accuse the UNIX world of overdoing it on the graphical user interface gig.

Simple Mail Transfer Protocol (SMTP) is a text-based communication protocol. It provides the means for users to exchange electronic messages, now called e-mail. The physical location on the hard disk drive where individual e-mail is stored is called the mailbox. User mailboxes are identified by a user name plus the full domain name of the host that sends, receives, and stores their e-mail. The user typically has a password that allows access to his/her e-mail that is stored on the host along with all other user mailboxes. We don't want anyone else reading our mail, right? Are you in for a BIG surprise! Not only is Big Brother watching, but he is also reading.

The text-based TCP/IP protocol suite was proven inadequate with the advent of computer graphics. To keep up with the times, the governing authorities added the Multipurpose Internet Mail Extensions (MIME) to the TCP/IP suite of protocols to allow the transmission and reception of binary imaging data as file attachments. While able to transfer binary imaging data, TCP/IP still does not provide for a rich graphical user interface. The computing platform running the TCP/IP protocol suite must provide the GUI.

The Domain Name System (DNS) implemented by the Domain Name Service is a distributed database system of IP addresses and aliases. It resolves addresses of hosts in order to establish contact with the target host. DNS was created to solve the problem of maintaining a host file with the associated addresses of all the hosts connected to the network on each host participating in a TCP/IP network. A host file consists of IP addresses and aliases, and each time a host or network is added or taken away the host file requires changing. DNS was designed to eliminate the constant updating of each host file.

Common Management Information Service (CMIS) is a management service offered by the Common Management Information Protocol (CMIP). CMIP is an OSI method of network management. When CMIP management functions are mapped to the TCP/IP suite of protocols, it is called Common Management Information Service over TCP/IP (CMOT). When it is mapped to the TCP/IP protocol suite, it uses TCP for a transport connection. CMIP uses Abstract Syntax Notation One (ASN.1), a language defined by Internet standard documents. ASN.1 is a language for writing clear and uniform data type definitions used in the management function.

X is a protocol and provides a distributed window environment. It permits requests and responses between X client applications and an X server. X includes the ability of an X client executing on one machine to operate against an X server on another machine, thus enabling a distributed windowing environment. The X technology has found its primary application in the UNIX environment. Some X basic components include:

- X Server—A program providing display services on a terminal supporting graphics at the request of an X client application.
- X Client—A program using the services provided by an X Server, such as a terminal emulation, for example.
- X Window Manager—This program helps in resizing, modifying, and relocating windows.
- X Library—This contains the interface for application programming. It consists of C language subroutines. One function of the XLIB is to convert X client requests into X protocol requests.

➤ X Toolkits—This is a software library providing high-level facilities for implementing buttons, menus, etc.

➤ Widgets—A widget is an X window, additional data, and procedures used to perform operations on that data.

Dynamic Host Configuration Protocol (DHCP) provides configuration information to Internet hosts. There are two DHCP components. One is a protocol for delivering host-specific configuration parameters from a DHCP server to a host and the other is a mechanism for allocation of network addresses to hosts. Designated DHCP servers allocate network addresses and deliver initialization and configuration parameters to dynamically configured clients. DHCP was originally designed to work in conjunction with BOOTP to configure diskless computers.

Bootstrap Protocol (BOOTP) was originally used to boot up diskless computers from a server. Long ago when disk space was very expensive, it made sense to use the remote services of a server to load boot programs into a computer that only had nonvolatile memory, i.e., random access memory (RAM). BOOTP is intended to garner all the information the computer needs to become fully operational on a TCP/IP network by querying a BOOTP server. The BOOTP server contains the diskless computer's operating system software and all the network configuration information the computer needs. These programs are downloaded to the diskless computer upon request.

Network Time Protocol (NTP) is used to synchronize time-sensitive functions and to set clocks for day, date, and time. The requester queries the time server on port 37 and receives back a 32-bit binary number representing the number of seconds that have passed since midnight, January 1, 1900. The centralization of a standard time-keeping server is absolutely necessary for the accurate transfer of data using transmission techniques that are time sensitive, such as time division multiplexing (TDM).

Trivial File Transfer Protocol (TFTP) is used in tandem with BOOTP to allow diskless computers to boot up an operating system using the boot and operating system file resources of a remote host. TFTP is implemented in a programmable read-only memory (PROM) device on the diskless computer. When the diskless computer is turned on, the TFTP contacts the remote host and downloads the appropriate boot software into random access memory (RAM).

TFTP was developed in a time when computing resources, and especially disk drives, were very expensive. Diskless computers booting from a remote host were a cost-cutting exercise. TFTP may still find some usefulness somewhere, but in the Age of Gates, with cheap computing, it is hard to imagine where (weight-sensitive applications such as satellites and cruise missiles?).

Hypertext Transfer Protocol (HTTP) is a means of communicating data across machine-dependent boundaries. Typically called hyperinformation or hyper-media, HTTP is basically a way of formatting information so that it is displayed on the monitor in a similar fashion regardless of the equipment it is viewed on. Messages are passed in a format similar to that used by Internet mail as defined by the Multipurpose Internet Mail Extensions (MIME).

Kerberos is a security protocol sometimes used with TCP/IP that operates by an authentication server and a "ticket"-granting server. For example, a client requests a "ticket" from the "ticket"-granting server, thus achieving authentication. Once authentication is achieved, the client is authorized to use a particular service.

Simple Network Management Protocol (SNMP) uses User Datagram Protocol (UDP) for a transport mechanism. UDP is TCP without certain reliability related features. Instead of the terms client and server, SNMP uses the terms managers and agents. Agents maintain information about the status of the node. A manager (application) communicates with agents throughout the network via messages. The information about the status of a device is maintained in a Management Information Base (MIB).

Network Disk (ND) provides the network disk services for diskless computers. The server designated as the BOOTP server performs the duties and functions of the ND. Network Disk was very useful years ago when computing costs were higher than we can imagine today.

HTTP, FTP, Telnet, and SMTP are considered DARPA services. DARPA maintains and updates these protocols as required. Additional proprietary and vendor-specific protocols used with TCP/IP include protocols from Hewlett-Packard, Sun, and a generic flavor called Remote UNIX. Hewlett-Packard Network Services TCP/IP protocols include Network File Transfer, Remote Database Access, and Remote File Access. Sun Networking Service TCP/IP protocols include Network File System (Statd Status Daemon), Network Information System (Mount), Port Mapper (Network Lock Manager), and Network File System (NFS). NFS is a collection of protocols produced by Sun Microsystems that uses a distributed file system allowing multiple computers supporting NFS to access each others' directories transparently. Remote UNIX Services TCP/IP protocols include Remote Print (lpr), Remote Copy (rcp), Remote Execution (rexec), Remote Login (login), and Remote Shell (rsh).

Presentation Layer Protocols

Lightweight Presentation Protocol (LPP) defines a way to provide network management functions (ACSE, ROSE) in a TCP/IP environment. The TCP/IP network management functions do not require the use of all of the ISO-compliant presentation layer services, hence the use of the term "lightweight" in the protocol name. See RFC 1085 and RFC 1095.

An additional proprietary presentation layer protocol is the Sun Networking Services External Data Representation (XDR).

Session Layer Protocols

Lightweight Directory Access Protocol provides the ability to access online directory services. LDAP does not provide all the functionality demanded by ISO, hence the use of the term "lightweight" in its name. See RFC 1777.

An additional Sun Network Services session layer protocol is Remote Procedure Calls. *Remote Procedure Calls* (RPCs) are programs permitting applications to call a routine executing on a server; in turn, the server returns variables and return codes to the requester. It is a mechanism implemented to support distributed computing via a client-server model used by Sun Networking. RPC works between the presentation layer's External Data Representation protocol and the transport layer's Transmission Control Protocol.

Transport Layer Protocols

Two different transport mechanisms are part of the TCP/IP protocol suite—Transmission Control Protocol (TCP) and User Datagram Protocol (UDP). TCP is connection oriented. TCP uses flow control, error checking, and retransmission as the mechanisms to provide reliable data transfer.

UDP is connectionless oriented. UDP does not make any provisions for error checking, flow control, or retransmission. UDP does not guarantee reliable data transfer. UDP is used by custom-written programs for specific purposes. These programs are individually responsible for ensuring reliable data transfer (checking to see if the data arrived at the intended destination) and retransmissions (repeating a transmission of data due to a loss caused by some problem). The focus of this book is TCP.

Network Layer Protocols

Internet Protocol (IP) transports datagrams across a network. A datagram consists of the data from the application layer and the transport level header and trailer information. IP resides at the network layer. It uses a 32-bit addressing scheme whereby the network and host are identified. IP was originally designed to accommodate routers and hosts produced by different vendors.

Internet Control Message Protocol (ICMP) provides messages concerning the status of nodes. These messages may reflect an error that has occurred or simply the status of a node. ICMP provides a way for certain commands to be issued against a target host to determine the status of the host, such as Packet Internet Groper (ping). ICMP and IP are implemented together because of how the two are intertwined in the routing and response mechanisms.

Address Resolution Protocol (ARP) determines the physical address (sometimes called a hard address) of a node given that node's IP address. ARP is the mapping link between 32-bit IP addresses and the underlying physical address, for example, the 40-bit Ethernet address. It is via ARP that a logical connection (BIND) occurs between the IP address and the hard address.

Reverse Address Resolution Protocol (RARP) enables a host to discover its own IP address by broadcasting its physical address. When the broadcast occurs, another node on the LAN answers back with the IP address of the requesting node. Hence, it is commonly called reverse ARP.

The Bootstrap Protocol (BOOTP) not only allows a host to discover its IP address by broadcasting its physical address, but it also provides a mechanism for downloading operating system boot images, allowing diskless machines to bootstrap themselves across a TCP/IP network. The Dynamic Host Configuration Protocol (DHCP) takes BOOTP a step further, providing a mechanism for dynamically assigning IP addresses to client computer systems.

Gateway protocols are a collection of protocols that allows routers to communicate. A variety of them exist; an example would be Routing Information Protocol (RIP). RIP is a basic protocol used to exchange information between routers. Again, this is a misnomer now because gateways are network devices performing a specific function which is usually not routing. Open Shortest Path First (OSPF) is another routing protocol.

Data Link Layer Protocols

TCP/IP does not define data link layer protocols. This is due to TCP/IP's original design intent to keep TCP/IP free from the issues involving the physical layer and its associated data flow. But a brief discussion of the data link layer interfaces is useful in orienting TCP/IP newcomers to the overall networking environment where TCP/IP performs its tasks so well.

TCP/IP can use different types of data link layer protocols including:

- Ethernet
- Token Ring
- Fiber Distributed Data Interface (FDDI)
- Integrated Services Digital Network (ISDN)
- X.25
- ATM
- DSL

Physical Layer Protocols

TCP/IP does not define physical layer protocols. TCP/IP will utilize whatever physical layer protocol implemented by the node. The physical layer is where the "rubber meets the road." All TCP/IP logic signals are converted to appropriate electrical, radio frequency, lightwave, or other signals for transport across the physical distances separating the network nodes. Some of the physical layer specifications governing specific types of physical layer media are listed in Figure 1.2.

Media Implementations

TCP/IP can be found implemented with multiple types of transmission media. For example, if TCP/IP is implemented with Ethernet, the media could be 50 ohm coaxial cable (narrowband), 75 ohm coaxial cable (broadband), 10 BASE-T twisted-pair copper cable, or 10 BASE-F (A or P) fiber optic cable. Ethernet provides a connectionless-oriented service for TCP/IP. The standard for Ethernet transmission media is IEEE 802.3

Although less popular, TCP/IP can also be implemented on top of a Token Ring network. With Token Ring, the transmission media is shielded twisted pair (4/16 Mbps), unshielded twisted pair (4/16 Mbps), or fiber optic cable. Token Ring provides a connection-oriented service for TCP/IP. The standard for Token Ring transmission is IEEE 802.5.

FDDI transmission media includes both shielded copper, shielded twisted pair, or fiber optic cable. FDDI provides a connection-oriented service for TCP/IP.

When TCP/IP is implemented using X.25 as the data link layer, Integrated Services Digital Network (ISDN at the basic rate of 64 Kbps) is the media utilized. After the information is converted to ISDN format, any combination of satellite, microwave, or serial telephone-type lines may be the transmission media used to get to the final destination.

With ATM or Frame Relay, DS1, DS3, or SONET may be the medium of choice. ATM transmission standards are governed by the ATM Forum.

Digital Subscriber Line (DSL) is an emerging analog transmission technology that is suited for high-speed (up to 133 Mbps) communication between the home and the central office via the humble twisted pair copper line connecting the two endpoints. The details of TCP/IP over DSL are yet to be resolved.

TCP/IP Protocol Suite Components

TCP/IP is a suite of software protocols as mentioned previously. It is software components used to build networks. Other components are needed to flesh out and complete a network, but the suite of TCP/IP software protocols is fundamental to any network.

Okay, but what is a software protocol? More fundamentally, just what is software? A software program is a step-by-step set of instructions that the computer must have to do something useful. A software program has one or more objectives to accomplish for the human users of the computer. The person or persons writing a software program must understand what the objectives are and how they can be accomplished with the computer performing the program steps. It is a lot like writing recipes. The "cook" must know what ingredients to use, when to add them to the mix, and how long to bake the mixture.

TCP/IP is a collection of software programs and defined ways of doing things like:

- Remote logon
- File transfers
- Information dissemination via the World Wide Web
- Electronic mail
- Providing support for custom-written programs
- Providing a mechanism for data transport throughout a network
- Routing data throughout a network
- Support for a distributed windowing system

Now, we will look a little closer at some of the tasks the TCP/IP suite of protocols can perform.

Remote Logons

If you are new to networking and TCP/IP, then the concept of a remote logon could be new also. It is, as the name implies, an application providing a function whereby a user can be on system A and log on to system B, wherever B might be located. The user has the perception that he or she is physically logged into system B. Actually, the appearance is a reflection of a logical connection established between system A and B.

The TCP/IP application that supports remote logon is called Telnet. It is often written in all capital letters, but other variations exist. Here, we will use Telnet. The Telnet protocol was one of the first Internet protocols, first proposed in RFC 0097 in February 1971. The Telnet protocol provides for a remote character-mode terminal emulation that operates over the network. Although fundamentally a character-mode service, most Telnet clients have been enhanced by hosting the character-mode interface in a graphical shell with drop-down menus which include point and click commands that execute common Telnet commands.

Most services that are available on a local character-mode terminal are also available across the network using the Telnet protocol. Historically, creative programmers wrote character-mode scripts (short lines of computer code designed to trigger specific responses) to provide custom information services through the Telnet interface. By accessing a remote computer with the Telnet protocol directed to a particular TCP/IP port, the user received a custom-programmed character-mode menu rather than a system login screen. However, the use of such interfaces has declined into obscurity with the availability of the rich, graphical interfaces provided by World Wide Web browsers.

File Transfers

TCP/IP supports file transfers from one system to another. This is similar to the remote logon capacity. A file transfer must support a remote logon to the target machine by default, but it does not provide the ability for the user to perform interactive work on the target system in the sense that Telnet does. The user is able to perform only file management functions on the remote system.

A specific program that is useful working with TCP/IP is the File Transfer Protocol (FTP). It provides a user on system A the ability to log on to system B and issue basic commands native to system B. For example, it would allow the user to issue commands to change a directory, delete a file, and perform other functions supported by the native operating system in system B.

FTP seems to imply, since it is called "File Transfer Protocol," a file is transferred from one system to another. This is not the case. FTP permits copying a file from, say, system B to system A. The original file being copied still exists on its original machine after the "file transfer" is performed. See Figure 1.3.

There are two software parts to the FTP system. One is the client and the other is the server. The server runs either as a stand-alone program, or as part of an operating service system such

How many copies?

Figure 1.3
A (very) busy FTP file server

as *inetd*. In other words, the server serves and the client requests to be served. The relationship is identical to the relationship between a restaurant patron and the individual taking the patron's meal order. See Figure 1.8 on page 22. The patron is the client and the waitress is the server. The patron/client can choose any one of many restaurants (computers) to patronize while the waitress/server must physically inhabit only one restaurant (computer) and serve all the patrons/clients coming through the door. The client/server relationship is discussed in more detail later in this chapter.

The full definition of the FTP protocol is specified in RFC 959. FTP was created to allow computers from different manufacturers, running different operating systems and using different systems of character representation (i.e., ASCII and EBCDIC), to exchange information in a vendor-neutral manner. The FTP specification defines four data transfer types:

ASCII—The default data type which must be accepted by all FTP implementations. It is intended primarily for the transfer of text files. The sender, which is the client in the case of an FTP "put" and the server in the case of an FTP "get," converts the data from an internal character representation to the standard 8-bit NVT-ASCII representation. The receiver converts the data from the standard form to the internal format appropriate for that hardware and operating system. The <CRLF> sequence is used to denote the end of a line of text. Note that NVT-ASCII is not US-ASCII text.

EBCDIC—This is the EBCDIC character data type, typically associated with IBM mainframe computing. This type is intended for efficient transfer between hosts which use EBCDIC for their internal character representation. For transmission, the data are represented as 8-bit EBCDIC characters. The character code is the only difference between the functional specifications of EBCDIC and ASCII types.

Image—Raw binary data using 8-bit bytes. Image type is intended for the efficient storage and retrieval of files and for the transfer of binary data. The FTP specification recommends that this type be accepted by all FTP implementations. This data type is used for transferring executable programs, compressed archives, graphics, and other binary data files.

Local—Binary data using variable byte sizes. This is designed for computers using other than an 8-bit byte size to exchange data more efficiently. It is less useful today, since computers using a byte size other than 8 bits are rare.

News

The Network News System, sometimes referred to as Usenet News in deference to its historical roots, provides a vehicle for the worldwide exchange of information. The News System can be considered either an advanced bulletin board system or a primitive groupware system. The Network News System uses the NNTP protocol and can be operated either as part of the worldwide Usenet News system or as a private information system. The most common access to Usenet is gained through Agent, a commercial software package readily available from the Internet. Usenet may have gained a certain notoriety due to the seemingly unlimited amount of sexually explicit material easily available through smut peddlers advertising their material in the Usenet newsgroups.

However, there is much to be said for Usenet. For the first time in the history of mankind (that is a bold statement), people from all over the world have easy access to the ideas of others through the posting of individual's ideas and opinions in the topical newsgroups on the Internet. While some governments have attempted to limit their citizens' access to the Internet, the fact is, the Internet just sprung up too fast for them to react adequately. Now, Usenet is a genie out of the bottle that will refuse to be recorked.

Gopher

The Gopher protocol was one of the first attempts to bring a user-friendly interface to information stored on servers dispersed across the Internet. Gopher is based on a hierarchical menu structure. Metaphorically, a Gopher server can be viewed as a "gopher hole" that is entered through a top-level menu and provides links to documents and submenus within the Gopher system.

Figure 1.4 A gopher (server) on the green

Tens of thousands of documents were placed on servers accessible by Gopher client software worldwide. This original, historical initiative perpetuates Gopher as an important protocol for accessing these documents. Although users originally accessed Gopher servers with Gopher client software, today's Web browsers are completely adept at handling the Gopher protocol—and most Internet access today is through a Web browser interface such as Netscape. So, although Gopher remains a powerful element in the Internet, its operation is now invisible to the general public.

In general, Gopher is an orphan in terms of the provision of information services. The majority of Gopher sites on the Internet today have not been recently updated. Those that continue to be maintained are maintained because the providers have determined that, at least for now, maintaining information in the Gopher format is easier than moving the documents to a Web-based format. The development of new Gopher-based information systems is basically nonexistent.

World Wide Web

The World Wide Web (WWW) has risen from relative obscurity at the beginning of the '90s to become one of the primary forces driving the adoption of TCP/IP in corporate networks. The power of the Web browser interface to access a wide variety of information resources, including not only static text and graphics but also business applications that access live data on corporate mainframes, has made TCP/IP networking a must-have commodity in the corporate world.

The World Wide Web, or Web for short, is by far the most popular, and fastest growing, service on the Internet. Figure 1.5 shows a realistic view of the WWW. At the center of the web are DARPA and the Internet Architecture Board and radiating out, like strands of the web, are the various countries that have a WWW point of presence (POP). Each POP is like the intersection of the strands where access to other countries' Web sites occurs. It is tempting to depict DARPA as the spider at the center of the Web; the metaphor is so appropriate.

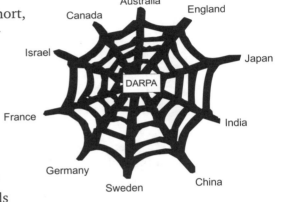

Figure 1.5 A realistic view of the WWW

The Web has opened up a whole new opportunity to deliver rich multimedia content to anyone in the world. In addition, Web content can be viewed on nearly any kind of computer platform, from Macintosh and IBM-compatible PCs to high-end UNIX workstations. Even though the Web is relatively young compared to the rest of the Internet, the variety and number of Web pages is staggering. Each month, the number of new Web servers across the world grows exponentially. Likewise, the number of Web sites being developed continues to grow daily.

Electronic Mail

TCP/IP supports electronic mail via Simple Mail Transfer Protocol (SMTP). See Figure 1.6. From an operational standpoint, it is similar to the remote logon and file transfer support in that a client and server are involved (clients and servers are explained in a later section).

Figure 1.6 Electronic mail—a better mousetrap

The electronic mail program enables users to exchange messages with one another. It also provides a way whereby a mass mailing can be performed. In the early days of TCP/IP services and the Internet, standards-based electronic mail systems were limited to ASCII text messages—making them far less desirable than the various proprietary e-mail systems in their support of impressive text, graphics, and multimedia attachments. However, the addition of the MIME (Multipurpose Internet Mail Extensions) standard to the baseline SMTP mail system now allows standards-based e-mail systems to exchange documents containing any data types.

Custom-Written Applications

TCP/IP provides support for those free-spirited souls who need to do something special that is not native to the TCP/IP protocol suite. For example, say a need exists to transfer data from one machine to another automatically without human intervention. It can be done, and there is support within TCP/IP for this.

An interesting current trend is the movement of programs traditionally based on proprietary protocols into the TCP/IP arena. Novell renamed its IPX/SPX-based netware product Intranetware and enhanced its ability to participate in TCP/IP networks. Novell has made it very clear that future versions of Netware will place the TCP/IP protocol on a complete par with its proprietary IPX/SPX system. Although Lotus Notes has always supported TCP/IP as one of its available protocols for the proprietary Notes client to communicate with the Notes server, Lotus has completely reformulated Notes with a TCP/IP-centric view—positioning the Notes server as a high-performance database back end accessible by generic TCP/IP World Wide Web clients. Additionally, Banyan Vines, Apple, Digital Equipment Corporation, IBM, Sun, Xerox, and Hewlett-Packard have developed customized applications for TCP/IP compatibility.

Data Transport Mechanisms

Figure 1.7 shows the TCP/IP protocols and how they correlate to the OSI model. Notice TCP/IP protocols start at layer three, which is defined by the OSI model as the network layer. TCP/IP is clearly not a full seven-layer network protocol. It really begins at the network layer and functions there and above.

| Transport |
| UDP TCP |
| Network |
| IP |
| Connection Connectionless |

Figure 1.7
TCP and IP protocols

As the figure shows, TCP/IP has two transport mechanisms. They are TCP and UDP. If we were to be completely accurate, we would probably talk about TCP/IP and UDP/IP—but nobody does that. Tradition specifies that we talk about the

TCP/IP protocol suite—and accept UDP as an alternative transport mechanism within the TCP/IP system. UDP is the acronym for User Datagram Protocol.

In general, TCP provides error-correction and retransmission services, where UDP does not. It would seem that you would always want error correction and retransmission of corrupted packets, but this is not always the case. For applications like Telnet, FTP, and Web access—the applications that come first to mind—the TCP protocol with its error detection and retransmission is the obvious choice. However, there are equally obvious applications where the error-detection and retransmission facilities of TCP are either unnecessary or undesirable. The foremost example of such applications relates to time-sensitive data including time inquiries and the transmission of isosynchronous data such as voice and video.

The TCP/IP protocol suite includes a protocol for making time-of-day inquiries of a time server. This protocol is frequently used for keeping computer clocks in synchronization. To facilitate this, the U.S. Naval Observatory maintains a time server that responds to time requests across the Internet. The time client on the user's machine sends a time packet across the Internet to the time server, noting internally when the packet was sent. When the return packet is received from the time server, the time returned is adjusted by half the time it took for the packet to make the trip from the client to the server and back again. In general, this provides a very accurate time source. Such time inquiries are typically made with the UDP protocol. If made with the TCP protocol, transmission errors could result in packet retransmission, providing a distorted measure of the time for a packet round trip from the client to the server—resulting in increased error. Use of the UDP protocol requires that the packet make its trip without retransmission. As a result, the value received is guaranteed to contain less error—although there is a risk of not receiving a response to an inquiry, requiring another time packet to be sent.

Another popular use of the UDP protocol is in the transmission of isosynchronous data—streaming audio and video transmitted across the network. In such a system, data received by the client is immediately converted to audio or video and displayed to the user. A retransmitted TCP packet containing, for example, a snippet of sound which arrives after the moment in time has passed when it should have been played for the listener is worthless. The retransmission only serves to diminish the bandwidth available for the transmission of current data.

Both TCP and UDP play an important role in the transmission of information in the TCP/IP network system. Judicious use of each results in maximum benefit within a given amount of network bandwidth.

IP Routing Mechanism

TCP/IP has within it a software module that performs routing of data throughout a TCP/IP network. It is that component which aids in setting up a logical connection with a target host, also called the destination, in the network. This component is called Internet Protocol (IP). Internet Protocol concerns itself with the assembly and disassembly of groups of data called packets. IP receives data segments from TCP and adds addressing information to the segments, which are then called packets. When IP receives a packet from the data link layer, it strips the address information from the packet, then sends the resultant data segment "upstairs" to the TCP module.

A Distributed Windowing System

Support for a windowing system is present within TCP/IP. It is not similar to Microsoft Windows, but it appears to be. The way the TCP/IP windowing works is entirely different. This windowing system is based on the X protocol, which sits on top of TCP at the application layer. This windowing system is different from Microsoft Windows if for no other reason than it supports programs running on different machines in a windowing environment.

The X Windows basically works by sending what-to-paint instructions from one computer to another. If computer B receives some data from computer A, computer A will also include some instructions on how to paint the window for displaying the data. It really is somewhat cumbersome, as the overhead required to transmit the painting instructions can be considerable.

What is Client/Server?

The terms "client" and "server" have risen from virtual obscurity not more than a half dozen years ago to the headlines in many trade magazines and weeklies today. In many instances the use of the terms defies explanation beyond some nebulous idea that is attempted to be conveyed. In many articles in the popular press where the terms client/server are used, the only ascertainable meaning you can derive from them is that a peer relationship exists between two computers. The point is these terms take on connotations usually contingent upon the vendor. However, with TCP/IP they mean something specific and definable. Before we define client/server, let's review some of the popular TCP/IP applications:

- Telnet
- File Transfer Protocol (FTP)
- World Wide Web (WWW)
- Simple Mail Transfer Protocol (SMTP)

All of these applications can be divided into two parts: a client and a server. Understanding their operation is easy. With respect to the TCP/IP applications mentioned above, you must only remember two things to master the concept of client/server: *Clients* always start a process and *servers* always respond to or "serve" a client's request. See Figure 1.8 for an everyday example of a real-life client/server relationship. The client starts the process by requesting something to eat and the waitress responds to the client's request by getting the client's order from the kitchen. So it is in the computing world, as illustrated in Figure 1.9.

Figure 1.8 A client/server relationship

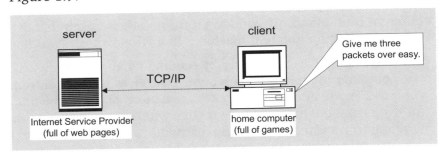

Figure 1.9 Another client/server relationship

Another term used interchangeably with client and/or server throughout the literature is "host." A *host* is a computer attached to a network. Hosts are the sources and destinations of packets. Hosts are the devices that execute processes. Processes are also called services. Processes and services are software programs that are executed to perform some particular task. In a network, the passage of data from one entity to another (host to host or layer to layer) is viewed as the execution of some process.

How Can TCP/IP Work With Different Operating Systems?

TCP/IP was originally conceived and developed over time to be software and hardware independent and open for general use. TCP/IP software itself must be modified to operate with different operating systems. This means vendors manufacturing and supporting operating systems must customize TCP/IP software to the particular operating system it is to operate under.

Competing with TCP/IP are other network protocols such as SNA. These types of network protocols are considered proprietary because they were developed by individual companies and typically operate only on the development company's equipment. They are not open in the sense another vendor can manipulate the protocol to operate on its equipment and maintain the native nature of the proprietary protocol.

Are All TCP/IP Protocol Implementations Alike?

No. Because of the open nature of TCP/IP, different vendors place varying twists on TCP/IP protocol implementations. Where this is the case, it is typically to support some particular functionality the vendor wants to add. It is not inherently bad or good, but buyers of TCP/IP products should ask how closely the particular product follows the official TCP/IP standards.

TCP/IP is generally considered open and not owned by any company or standards-making body. However, TCP/IP components and its general direction are guided by different groups and agencies that serve more of a steering role than a mandating one.

TCP/IP Standards

When TCP/IP standards are discussed, one cannot ignore the source of the standards—the documentation establishing the well-known Internet. TCP/IP is the foundation upon which rests the Internet, and the Internet standards include the TCP/IP protocols. We cannot have one without the other. The following discussion endeavors to explain where the standards come from.

The Internet Architecture Board

Why are we interested in the Internet Architecture Board (IAB)? Because the IAB is the governing body of the Internet and the Internet's suite of protocols which includes TCP/IP. The Internet Architecture Board maintains the documents that define the standards for the TCP/IP and Internet protocol suite. The IAB includes several groups engaged in the development of standards with the stated goal of coordinating the evolution of the Internet protocols. As the Internet gained popularity in the early '90s, and the demand for services increased exponentially, the coordination of standards became imperative. As the Internet becomes more commercialized, the importance of maintaining a robust and coherent platform for the Internet to rest on cannot be overstated.

One IAB group is the Internet Research Task Force (IRTF) which includes its steering group, the Internet Research Steering Group (IRSG). Another IAB group is the Internet Engineering Task Force (IETF), which includes a steering group called the Internet Engineering Steering Group (IESG). The IETF is responsible for developing Internet standards. A stated goal of the IETF is the coherent evolution of Internet standards that ensure future compatibility among the various protocols. Most of the Internet protocol development and standardization activity occurs in the working groups of the IETF.

The foundation of the Internet rules is contained in RFCs, or Requests for Comment. Appendix C contains references to most of the RFCs. These are protocol descriptions, ideas, and other comments from individuals interested in the Internet, and in a real sense this is part of what places TCP/IP in the public domain. All the RFCs current at publication are included on the accompanying CD-ROM. The full text of all RFCs in existence is located on the Web at **ftp://ds.internic.net**. The charter of the IAB is detailed in RFC 1601. The role of the IAB in the formation and management of the Internet and the organization of the IAB is detailed in RFC 1160. The road map for establishing Internet standards is detailed in RFC 1602.

Individual RFCs have a state and status assigned to them. The RFC states and status are self-explanatory. RFC states include:

- Standard
- Draft
- Proposal
- Experimental

RFC status includes:

- Required
- Recommended
- Elective
- Limited use
- Not recommended

The "experimental standard" stage is not required of all standards, only those standards whose authors wish to be able to go online while conducting trials of the protocol.

The process of going from a proposed standard to an accepted standard involves several stages of development. The formalized development stages are "proposed standard," "draft standard," and "standard." Also, each document has a status associated with it at each stage of development. The IETF recognized statuses are "required," "recommended," "elective," "limited use," and "not recommended."

The "required protocol" status specifies that all systems must implement the required protocol. The "recommended protocol" status specifies a system should implement the recommended protocol. The "elective protocol" status specifies a system may or may not implement the protocol, but if the protocol is implemented, it must be compliant to the standard requirements. The "limited use protocol" status specifies a protocol for use in a limited circumstance. The assignment of this status may result from the protocol's experimental state, specialized nature, limited functionality, or historic value. The "not recommended" status specifies a protocol that is not recommended for general use. The assignment of this status may result from the protocol's limited functionality, specialized nature, experimental state, or historic value.

As a document progresses from the proposed to standard state, the IESG must make a recommendation that the proposed standard move on to the next stage. The IESG makes its recommendation based upon test results and evaluation of the proposed standard. The actual tests and evaluations may be performed by individual bodies and members of the IETF. Upon completion of the development process, the standard is assigned an STD number. STD numbers are assigned per RFC 1311. There is a minimum six-month waiting period before a document can advance from proposed standard to draft standard. There is a minimum four-month waiting period before a document can advance from draft standard to standard. The waiting periods are designed to allow interested parties to test, evaluate, and/or comment upon the standard.

Who are the interested parties? Well, companies that produce networking equipment and software are very much interested in proposed standards, and even propose many of them. Also, academia and users are interested parties, both in proposing standards and implementing them. Internet service providers have a great financial stake in the ramifications of any new proposed standards.

Three additional categories of RFCs exist. They are "experimental," "informational," and "historical." The experimental category is used to solicit additional insight and comment upon the subject of the document listed as experimental. The informational category is just that, informational in nature with no authority for adoption of the content. The historical category includes those documents that are superseded by revised documents and perhaps documents that just do not have any impact anymore, such as early (circa 1970s) Internet meeting notes.

Protocol	Name	State	Status	RFC
IP	Internet Protocol	Std	Rqd	791
ICMP	Internet Control Message Protocol	Std	Rqd	792
UDP	User Datagram Protocol	Std	Rec	768
TCP	Transmission Control Protocol	Std	Rec	793
TELNET	Telnet protocol	Std	Rec	855
FTP	File Transfer Protocol	Std	Rec	959
SMTP	Simple Mail Transfer Protocol	Std	Rec	821

Protocol	Name	State	Status	RFC
NTP	Network Time Protocol	Std	Rec	1119
DOMAIN	Domain Name System	Std	Rec	1035
SNMP	Simple Network Management Protocol	Std	Rec	1157
TFTP	Trivial File Transfer Protocol	Std	Elec	1350

Table 1.1 Status of some TCP/IP protocols

Table 1.1 lists the state and status of some of the TCP/IP protocols. In the table, "Std" is a standard state, "Rqd" is a required status, "Rec" is a recommended status, and "Elec" is an elective status. RFC 1360 contains the complete list of protocols and their state and status.

Proposed standards are advanced from stage to stage only upon completion of demonstrated operational effectiveness using two or more implementations of the proposed standard. And, of course, upon the recommendation of the IESG.

A possible point of confusion might be the relationship between RFCs and STDs. Standards (STDs) define protocols while RFCs are a combination of IAB "notes," STDs, and any other information the IAB deems appropriate for the Internet community. All STDs become an RFC, but all RFCs are not STDs. Anyone can submit a request to the RFC editor at the IAB for an RFC to be assigned to their document for publication.

RFCs are never revised. Once an RFC number is assigned, the document it represents is never changed. If the document requires changes, a new RFC number is assigned to the document after the changes are incorporated. For some strange reason, the IAB thinks it is easier to track change history in this manner. Any ex-defense configuration control contractor can vouch for the morass this approach soon leads one into. The determination of the most current revision is much easier to track when revision levels (A–first revision, B–second revision, C–third revision, etc.) are used. The IAB's purported reasoning is that with a new number each time "there is never a question of having the most recent version of a particular RFC." No, there isn't, as long as you can find out what the latest number is. So, you must always contact the IAB to determine if you are holding the latest copy. If revision numbers were used, contacting the IAB to determine the latest revision would be unnecessary. However, it becomes very easy to track the revision history using revision numbers. If I am holding a Rev C document, then I know without doubt (I am a trusting soul!) this document has been revised three times (A, B, C) and I can easily locate the previous revisions. But, with the number changing each time, say from RFC 882 to RFC 883 to RFC 973 to RFC 1035, the ability to easily follow the history becomes problematic.

The RFCs are available from the InterNIC Web site and from any number of other sites, particularly as ftp files from universities. But the InterNIC Web site is the official site that should have the latest versions. There is another source of Internet standards, including TCP/IP, that should almost be a hysterical footnote—absolutely no pun intended. The source is the official Department of Defense's military standards, also known as MIL-STDs. These Internet standards are so far behind the times as to be almost laughable. I do not think the Department of Defense even attempts to keep them updated any more. The Internet ship just moves too fast for the world's greatest military force to get on board.

TCP/IP Over Ethernet

A term frequently heard when TCP/IP is discussed is Ethernet. Created at PARC and refined by Digital, Intel, and Xerox, Ethernet has become the most common, but not only, data link level protocol used with TCP/IP networks. A broadcast technology capable of being implemented over different types of media, Ethernet has permeated the marketplace. It is mature and inexpensive, and this has also contributed to its success. Advanced Ethernet technologies have continued to allow the fundamental Ethernet technologies to scale to meet the bandwidth needs of our insatiable appetite for network capacity.

Together, TCP/IP and Ethernet are a good choice to provide LAN services. Both accommodate the needs of both the novice and the network technocrat. Together they provide not only networking basics but also the foundation to exploit advanced networking techniques including distributed databases, network management, and even file systems. Their proven effectiveness continues to make them a network of choice for many network implementations.

Summary

TCP/IP is a mature networking protocol dating back to the 1960s. Its proliferation among universities, government institutions, and organizations of all types has contributed to its dominance in the marketplace. TCP/IP is best defined as an evolving network protocol with core components capable of networking heterogeneous hosts. TCP/IP's power lies in the following:

- It can operate on different vendor computers.
- Remote logons, file transfers, electronic mail, and the World Wide Web are some major applications it provides.
- Its IP addressing scheme makes connecting multiple networks relatively easy.

- ► It offers two distinct transport mechanisms (TCP and UDP).
- ► It has relatively low overhead from the standpoint of amount of software code required to provide a particular function.
- ► It is relatively inexpensive.
- ► A broad base of technical people has experience with it.
- ► It can operate with multiple data link level protocols and different types of media.

TCP/IP is based on a client/server relationship at an application layer. This client/server technology makes its applications fundamentally user friendly. Other components make up TCP/IP including network management and a distributed windowing mechanism.

Associated with TCP/IP are the Internet and the Intranet. The Internet is comprised of ARPANET, NSFNET, and other networks connected to it, making a virtual network spanning the globe. Intranets are implemented in locally administered networks. Institutions, businesses, organizations, and individuals can connect either single computers or intranets to the worldwide Internet.

Networks can be built with different network protocols. TCP/IP is a network protocol that is popular today. It is mature in the sense that it has now been in operation for many years. As a result, it has become relatively inexpensive. Basic TCP/IP client services are now bundled with leading operating systems on systems used as both clients and servers. Windows 95, Windows NT, Macintosh, OS/2, Netware, and the various flavors of UNIX all come with TCP/IP capabilities right out of the box. TCP/IP's past has been rooted in governmental agencies, universities, and other non-corporate entities. But because of the explosive growth TCP/IP has experienced in the corporate community worldwide in the past half dozen years, it has come to the forefront of many networking conversations. Today, most users have had at least some exposure to TCP/IP because of the pervasive nature of the World Wide Web and the Internet.

TCP/IP is a client/server technology at the application layer. In TCP/IP, clients always invoke a process and servers always serve the request of clients. Other references are prevalent today using the terms client/server, usually to indicate something peer oriented.

TCP/IP was originally conceived to be software and hardware independent. Evolutionary refinements and extensions reinforce the software and hardware independence of the TCP/IP protocol. Of course, somewhere, someone must account for the software and hardware differences.

Originally, TCP/IP was intended to be the glue in a network to connect heterogeneous devices. To that end it has had a long and prosperous life with no end in sight. TCP/IP must be modified to operate with various operating systems, but a consensus exists to modify it only so it can operate with a different operating system, thus leaving its fundamental characteristics intact.

Because of the robust design and flexibility inherent in TCP/IP, developers who sell it can customize it to provide certain services. This is not necessarily good or bad. The point is, buyers should understand what is generally considered standard TCP/IP. Being able to recognize any variation that might exist is important; it can make the difference between a smooth implementation and an unpleasant surprise when performance is not consistent with expectations.

Chapter 2

Networks

Questions answered in this chapter:

What is a network?

What are network topologies?

What is an intranet?

What is an Internet?

What is a network backbone?

Introduction

TCP/IP is an internetworking protocol. It may be impossible to completely comprehend the workings of TCP/IP without some degree of network knowledge. After all, you can take the protocol out of the environment, but you cannot take the environment out of the protocol. TCP/IP is a homeless refuge without the shelter provided by networks. To understand what TCP/IP can do for you, and for society, an understanding of basic network technology is imperative. Otherwise, it is nothing more than gibberish.

This chapter seeks to give the reader a basic understanding of network technology. In some respects, networking is very complicated if you consider every single possible technical facet of the networking environment. However, it is not the intent of this book to give the reader such a grounding in communications. Rather, we seek a fundamental networking knowledge that provides a solid foundation for further reading. Hopefully, after reading this chapter, the networking novice will be able to understand the context of the remaining chapters.

Perhaps now is a good time to mention something about the often confusing terminology of networking communications. In the networking literature, you will find the terms "node" and "host." The only discernible difference between the two terms is this: A *node* is any computing device, such as a computer, a printer, a shared hard drive, or a server, that is connected to a network, while a *host* is any computing device that is capable of performing multiple functions for a user. In other words, a host is a personal computer, laptop, mini-computer, etc., while a node is any computing device. So, hosts are a subset of nodes. Nodes encompass all networking computing devices while hosts are more specific networking components.

Now for the tricky part. A *local host* means the computer in your cubicle (the computer right in front of you when you are reading your e-mail). A *remote host* is the computer in the other cubicle, in the other building, or in the other city. Now, a local TCP or local IP means the TCP/IP running on your computer (the computer right in front of you when you are reading your e-mail), while the remote TCP or remote IP is the TCP/IP running on the computer that sent you the e-mail. Important stuff for growing minds.

Network Topologies

It is important to know how networks are built because this provides a framework for discussions about how networks operate. One way to explain how networks are built is to explore how network devices are physically connected to a common transmission medium. The idea of a common medium is fundamental to many networks. Granted this common medium may span great distances and be comprised of "different" types of media. Collectively, the medium can be considered as a whole.

Networks may consist of devices such as computers, printers, servers, etc., connected together. These devices connect to the medium directly or indirectly. The medium may consist of different types, but the common thread is the connection of these devices to the medium, thus forming a network. The devices may be spread out physically around the world. There are various physical layouts in use. Each layout has unique characteristics that make it desirable for a particular networking application. A layout is called a *topology*. A number of topologies exist, but our focus here will include:

- Star
- Bus
- Ring
- Hub
- Switch
- Mesh

Two terms frequently used in discussions about networks are "physical" and "logical." The term *physical*, in networking, is used to describe the physical characteristics of the network, such as connections, wiring, equipment placement, etc. When used, physical may describe how the interconnecting network wiring snakes around and through walls, ceilings, and floors, or perhaps from business location to central office, or central office to the trunking office. Accurately depicting the physical wiring of a network is very important for current and future reference. Installers and technicians must have adequate documentation to show where to place the wiring, drops, and network equipment. And when it is necessary to troubleshoot the network, adequate documentation depicting the network physical resources is almost mandatory. Granted, connecting two computers together to form a network is no big deal. But what about a hundred computers that are also connected to bridges, routers, and/or switches that might be connected to the public switched telephone network (PSTN)? Can a person describe, in such a network, where the demarcation is between the PSTN and the customer premises equipment (CPE) without a detailed physical wiring and connection diagram? No.

However, for a network manager, such detailed network drawings are very cumbersome to use. For a network manager to manage the network, the physical placement of cables is not important, assuming the network wiring was installed correctly. But the manager must know how the equipment is connected in a particular fashion. That is, what are the port assignments? Such an overview of the network is called a logic diagram and the shorthand representations of the network connections are called *logical connections*. When an individual mentions logical connections, he is concerned with the two (or more) ends of interconnecting devices and ignores the intervening hardware. So, "logical" is function related where "physical" is form related.

Confused? Take a look at the bus topology shown in Figure 2.2. The diagram depicting the bus topology is a logical diagram. You do not see how the interconnecting cabling snakes through the physical environment. What you do see is an "idealized" drawing depicting, at a high level, the interconnection of the network devices. This is a *high-level* logical drawing in the sense that the drawing does not show port assignments.

The Star

A star network was common in the 1960s and 1970s. During this time period, virtually all networks were owned by either the military or the defense-industrial complex. Distributed computing was not the mainstay of military networks. A typical military network consisted of a master node (or station, as they were called at the time) and one or more slave nodes, as illustrated in Figure 2.1.

The master node would query each remote slave node in turn for downloads and uploads of data. The maximum data rate achievable using the star topology is not very high since each remote slave node must wait until the master node has transmitted updates and received updates from all the other remote slave nodes before it can query a particular remote slave node again. But the network is very reliable since each slave node is capable of assuming the role of master node if the master node is silenced—a very real possibility in combat situations.

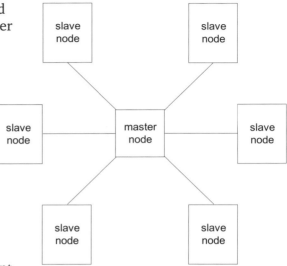

Figure 2.1 Star network topology

The Bus

In the bus topology, the bus is a cable that serves as an access point for all network devices. A bus-based network can best be understood by analogy. A bus can be thought of as a street. Each house on the street has physical access to the street. For the sake of simplicity, let us assume all driveways are connected from the garage to the street at the front of the house. It really does not matter, but the visualization may be easier if considered in this manner.

The bus topology is similar to a street because each network device has access to the bus in the same fashion that each house has access to the street. But there is a significant difference in the street/bus traffic analogy. Any number of autos may be present at any given time on the two-way street with several autos traveling in each direction. On the bus, only one device may be sending or receiving a signal at any particular moment of time. The bus may be thought of as a "one-way" street for each individual electrical signal transmission. If two or more electrical signals are present on the bus at the same time, they interfere with each other in a destructive

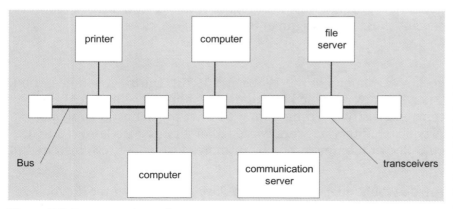

Figure 2.2 Bus network topology

way—kind of like hitting another car head-on when traveling down the street at a high rate of speed. What is left is not pretty to look at, is probably not even recognizable as the original human, auto, or electrical signal, and is no longer of any use.

Consider Figure 2.2, which depicts a bus with computers, printers, file servers, and communication servers. The transceivers act as the interface between the bus devices, such as printers and computers, and the bus itself. All electrical signals to and from a bus device pass through its transceiver. Also, all electrical signals on the bus itself pass through every transceiver. The transceiver maintains the bus address of its bus device and pulls off the bus those signals that are addressed to its bus device.

The figure shows a straight line as the common link between all participating network devices. Notice the bus is displayed as a straight line. In reality this is generally not the case. Because the bus is a cable, it usually gets shaped to fit the physical environment where it is installed.

One example of a bus topology is where network devices attach to the cable via a transceiver. The transceiver serves as a connection point for network devices. Transceivers do more than serve as a connection point, but this is not the focus here. Historically, these transceivers have a cable that connects them to the network device interface card. This cable is typically called a drop cable. However, most currently manufactured network interface cards integrate the transceiver onto the interface card itself. A number of computers ship from the factory with a network interface and transceiver integral to the system board. Therefore, it may not be possible to identify a separate transceiver for each piece of network equipment in a bus network.

A bus could be considered a data highway. It is the medium where data is passed from source to destination. Devices attached to the bus can access it and send or receive data. In a very real sense, it is a data highway.

The Ring

When a ring topology is mentioned, token ring may come to mind. Token ring is a protocol (way of passing data) at lower layers within a network, specifically the data link layer. The ring topology uses a cable in a ring fashion and serves as the data highway for data to get from source to destination. A token ring network schematic looks like Figure 2.3, as shown on the following page.

Figure 2.3 is a "logical" example of a network based on a ring topology. It does not depict how a token ring network appears physically. A token ring network is built around a device called a Media (some call it a Medium) Access Unit (MAU), depicted in Figure 2.4. If one goes looking for a token ring network, Figure 2.4 is an example of what will be found.

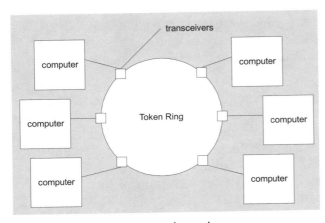

Figure 2.3 Token ring network topology

Figure 2.4 Media Access Unit

The MAU has a physical ring inside. Unfortunately, many diagrams and explanations depicting a ring network either assume the reader possesses this knowledge, or for whatever reason it is omitted.

This could be funny. Can you imagine someone new to token ring networks being asked to isolate a problem with a token ring network? If nobody told the individual there is no visible "ring" to be found (outside of disassembling the MAU), they could look for days! Sort of like asking a new recruit to go to the supply shop and pick up ten yards of flight line or five gallons of prop wash.

There is an important reason for constructing the network ring with a return cable run to the MAU between every device. If a network device fails, the circuits in the MAU can isolate the defective device and continue the network operation with the remaining devices without bringing down the complete network. This reliability feature has always been a strong selling point of ring-based networks.

Other types of ring-based networks exist; however, they are based on the same fundamental premise. They have a ring (or two) used to pass data.

The Hub

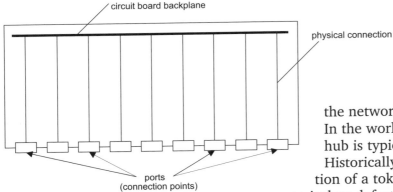

Figure 2.5 Hub network topology

A hub topology is like its name connotes. It is a central point of connection. Figure 2.5 shows how a hub topology appears.

A hub is the central point of the network from a physical connection. In the world of Ethernet networks, the hub is typically called a "concentrator." Historically, the physical star configuration of a token ring network and its ability to isolate defective nodes were strong selling points over Ethernet, which in its original definition was based on connecting a single wire from computer to computer. The bus-topology Ethernet system was vulnerable to breaks in the cable. Any cable fault would disable all the computer systems attached to the Ethernet segment containing the fault.

The Ethernet concentrator maintains the bus topology of the Ethernet system from an electrical perspective but implements it physically as a star network where every computer connects to the concentrator via two twisted pairs of wire. Combining the low-cost manufacturing of standards-based Ethernet cards with the reliability of a hub-based cable plant allowed Ethernet to become the dominant network technology in the 1990s. Additionally, adding intelligence to the hub electronics allows them to communicate with SNMP management consoles so that the network infrastructure can be centrally managed by technical support personnel.

The Switch

From the outside, you can't tell a hub topology from a switch topology. Both sit at the core of a star-shaped wiring scheme, as shown in Figure 2.6. The difference is on the inside. A network hub, or concentrator, implements a physical star wiring scheme—but using an electrical bus. In the case of Ethernet, the hub bus operates at 10 megabits per second (Mbps) or 100 Mbps.

All of the devices connected to the hub take turns sharing the single 10 megabit bus. An Ethernet switch, in contrast, provides a 10 megabit data path to each network device, allowing multiple, simultaneous connections. The limiting factor of the switch is the speed of its backplane, which in an Ethernet switch is typically in the neighborhood of 600 megabits per second.

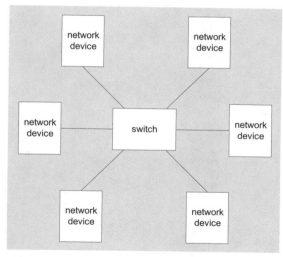

Figure 2.6 Switch network topology

An additional performance boost can be gained in Ethernet switching by operating the switch in a full-duplex mode rather than a half-duplex mode. In the original Ethernet system, at a particular point in time a single Ethernet card could either transmit or receive—but could not do both at the same time. Once every Ethernet device has its own dedicated set of wires to the switch backplane, it is possible to configure the system so that a single card can both transmit and receive at the same time. In considering, for example, the connection to a server, it is easy to see where the ability to receive a request from one client while simultaneously sending data to another client would provide a real performance boost. There is a small downside to full-duplex switching however. While any Ethernet card can participate in a half-duplex switched environment, the ability to operate in full-duplex mode is a feature that is only available on premium-quality, current-technology cards. Fortunately, full-duplex switches can generally be configured to work simultaneously with a mixture of half-duplex and full-duplex devices.

Switching additionally serves as the foundation of some of our highest-speed network technologies. The ATM (Asynchronous Transfer Mode) network system is based on the rapid switching of small, 53-byte data packets. Asynchronous Transfer Mode networks range from 25 megabit per second switches typically used for providing high-speed connectivity to the desktop to 2 gigabit ATM switches for exceptionally demanding high-bandwidth environments.

Mesh

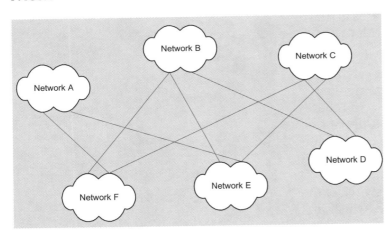

Figure 2.7 Partial mesh network topology

Figure 2.7 depicts a partial mesh topology consisting of unrelated networks. The partial mesh network does not have a physical connection to every single other network. Hence, it is partial. A mesh network that connects to every single node in the overall network is called a full mesh network. The Internet is not a full mesh network. To achieve complete connectivity among Internet users, routers pass the information on down the line until the information reaches a router connected to the destination network. Of course, to achieve such connectivity, routers must be able to determine which router, of possibly many routers they are connected to, is the appropriate router to forward the information to.

The individual networks depicted in Figure 2.7 may consist of any combination of network topologies previously defined (bus, ring, etc.) and may be LANs, WANs, or GANs. A great example of a mesh network is the popular

Internet. If the figure represents the Internet, then the individual networks could represent defense, government, university, and company intranetworks.

The salient characteristic of mesh networks is the variety of connections between networks, or nodes. Any network may connect to any other network without constraint. Well, actually, there are some constraints, such as the number of ports available to use which is directly related to the financial means and perceived necessity of the owning organization. But let us assume an unlimited bank account and necessity. Then, any network may connect to any other network. The resultant mesh network then may appear to be a confusing and totally unmanageable mass of interconnecting networks. In the case of the Internet, appearances are very realistic. Yet TCP/IP does manage the process quite well.

The mesh topology makes the Internet possible. What makes a mesh network possible is state-of-the-art network routers and their routing algorithms. An algorithm is the step-by-step approach used by engineers to solve a problem. For Internet routers, the routing algorithm of choice is Open Shortest Path First (OSPF), which is covered in a later chapter.

A note about routers: For high-capacity communication links, used by large owning organizations such as telephone companies (as part of their national commercial backbone), major corporations, and governments, routers are replaced with switches. While routers are complicated enough, switches are very complex electronic devices capable of switching from small data streams to massive gigabit streams.

Networks

Computer communication networks play an important role in military, government, and civilian environments. Seems we are inundated with the term "network." Forty years ago only television stations networked, forming the familiar NBC, CBS, and ABC television networks. Thirty years ago computers began forming networks, twenty years ago countries began networking, and ten years ago people began to network. One wonders if people felt compelled to keep up with computers. Now, computer networks are networked, forming hierarchical systems of computer networks.

In a larger sense, networks, whether television, computers, countries, or people, share a common goal. Each type of network has as its primary purpose the sharing of information for the benefit of at least one of the parties involved in the sharing. The methodology for storing, retrieving, and transmitting the information is all that differentiates one network type from another. But what exactly is a computer network?

What is a Computer Network?

Webster's New World Dictionary defines network as "any arrangement or fabric of parallel wires, threads, etc., crossed at regular intervals by others so as to leave open spaces." In the world of computing, a network is "an arrangement of interconnected computing devices." A computer network exists when two or more computing devices are electronically connected together so that the devices may share their computing resources with each other in some deterministic fashion. Of course, it must be deterministic. After all, we do know what we are doing, eh?

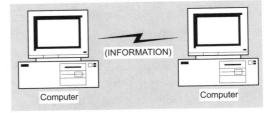

Figure 2.8 A simple network

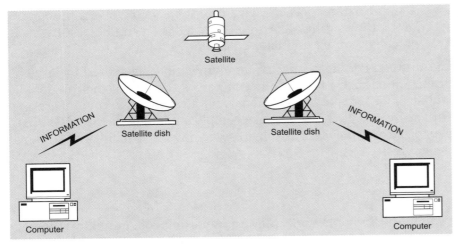

Figure 2.9 Still a simple network

A physical connection that provides an electrical path between some or all the network devices may or may not exist. If there is no physical connection, i.e., wires, cables, optical fiber, etc., then electrical continuity must be established in some other manner, usually via RF wave propagation, such as found in satellite communication links. Figures 2.8 and 2.9 illustrate simple networks.

The desire to move information quickly and efficiently across a network, from source to destination, is the underlying driving force behind networking computers. Of course, at the heart of the matter is economics. As we gain access to more and more information with less and less physical resources we become more cost efficient, keeping us in the race for self-preservation. Perhaps someday, as we take the physical limit of the self-preservation equation, we will know everything about nothing at an affordable price.

Anyone can own and operate a network. No network wizards are necessary. All that is required for a person to understand networking is a desire to understand and the ability to read. Who has networks and where are they? The technical junkie with two or more interconnected computers at home possesses a bona fide computer network. The small business with two or three or more computers interconnected at the office possesses a bona fide computer network. The Fortune 500 company with hundreds of interconnected computers scattered across the nation and perhaps the world possesses one or more bona fide networks. Just as there are many different tastes in the world, so are there many different sizes and types of networks. See Figure 2.10.

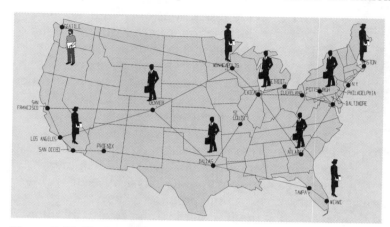

It is easy to distinguish between two functionally different but physically similar networks. One network type is an "intranet" and the other is an "internet." Each type of network has its own special purpose and usefulness as explained in greater detail in the following sections.

Figure 2.10 "Packet-men" and "packet-women" carrying the (e-) mail

What is an Intranet?

An intranet is composed of locally administered local area networks (LANs) utilizing TCP/IP for their upper layer transmission protocols. An intranet does not have all of the restrictions and requirements an internet must abide by because it is a "local" network in scope. That is, the LANs comprising intranets are physically confined to small geographical areas with access limited to those computers either connected directly together and/or to a server and those computer users authorized to "dial in" via "remote node access." An intranet may consist of a single LAN or several LANs interconnected via private or public switched network lines. Several interconnected LANs form a wide area network (WAN).

An *intranet*, as illustrated in Figure 2.11, is not necessarily a geographically small network. The private networks, or intranets, maintained by multinational corporations such as Texas Instruments, IBM, EDS, and NASDAQ span the country and even the globe. While they may not have as many users as the much larger and now commercialized Internet, they are certainly global in their reach. Employees from IBM can access their company's network from any location on the globe where dial-up capabilities exist, assuming the employee has the proper authorization to use IBM's intranet. And even some

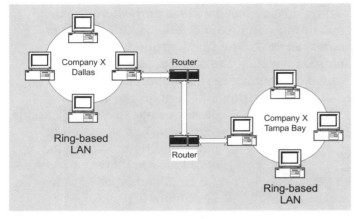

Figure 2.11 An intranet

individuals without permission, called hackers, occasionally penetrate a company or government's intranet and may or may not cause damage or alarm.

While an intranet does not have all the restrictions of an internet, an intranet does have restrictions and requirements in order for it to be functional. One very important restriction is access, especially if the intranet is connected to an internet. Intranet owners, typically corporations, do not want unauthorized users gaining access to privileged corporate information. For intranet security, it is relatively easy for corporate information technology (IT) bit counters (programmers) to limit intranet access since corporate physical security prevents unwanted users from gaining access to the premises where the computers are located. However, when the intranet is connected to an internet via a gateway, physical access limitations to the company network (and the associated data) disappear. To prevent unwanted users from gaining access to the intranet via the internet, corporations erect software barriers called firewalls. Sometimes the existence of a corporate firewall makes it easy to determine where the internet leaves off and the intranet begins. Other times, the point of demarcation (where an "internet" begins/ends and an "intranet" ends/begins) may simply be a router that provides the connection between the company or organization and the world at large.

What is an Internetwork?

An *internetwork* consists of hosts connected to networks. These networks are connected together via gateways. The networks forming the internetwork may be any combination of local networks (such as Ethernets and/or token rings) or large networks (ARPANET, Intranetworks). It was fashionable in times gone by to limit the internetwork definition to networks based upon packet-switching technology. However, with the advent of new networking and communications technologies, the packet-switching limitation no longer applies. As an example, it is quite convenient to connect packet-switched networks together via cell-switched backbone networks using a relatively new communications technology called Asynchronous Transfer Mode (ATM). Networks based upon the native ATM communications protocol are quite capable of replacing the packet-switched networks, resulting in faster and leaner communications. But that is really the subject of another book, such as *Demystifying ATM/ADSL* (Wordware Publishing).

Internet is a shortened form of internetwork. An internet in the purest sense of the term is just the interconnection of two or more networks and/or the interconnection of other computing resources that may or may not be a part of a network. An example is, of course, the home computer connected to the Internet. While the home computer is connected to the Internet, it is a part of the network comprising the Internet, although by itself it is not necessarily a part of another network. But, from a purist's perspective, any two or more networks connected together form an internet.

Many globally connected intranets are connected to the Internet. Special restrictions apply to intranets connected to the Internet. Typically, the connection of individual intranets to the Internet must be accomplished by having a router or a multihomed host, a host attached to two or more LANs. A multihomed host connecting an intranet to the Internet has a local IP address and another IP address assigned to it so it can be known by both networks. Figure 2.12 depicts multiple intranets and Internet service providers connected, in a mesh topology, as the Internet. Of course, the real Internet has thousands of service providers and hundreds or perhaps thousands of intranets connected together in a mesh network, so this is a simplified diagram of the Internet.

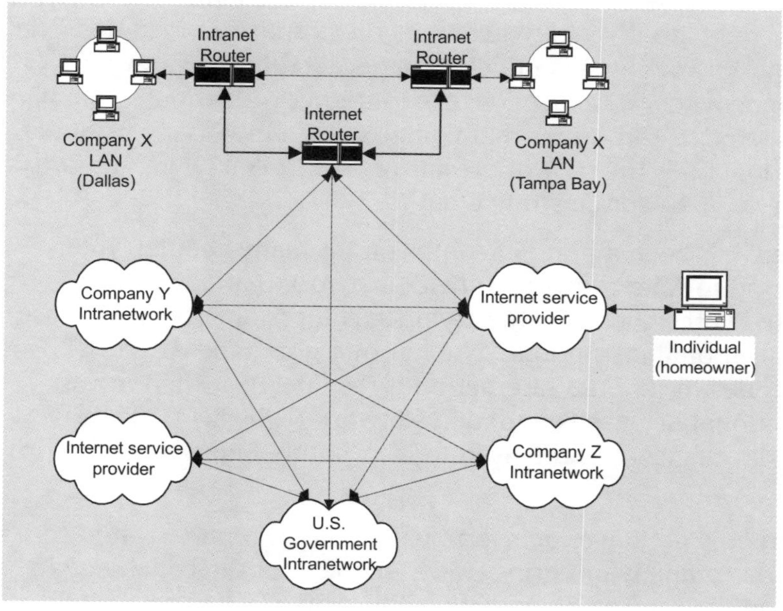

Figure 2.12 Intranets connected as an internet

Each "cloud" in Figure 2.12 represents an intranet of the type depicted at the top of the figure as Company X. Each of these intranets and the Internet service providers connect to the mesh through on-site routers, or switches. These intranets must be physically connected together somehow. The somehow, most often, is public switched network (the telephone companies) leased lines. However, some connections exist through privately owned telephone lines.

Notice the humble individual/homeowner who gets into the internetworking act through a modem connection to a commercial Internet service provider.

Employees of companies with sufficient resources connect to the Internet through the service provided by their company, not through commercial Internet service providers. However, small companies without the resources may use a commercial Internet service provider to put up a web page and to send/receive e-mail.

Why is all this important to understanding TCP/IP? Figure 2.12 depicts the environment where TCP/IP is used. All those intranets, Internet service providers, and homeowners are able to communicate with each other because of TCP/IP. Each individual intranet may communicate using a proprietary communications protocol but they talk to the outside world using TCP/IP. Multiple communications protocols were the norm but more and more companies are migrating to TCP/IP for their intranet communications since TCP/IP is a public domain protocol and no one manufacturer can hold a company hostage, price-wise. Millions of people use TCP/IP on a daily basis, and soon we can boast hundreds of millions will use it.

What is *the* Internet?

The Internet is usually modeled as a collection of computers and "intelligent" devices interconnected with diverse switching and transmission facilities. The collection of computers and intelligent devices are called hosts, gateways, bridges, routers, and switches. Control over the Internet is distributed among the various administrative authorities that comprise the networking resources of the Internet. A domain is the network resources controlled by an authority. DARPA is an example of an administrative authority.

The word "Internet" has been a point of confusion for many people. "Internet" is the name used to refer to the worldwide network that began when ARPANET connected with other private networks, comprising mainly defense companies and educational institutions. The Internet grew, and ARPANET remained the main network of the Internet until the late '80s when it was replaced by the National Science Foundation Network (NSFNET). The primary purpose for the change was the need to incorporate high-speed links in various places.

Although the Internet is no longer a government-sponsored project, it is not owned by any single company or entity. However, many of the collaborative structures, including the Internet Engineering Task Force (IETF) that established the initial rules for the operation of the Internet, are still in operation. The IETF both solicits and proposes changes to the Internet to accommodate changing needs. The IETF home page is **http://www.ietf.org/**.

For anyone wishing to get a really good grip on just what the (commercial) Internet is, or is not, please read RFC 1935, "What is the Internet, Anyway?" by J. Quarterman, April 1996.

How are Computers Networked?

Computers, and computing devices, are networked by physically linking the devices together in such a manner that they can transfer information from one to another using electrical signals. Some of the computing devices may act as repositories of large amounts of information and also act to connect other computers together into a network. These special computers are called servers. Computers that use server services, such as file management and electronic mail service, are called clients. Some networks require servers and some do not, depending upon the topology, or structure, of the network.

The active agents residing within computing hosts that produce and consume messages are called processes. Various levels of communications protocols in the networks, the gateways, and the hosts work together to support a data communications system that provides bidirectional data flow on logical connections established between process ports on computing hosts.

A common use of networks is the transfer of large files from one host to another. In the rich, graphical world of computing today, files can easily be 1 MB or larger. It is not convenient, or economical, to transfer such files as one massive file in a single transaction. Such a herculean effort would certainly fail due to the vagaries of computer communications. Rather, transferring files, or any other type of data is much more manageable when the job is divided into smaller pieces or tasks. When the data is divided into smaller portions, the resultant data pieces are called data segments. Routing and flow control information is then added to data segments to form datagrams. The local network may take the datagrams, now called a packet, and add additional routing information if the datagram is destined to traverse another network. The additional routing information, addresses, flow control, etc., to the original data segment is called *overhead*. See Figure 2.13.

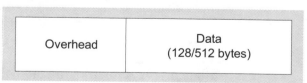

Figure 2.13 A packet

What is a packet? A group of data bits attached to a group of overhead bits. The data bits are typically either 128 bytes or 512 bytes in length. Networks that package data in this manner into "packets" are called packet-switched networks, as shown in Figure 2.14. The packet contains all the information necessary for the data segment to get from source to destination anywhere in the world.

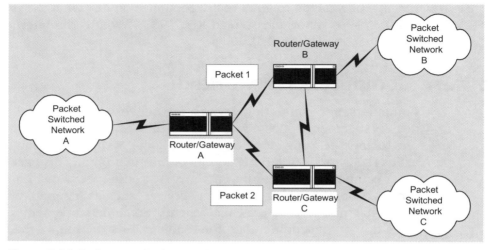

Figure 2.14 Packet-switched network

The original ARPANET was, and still is, a packet-switched network. What is a packet-switched network? A network that provides for transmission of packets from node to node using the packet addressing information included in the packet header to route the packet to the next node. Packets continue on down the network in this manner until they finally reach their destination. Yes, in the olden days packets got lost. Now, with intelligent routing, fewer packets get lost.

Packet Gateways/Switches

A model of internet communications includes the internet protocol module and its associated TCP module functioning as the interface between higher level processes, i.e., applications, and the physical local network. The TCP segments data while the IP packages the segments into datagrams. The datagrams are then routed to a destination internet protocol module or to an intermediate router or switch which may be a gateway to another network. If the datagram does not go directly from the source IP to the destination IP, but must pass through two or more network routers, it is repackaged into a packet. These "packet switches" are capable of performing additional operations on the datagram, including manipulating the data, to pass the datagram through the packet switch. A good example of the datagram manipulation by packet switches is the fragmentation of datagrams to accommodate the packet switch's smaller throughput buffer.

At each gateway, which may be a router or a switch, the internet protocol datagram is stripped of its local packet. The gateway examines the datagram and determines the optimum route of the packet through the adjoining network. The datagram is then repackaged with the new network's packet and sent on to either the next gateway or the destination if the destination resides in the current network.

Each gateway is capable of segmenting the datagram into smaller fragments of the original datagram. This may be necessary because the routers in the new network may not be able to accommodate the larger datagram size. Further fragmentation may occur at downstream gateways. The destination internet protocol is responsible for reassembling the fragmented datagrams into the original IP datagram before passing it on to the TCP module.

Why Do I Need a Network?

As pointed out at the beginning of this chapter, networks exist to share information. You need a network to gain access to information on computers other than the computer you are physically near to help you do your job, or to educate or entertain yourself.

Even with gigabyte-sized hard drives, a single computer cannot store all the information available to the general public. Information is created in a distributed fashion across the nation and the world.

If you ask ten people this question, you will probably get ten different answers. Some consensus exists, however. Ask this question to financial people or managers in corporations and they may respond by saying networking will help them maximize technical resources within their company. Networking can do this if properly implemented. Ask a documentation or training department the same question and the response may be entirely different. A typical response from such a department might be something like, "It would enable all workers in the department to exchange files, have electronic mail, and have remote logon access to hosts not located on their desks."

There are many reasons for having a network. Commonalities exist among most networks, but differences also exist. Additionally, the reasons for building networks have changed over time. In the earliest days of networking, when networks were confined to workgroups or departments, the primary driving factor for building networks was sharing expensive computer resources. When a 5 MB hard disk cost $6,000 and the least expensive printer on the market that could be called "letter quality" cost $3,500, sharing disk space and print services was the most important driving force in many organizations. However, with $99 gigabyte hard disks and $199 inkjet printers that make the old typewriter-technology letter quality jobs look prehistoric, the driving forces behind networking are no longer basic sharing of peripherals. Today, the driving forces behind the implementation of networks certainly include the provision of basic file and print services, but the sharing of information itself has become the primary force. Several of the common reasons for installing a network are the following:

Remote Logon—This service permits a user on his/her host to log on "remotely" to a host in a different location.

File Transfer—This service permits network users to exchange files. It saves time and can eliminate duplication of resources. And, most of all, it is convenient for users.

File Services—Different from file transfer, file service allows disk space that physically exists on another computer on the network to function identically to local disk space, either through the assignment of drive letters or named volumes, whichever is appropriate for the operating system of the user's computer.

Electronic Mail—This service allows all users on the network to exchange mail electronically.

Shared Printers—Print services allow multiple users to share a printer. Shared printers are typically either faster than inexpensive desktop printers, or have special capabilities, such as extremely fine resolution, large paper size, or the ability to print in color.

Information Services—Information services take many forms: the World Wide Web, Gopher, Usenet News, and Lotus Notes. Each of these information resources has its own system for presentation and navigation—but all are characterized by having a piece of client software on the user's computer (i.e., Web browser, Newsreader, Notes client) that interacts with a corresponding piece of server software on the network to allow the user to interact with the information resource.

Electronic Commerce—The Internet provides every individual the opportunity to sell any product and be competitive with established businesses. And the Internet is fast becoming every shopaholic's dream, an electronic mail order mall. Original equipment manufacturers (OEMs) and value-added resellers can place orders for materials directly with vendor companies, reducing paperwork and man-hours, and speeding the ordering and delivery process.

The type of network utilized depends upon the particular needs of the user. An advantage networks offer is that some networks support different vendor equipment, thus providing interoperability between unlike equipment. Making computer systems from different manufacturers running different operating systems communicate with each other is often reason enough to install a network.

The Backbone is Connected to the...

The term "backbone" can be most confusing, especially if the speaker or writer does not communicate precisely the intended meaning. The term backbone is used frequently in conversations about networking and the meaning is usually fuzzy. It means different things depending upon the context and point trying to be made. For example, the backbone could be used in reference to the topology of a network. If such is the case, the meaning conveyed is the physical connections, primarily the common point of connection, for devices attached to the network. See Figure 2.15.

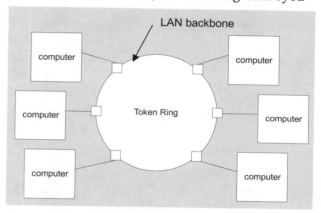

Figure 2.15 Topology backbone

Backbone is also used to refer to a network protocol. When this is the case, a larger concept is usually conveyed. An example of this is using the term to refer to routing from network A to network C <u>through</u> an unlike network, say network B. An example of this is Figure 2.16 on the following page. In this instance, the network backbone is network B. Included as part of the backbone is the interconnecting transmission media between network B and network A and the interconnecting transmission media between network B and network C.

Figure 2.17 depicts the Internet, or at least two Internet servers, as connected through the public switched network (PSN). To get a clearer picture of the real Internet, all you need do is add more Internet servers, more Local Access Transport Areas (LATAs), and more Interexchange Carriers.

In the figure, the Internet backbone is either easy to discern or difficult (isn't that peachy keen?), depending upon the perspective one takes. Either it is all backbone, or pieces of it are. Actually most, but not all, of it is backbone. It is perhaps most convenient to describe what is not network backbone. In this case, it is the Internet servers, their associated routers, and the subscribers. Everything else is backbone.

Now you should be getting the idea that network backbone really refers to the transport medium that a device, either an individual computer or an individual network comprised of two or more computers, uses to pass data from itself to whatever destination (computer or network) is intended.

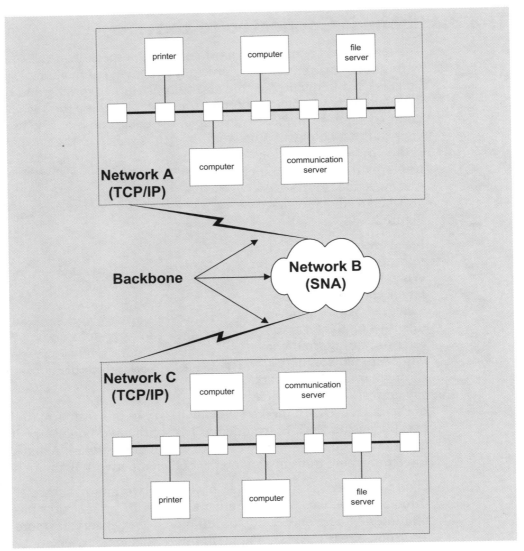

Figure 2.16 Network-network (intranet) backbone

As networks proliferated during the first part of the 1990s, the backbone of a network system was typically implemented as a series of network connections between routers. In the late '90s, advances in switch technology challenged some of the fundamental assumptions associated with the traditional construction of networks, especially in the context of a building or campus network. When a traditional router-based network system is drawn on paper, it is typically possible to identify the primary communications links that constitute the backbone of the network. If these core routers and communications links are replaced with a high-capacity switch, the network backbone

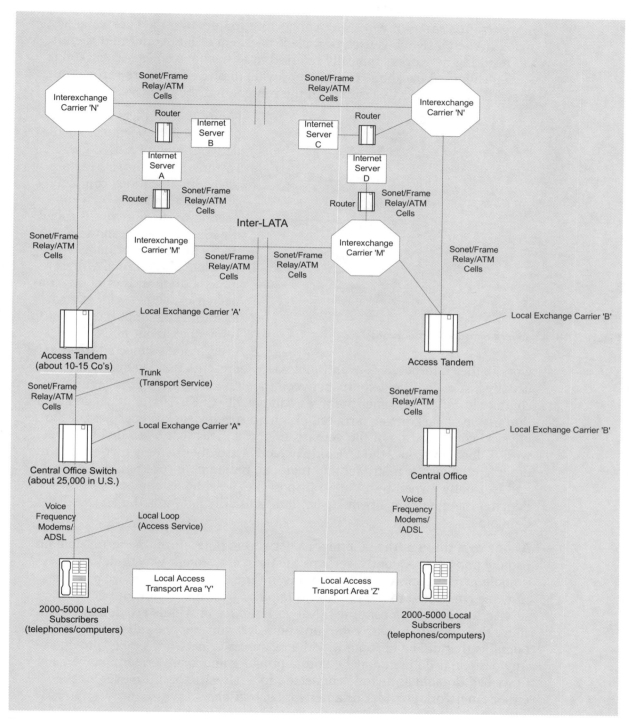

Figure 2.17 Internet backbone

moves from a series of wires interconnecting routers into the backplane of a switch. When a switch is used to replace a system of interconnected routers, the resulting network is typically referred to as having a collapsed backbone. Such a collapsed backbone can often provide improved network throughput, as switches are typically faster than the routers that they replace.

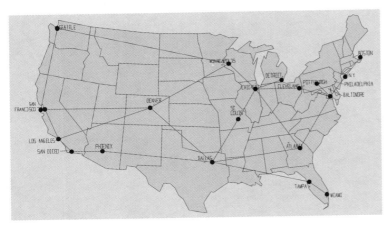

Figure 2.18 A network of national proportions

Figure 2.18 depicts a network of national proportions. Such a network might be used by a Fortune 500 company, say a telecommunications company, or the government. Each connection to the network is called a node. The figure shows all nodes in each location as a single black dot. In reality there may be thousands of nodes connected to the network at each location. One important point to remember about networks is every node connected to a network, either internetwork or intranetwork, represents the demarcation, usually just called the demarc, between the network and the local equipment, commonly called customer premises equipment (CPE). The physical demarcation may be a jack panel, a router, or a high-speed switch. Regardless of the physical configuration of the demarcation, it is clear that one side of the network is local in scope, the CPE side, which is usually privately owned, and the other side, which is metropolitan, regional, national, or international in scope and is usually owned by a data transport, i.e., telephone, company. At the demarc, the upstream/downstream data is usually fed into a larger/smaller data pipe.

As one digs through the voluminous networking literature, the term "domain" usually pops up frequently. Perhaps the most convenient way to define a domain is to explain what a domain is in terms of network service providers (anyone connected to the Internet is familiar with that term) and network service subscribers (most of us). Network service providers are domains that share their resources with other domains. Network service subscribers are domains that utilize in some way the resources of network service providers. Any particular domain may be both a provider and a subscriber. So, we have described domain as anyone connected to a network, because everyone is either a network provider or a network subscriber.

Summary

Networks can be a valued addition to a corporation or even a small company. The type of network chosen will dictate features and functions available for users, programmers, and others accessing the network.

Networks are comprised of protocols. Network protocols themselves are rules defining how things will be done such as remote logons, file transfers, and electronic mail, for example.

The protocol chosen for a network should be based upon the one that best meets users' needs. Consideration for interoperability among different vendor equipment should be taken into account also. Other issues may need evaluation, and each site should be able to define its own needs.

The physical layout of a network can vary. The site can dictate this to some degree, but many protocols dictate which physical arrangement must be used with network implementations. In any case, economics always plays a major role in which network topology is used.

The difference between the physical layout of a network and the logical implementation can be confusing, but it is nevertheless important. The term backbone should be understood in light of how vendors use it to explain their equipment. Various meanings are currently associated with the term, and as a result confusion abounds.

Getting acclimated to computer networks is half the battle. The remainder of the battle is the constant challenge to remain current, understanding the technology used and changes to existing equipment. The pace of change in network technology continues to escalate with technologies such as ATM and Gigabit Ethernet now on the market.

Now more than ever companies are harnessing the power in networks to leverage company resources. The explosion of the World Wide Web has demonstrated the worldwide scalability of open information systems based on TCP/IP. In its wake, organizations around the world are looking at ways of applying TCP/IP-based technologies to their internal as well as their external networks.

Chapter 3

Network Protocols

Questions answered in this chapter:

What is a networking protocol?

What are some networking protocols?

What is the relationship between TCP/IP and network protocols?

Introduction

What is a protocol? Diplomatic protocols are the established ceremonial forms and courtesies used by diplomats in the exercise of diplomacy. Deviations in the established diplomatic protocol are considered serious breaches of convention and can lead to unfortunate consequences, perhaps even wars. Similarly, communications protocols define acceptable queries and responses between users of a particular network type. The objective, of course, is to provide for the orderly and predictable behavior of hardware and software used in the network.

While governing bodies have established communications protocols to be machine independent, setting down rules and guidelines for the general cases without regard to the specific platforms performing the communications tasks, protocols, in a sense, are very environment oriented. Designers must consider the specific equipment and their peculiarities, or uniqueness, used in assembling network components. A DOS-based machine will not behave identically to a UNIX-based machine in a network unless such behavior differences are accounted for in the design of the network. Currently, the most common method of accounting for machine dependencies in network communications is to purchase third-party software and hardware. Protocols are concerned with every aspect of communications, from equipment physical interfaces and data formats to communication speeds and high-level software interfaces. The objective is to provide users a communications service that is reliable.

Communications protocols are rules that attempt to define specific events that are intended to control, in some acceptable and understandable manner relative to the objective to be accomplished, the devices that are involved in a communications network. The events of interest and the sequence or manner in which they occur define the protocol. Numerous communications protocols exist today. Among these are IEEE 488, RS-232, and IEEE 803.

Why does the world need communications protocols? Variety. Someone said variety is the spice of life. I do not know the context of the statement, but I can certainly see how it may be applicable in some settings and totally inappropriate in others. Variety is certainly the norm in communications. There are many different ways to transport information from end to end, and there are many different ways of encoding information for transport. For any two similar transport or encoding systems to work, a defined set of rules must specify all the particulars of any importance. Two similar transport or encoding systems will provide gibberish, i.e., garbage, results unless all the rules are followed within any specified tolerances. Just as humans need varied behavioral protocols to define acceptable behavior in varied social settings so that human actions may be interpreted with a certain degree of accuracy, so do communications systems need protocols to define acceptable behavior, that all communications between end users of a similar system will be understandable.

What if a rebel, with or without a cause, decides to flaunt convention and attempt to communicate outside the established protocol? A communication outside the established protocol may go unrecognized or result in a message to the sender, and perhaps to the intended recipient, that an unacceptable or unrecognizable communiqué was attempted. Totally unexpected results may occur or, in poorly designed systems, equipment may crash.

OSI Networking Protocol Model

What is a network protocol and which network protocol is needed? To decide this expansive question, a point of reference is needed. A good reference point is a model of what parts should exist in networks. A standards-making body called the International Organization for Standardization has what it calls the Open Systems Interconnection (OSI) model.

This OSI model defines elements that should exist in any network. The OSI model used here will be a reference point to explain basic aspects about network protocols. The OSI model consists of seven layers. To better understand this, picture a cake with seven layers, as shown in Chapter 1, and envision the cake cut in half; the seven layers would be identifiable. The OSI model is similar to the seven-layered cake cut in half. OSI network layers have names and perform specific functions. This model, including the layers and their names, was identified in Figure 1.1.

Before we examine what each layer does, consider this: Envision a network consisting of computers, software, cables, and everything that goes into making a network. Most networks can be divided into layers. Network layers can be explained in accordance with their function. Usually, there is not a one-to-one correspondence when attempting to explain different networks by layers. Some protocols, like TCP/IP, predate the OSI model. In other cases, vendors developing protocols have found that there are advantages in terms of speed, memory, or other efficiency that made it to their advantage to not strictly adhere to the OSI model. Many network protocols do not appear like the OSI model.

A protocol template to use for modeling communications systems is beneficial that we might more easily visualize the underlying concepts. ITU-T (formerly CCITT) developed the Open Systems Interconnection (OSI) model that serves the purpose of a protocol template very well. See Figure 3.1. The OSI model represents a stack of seven layers that can be considered as gradations from simpler to more complex functionality as one goes up the stack. This does not mean that one layer is simpler than another. In fact, each layer in its own right is a complex interworking of rules, hardware, software, and human endeavor.

| Application |
| FTP TELNET SMTP HTTP |
| **Presentation** |
| PAD |
| **Session** |
| DAP SAP PAP |
| **Transport** |
| TCP |
| **Network** |
| IP IPX |
| Connection Connectionless |
| **Data Link** |
| 802.2 802.3 802.4 802.5 |
| HDLC X.25 |
| ATM AAL |
| Media Access Control |
| **Physical** |
| RS422A RS232D RS449 |
| X.21 V.35 V.42 |
| DS-1 DS-3 SONET |

Figure 3.1 Open Systems Interconnection (OSI) model

The OSI model, especially above the physical layer, is really a hierarchical software model that provides for coherent communications between groups of software procedures and/or programs. Each layer can be represented by a software program that communicates only with the layer above and below it. Typically, each layer is comprised of software routines that are called by the next higher or lower layer, when appropriate. The software routines are written for specific communications applications. The interface between higher and lower layer routines is performed by procedure calls known as application programming interface (API) calls.

The first three layers—the physical layer, the data link layer, and the network layer—are closely linked together. Kind of a "you can't have one without the other" sort of thing. The three layers comprise the minimum structure required to establish and maintain communications between two entities (nodes). These three layers, in a sense, pass from node to node in the transmission path and contain, besides the data, source and destination addresses and error-detection information necessary to ensure error-free routing to the correct destination. The control and routing information is called Operations Administration and Management (OAM) data and is added to the user data stream in quantities called headers and trailers. Each layer adds its own headers and trailers to the data "packet." A complete package of data, headers, and trailers that is ready for transmission is called a *datagram*.

The control and routing information is interpreted by switches, routers, gateways, and bridges along the transmission path. The control information and data are bound together until received by the destination, where the control information and data are separated. Generally, the first three layers represented by the OSI model comprise the fundamental ISDN/BISDN software package running on a host processor responsible for the physical switching duties. The user provides the application-specific software package, comprising the remaining OSI layers, that typically runs on a remote host computer.

layer	functionality
1	physical (repeaters)
2	data link/subnetwork (bridges)
3	network/internetwork (IP gateways)
4	transport/end-to-end (IP hosts)
5	session (remote procedure calls)
6	presentation (data representation)
7	application (mail relays)

Table 3.1 ISO/OSI layers and functionality

Table 3.1 shows the functionality of each layer of the OSI model. The layer function examples shown in the table are not all-inclusive. There is much networking functionality that is not covered in this table. It is intended as a representation only of what types of software modules one will find at each layer.

A layer synopsis from bottom to top includes:

Physical This layer is an interface between the medium and the device. This layer transmits bits (ones and zeroes). Specifically, it transmits voltage or light pulses.

Data Link The main goal of the data link layer is to provide reliable data transfer across a physical link. This layer puts data into frames, transmits these frames sequentially, and ensures they have been received in order by the target host.

Network This layer routes data from one location to another (source to destination). The network protocol in use determines how this layer works. In the case of TCP/IP, this is Internet Protocol (IP).

Transport On the sending node in a network the transport layer takes data from the session layer and puts a header and trailer around the data itself. Some transport protocols ensure the data arrives correctly at the destination; this type of protocol is connection oriented. Conversely, connectionless-oriented protocols do not ensure this. On the receiving node, the transport layer removes the header and trailer and passes the data to the session layer.

Session This layer is considered the user's interface into the network. However, the user is not aware of it. This layer is where logical connections are made with applications. The session layer has addressable endpoints that relate to programs or a user.

Presentation This layer determines data syntax. In short, whether data is ASCII or EBCDIC is determined here. This layer performs encoding values that represent data types being transferred.

Application This layer provides services that software applications require. For example, it provides services necessary for a file transfer program to operate. It is called the application layer because it works with or is a provider of services to applications (in certain network protocols).

Different network protocols can be evaluated with the OSI model serving as a baseline. OSI itself is a network protocol, but the focus here is TCP/IP. It was once thought that everyone might switch to the OSI network protocol. Various parts of the federal government issued mandates for future compliance. State governments mandated state agencies to plan for a conversion to OSI. However, very few organizations actually built an OSI network. Sensing a lack of a sizable market, network vendors developed hardware and software to build the kind of networks that their customers would purchase today. The OSI protocol may be the protocol of the future that ends up as a historical footnote. The OSI model, however, provides an excellent framework for discussion of how various parts of other protocols work. The OSI model will be used later in the book to explore further aspects of TCP/IP.

Data Flow Through a Network

In a network, data flows from the sending node from top to bottom (with respect to layers in the network). This means that as data passes down the network protocol stack, headers and trailers are added to the data at each layer. Likewise, in a network the receiving node's data flows from bottom to top (with respect to the network layers). These headers and trailers are removed by layer as the data moves up the protocol stack.

In some cases the sending node is a terminal user and the receiving entity is an application program. In other cases, both sending and receiving entities can be application programs.

These headers and trailers wrapped around the data include information particular to the needs of a specific layer. For example, the network layer header includes routing information. Consider Figure 1.2, which depicts the OSI model and how headers are added to data as it passes down the OSI protocol stack.

Why Do I Need a Protocol?

Connecting computers, printers, disk drives, terminal servers, communications servers, and other devices requires some form of a network. For a network to function, rules and regulations must be followed. In the technical community, these rules and regulations are called protocols.

During the first decades of computer and network development, vendors tried to use their own protocols to establish a competitive advantage. Apple has AppleTalk; Novell has IPX/SPX; IBM has SNA; Microsoft has NetBIOS; and the list goes on. Vendors call this lock on their customers' computing environment "account control." Users call it an excuse to charge prices that are too high and limit their flexibility in constructing a computer environment that takes the best products from several vendors to meet the diverse computing needs of their organization.

One of the world's largest computing customers, the U.S. Department of Defense, began insisting that the computers it bought be able to communicate using a single common protocol, Transmission Control Protocol/Internet Protocol, or TCP/IP. This didn't mean that the vendors couldn't also offer their own proprietary protocols; it just meant that TCP/IP must also be available. Vendors doing business with the government began offering TCP/IP options—and brought along the purchasing power of the nation's research universities who needed TCP/IP networks to be competitive in their quest for federal research dollars.

Today, the TCP/IP network protocol has grown from one that was primarily of interest to the government, military, universities, and agencies doing business with the government squarely into the mainstream and future direction for computer networks. Because the TCP/IP protocol was developed to be open to all vendors, and not favor one vendor over another, it provides a solid basis to permit different vendor equipment to interoperate. This is a powerful statement. Examples will be provided later, but for now it means if a network is based upon TCP/IP, a DEC computer can communicate with an IBM, Apple, Sun, Silicon Graphics, Hewlett Packard, or just about any vendor's equipment.

A Closer Look at the OSI Model

The layers of the OSI model can be viewed as a "trickle down" hierarchy of software procedures but must also include a "trickle up" hierarchical view as well. While a thorough description and analysis of each OSI model layer is beyond the scope of this book, knowledge of the basic purpose of each layer is useful. In the communications literature, there is often reference to the OSI model and the interworking relationships of the layers. The following discussion serves only as an introduction to the OSI model. The interested reader is encouraged to seek additional information and understanding.

Physical Layer

The physical layer interface of the OSI model is concerned with the various physical interfaces of the equipment. Some of the issues this layer is concerned with are: voltages, electrical currents, frequencies, connectors, and transmission media, such as fiber, coaxial, or twisted-pair. This layer is responsible for the physical generation and transmission of information and control signals. The physical layer interacts with the layer immediately above, the data link layer. Control and data information is passed between layers through a software and hardware

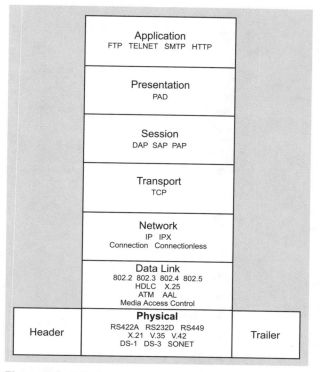

Figure 3.2 OSI physical layer

combination called a Low Level Driver (LLD). The LLD is an electrical circuit that responds to low-level (basic) software commands.

The physical layer controls the physical link between nodes of the communication path. The connections are called physical service access points (PSAPs). It also supervises the specific medium—coaxial, fiber, RF wave, twisted-pair—of the transmission path. And it transmits the bits between nodes. The controlling aspect of the physical layer's job includes such mundane activities as turning things off and on, as appropriate. The supervisory aspect includes monitoring the path and the data to detect conditions conducive to error generation. The transmission portion of its job is to cause the transmission medium to physically emit or receive the signal, either light wave, electrical, or RF wave, that represents the data.

The physical layer responsibilities include the following functions:

- provide the correct electrical signals for the proper transmission medium which can be:

  fiber-optic cable
  coaxial cable
  unshielded twisted-pair wire (UTP)
  shielded twisted-pair (STP)
  RF (satellite, microwave)

- managing the medium before, during, and after the transmission including:

  data (bit) transmission
  physical link control

Some of the specifications that define physical layers for specific types of networks include:

- DS-1 Basic Rate Interface (BRI)
- DS-1 Primary Rate Interface (PRI)
- DS-3
- SONET
- RS-422A
- RS-423
- RS-232D
- RS-449
- B-ISDN
- N-ISDN
- V.xx (21, 22, 26, 27, 29, 32, 42, etc.)

The physical layer interface may attach a trailer, header, or both to the data element. The trailer/header includes control information about the source and destination address, and error-control information.

Data Link Layer

The data link layer is responsible for establishing a connection between networks, framing the data and control bits, and ensuring data integrity. The data integrity function provides flow and error control of the data transmitted over the physical link. The data link layer operates on the physical devices involved in the electrical transmission of the data.

A primitive is a term used to describe a "request for circuit connection," "request for circuit deactivation," or a "request to transfer data." *Primitives* are software routines of the lowest kind, in a manner of speaking. The data link layer uses a defined set of primitives (basic software routines) that control the physical devices. An LLD interprets the primitives and manipulates the appropriate control circuits, typically called registers, that activate the circuit devices involved in determining the actual physical transmission path.

	Application FTP TELNET SMTP HTTP	
	Presentation PAD	
	Session DAP SAP PAP	
	Transport TCP	
	Network IP IPX Connection Connectionless	
Header	**Data Link** 802.2 802.3 802.4 802.5 HDLC X.25 ATM AAL Media Access Control	Trailer
Header	Physical RS422A RS232D RS449 X.21 V.35 V.42 DS-1 DS-3 SONET	Trailer

Figure 3.3 OSI data link layer

The data link layer includes the media access control (MAC). The MAC is just what it says it is. It is responsible for loading data into the transmission medium and unloading data received by the transmission medium. The MAC includes buffers (bit buckets or, more appropriately nowadays, byte barrels) to hold data going to/from the transmit and receive paths. The MAC is able to accommodate differences in speed between applications and mediums to some degree. Also, the MAC frames the bits into ATM cells, both coming and going. And the MAC can request retransmission of data, if required.

The data link layer also includes the Logical Link Control (LLC) sublayer. The LLC is the logical element that controls acknowledged, unacknowledged, connection-oriented, and connectionless-oriented services for the network node. The LLC manages and controls the flow of information into and out of the node based on the type of network connection bought and paid for.

The data link layer responsibilities include:

- Establishing a physical connection (called building a connection) between nodes
- Deactivating a physical connection (called tearing down a connection) between nodes
- Framing the individual bits before transmission
- Framing the individual bits after reception
- Retransmission service for protocol data units (PDUs)
- Detecting transmission errors
- Ensuring proper addressing
- Controlling the flow (speed) of data

Some data link layer specifications include:

- ATM Adaptation Layer (AAL)
- ATM Layer
- IEEE 802.2
- IEEE 802.3
- IEEE 802.4
- IEEE 802.5
- HDLC
- X.25
- ISDN

The data link layer attaches a trailer, header, or both to the data element. The trailer/header includes control information about the source and destination address, and error-control information.

Network Layer

The network layer is intended to provide the upper layers a high degree of freedom from specific network connection protocols such as voice analog modem protocols V.xx. The network layer is therefore involved in the setup and teardown of connections. Also, the network layer identifies the connection as connection oriented or connectionless oriented. Sometimes, it is also used in data transfer. The network layer provides routing and addressing information to its adjacent layers. It is the uppermost layer of the three chained layers. The network layer also provides for the orderly interconnecting of both similar and dissimilar networks.

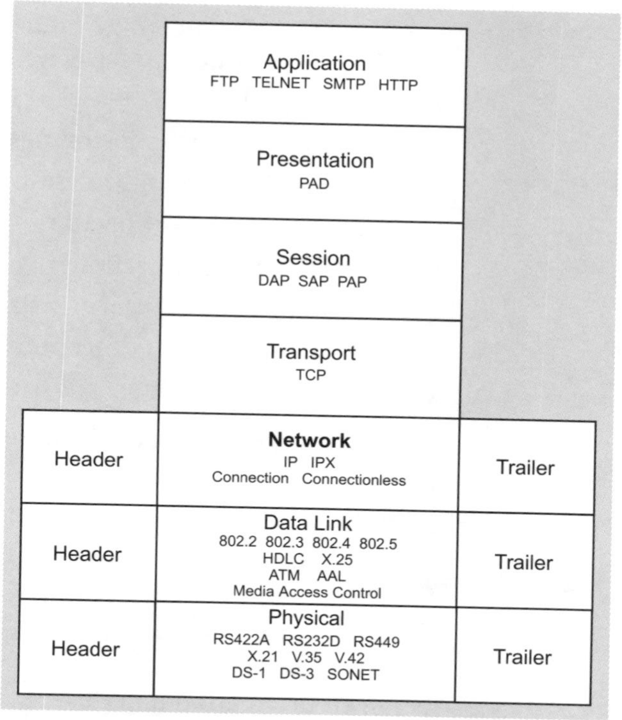

The network layer, which includes a predefined set of route tables, will calculate the open-shortest-path-first route used to identify the route the data will take from source to destination. In order to minimize the number of blocked transmissions (and therefore maximize revenue), the open-shortest-path-first routine examines the current connections and determines an appropriate transmission path that is not currently in use. As the name states, the routine looks for the shortest

Header	Application FTP TELNET SMTP HTTP	
	Presentation PAD	
	Session DAP SAP PAP	
	Transport TCP	
Header	**Network** IP IPX Connection Connectionless	Trailer
Header	Data Link 802.2 802.3 802.4 802.5 HDLC X.25 ATM AAL Media Access Control	Trailer
Header	Physical RS422A RS232D RS449 X.21 V.35 V.42 DS-1 DS-3 SONET	Trailer

Figure 3.4 OSI network layer

path available. In many instances, particularly in LAN applications, there may be only one choice and the calculation really does not exist. However, in the public sector, there could be thousands of choices available. Do you want the Russian operator or the Chinese operator to listen to your Washington, D.C.-Bombay conversation?

This aspect of communications has extremely important implications for video applications. And ATM/ADSL are very much concerned with video applications. Video that is sent to a user destination, stored, then played back at the user's leisure is not too worrisome. But live video must traverse the transmission path in the exact order sent and the transmission delay from source to destination must be negligible; otherwise the quality of the picture suffers dramatically. While the shortest path available may be okay for voice and bursty data communications, it probably is not any good for live video.

Here is $10,000 worth of consulting advice. The network layer includes the Management Information Base (MIB). The MIB is a difficult-to-read (and understand) software database that includes all of the known information regarding the network node. If you want the network to provide you any particular information, reports, etc., concerning the status of individual connections or group of connections (by location, SVC, PVC, port, switch, etc.), ask someone (Engineering? Sometimes they do not understand the MIB.) if it is in the MIB. If the answer is no, don't waste your time trying to get network information that does not exist.

The network layer responsibilities include:

▸ Determining the transmission path

▸ Establishing the connection

▸ Releasing the connection

▸ Transmitting and receiving data

▸ Acknowledging data reception

▸ Requesting data retransmission

Some network layer specifications include:

▸ IP

▸ IPX

Transport Layer

The transport layer is responsible for the delivery of data between origination and destination within the bounds of established reliability levels. There are five defined levels of reliability. The reliability level is established by the type of service requested from the service provider. This layer is also responsible for data multiplexing and demultiplexing. ATM does not utilize the transport layer functionality. ADSL does.

The five reliability levels are simple, multiplexing, basic error recovery, error recovery and multiplexing, and error detection and recovery class. For simple reliability, flow control and connection

	Application FTP TELNET SMTP HTTP	
	Presentation PAD	
	Session DAP SAP PAP	
Header	**Transport** TCP	Trailer
Header	Network IP IPX Connection Connectionless	Trailer
Header	Data Link 802.2 802.3 802.4 802.5 HDLC X.25 ATM AAL Media Access Control	Trailer
Header	Physical RS422A RS232D RS449 X.21 V.35 V.42 DS-1 DS-3 SONET	Trailer

Figure 3.5 OSI transport layer

release are provided by the underlying network layers. Multiplexing utilizes flow control but does not specifically utilize error control which is provided by the underlying layers. Basic error recovery does not utilize flow control but can detect errors and provide some error control functionality. Error recovery and multiplexing utilizes flow control, error detection, and correction. Error detection, and recovery utilizes flow control, error detection and correction including retransmission, routing around network path failures, and detecting and reacting to link inactivity.

The transport layer responsibilities include:

▲ Ordering the establishment of connections

▲ Ordering the release of connections

▲ Notifying the source of errors

▲ Establishing the priority order of multiple users

▲ Multiplexing and demultiplexing data

Some transport layer specifications include:

▲ TCP

▲ UDP

▲ SPX

▲ TP0, TP1, TP2, TP3, TP4

▲ SPP

▲ SEP

▲ ADSP

▲ VIPC

▲ VSPP

Session Layer

The session layer establishes and maintains the exchange of data between origination and destination. Also, the session layer must provide for an orderly recovery from failures caused by any number of predictable and unpredictable events. This layer is the lowest layer of an application-oriented communications software program.

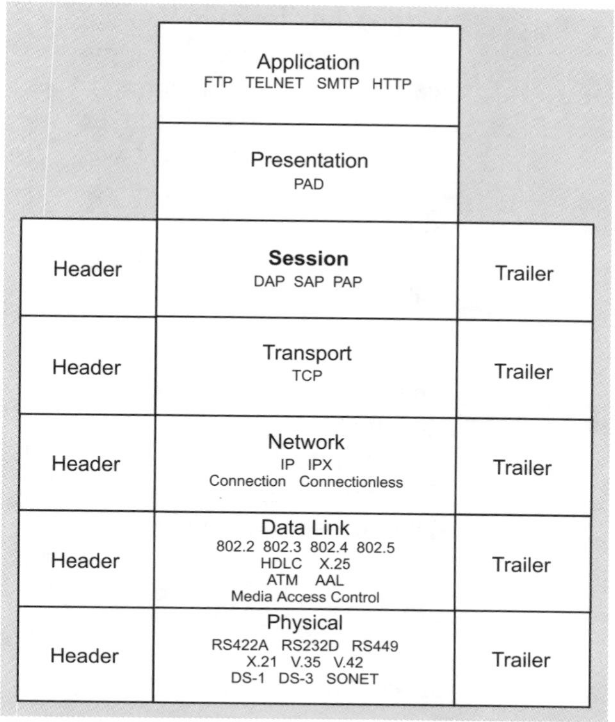

Header	Application FTP TELNET SMTP HTTP	
	Presentation PAD	
Header	**Session** DAP SAP PAP	Trailer
Header	Transport TCP	Trailer
Header	Network IP IPX Connection Connectionless	Trailer
Header	Data Link 802.2 802.3 802.4 802.5 HDLC X.25 ATM AAL Media Access Control	Trailer
Header	Physical RS422A RS232D RS449 X.21 V.35 V.42 DS-1 DS-3 SONET	Trailer

Figure 3.6 OSI session layer

The session layer is responsible for:

▶ Data transfer to/from the lower layers

▶ Establishing the connection

▶ Releasing the connection

▶ Re-establishing a broken connection

▶ Enforcing protocols between applications

Some session layer specifications include:

▶ DAP

▶ RPC

▶ SAP

▶ DNS

▶ SCP

▶ ASP

▶ PAP

Presentation Layer

The presentation layer is responsible for manipulating the data such that the application host will understand it. As an example, this layer residing on a UNIX host will interpret DOS formatted data so that the UNIX machine will understand the data correctly. A common interpretation issue addressed by this layer is the different method of using the carriage return/line feed in files between UNIX- and DOS-based machines.

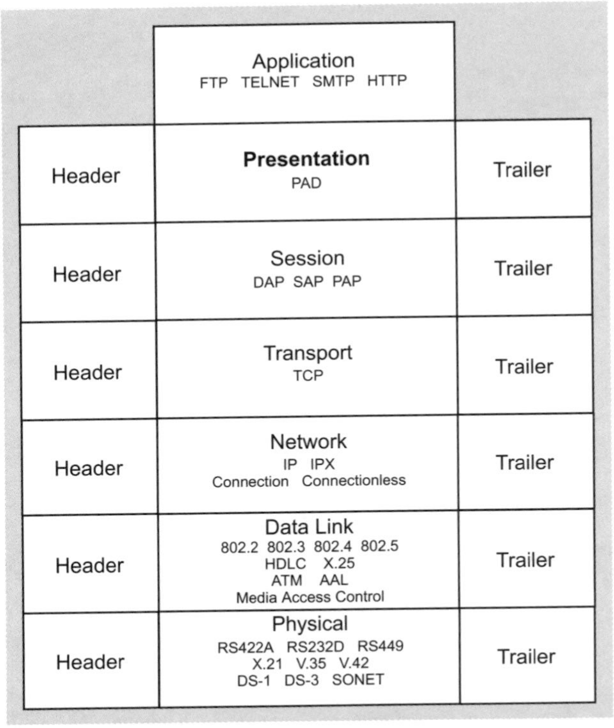

Some presentation layer responsibilities are:

▶ Establishing the connection

	Application FTP TELNET SMTP HTTP	
Header	**Presentation** PAD	Trailer
Header	Session DAP SAP PAP	Trailer
Header	Transport TCP	Trailer
Header	Network IP IPX Connection Connectionless	Trailer
Header	Data Link 802.2 802.3 802.4 802.5 HDLC X.25 ATM AAL Media Access Control	Trailer
Header	Physical RS422A RS232D RS449 X.21 V.35 V.42 DS-1 DS-3 SONET	Trailer

Figure 3.7 OSI presentation layer

▲ Releasing the connection

▲ Negotiating and formatting platform-independent data syntax (i.e., DOS vs. UNIX)

▲ Encrypting and decrypting the data

Some presentation layer specifications are:

▲ LPP

▲ NCP

▲ NetBIOS

▲ X.25 PAD (Packet Assembler/Disassembler)

Application Layer

The application layer is responsible for providing the interface between lower layers and the user's application programs. It is rich with application programming interface (API) function calls. The application layer utilizes the API function calls to pass data and control information to and from the lower layers.

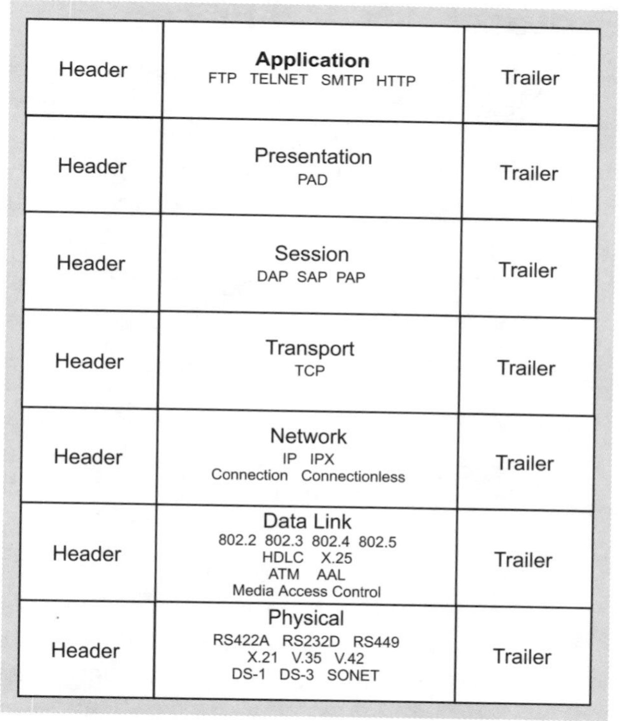

Some application layer responsibilities include:

▲ Providing an interface between the network and user applications

▲ Requesting the execution of an operation (i.e., file transfer to a printer)

▲ Reporting the results of operation execution (file sent to printer)

Header	**Application** FTP TELNET SMTP HTTP	Trailer
Header	Presentation PAD	Trailer
Header	Session DAP SAP PAP	Trailer
Header	Transport TCP	Trailer
Header	Network IP IPX Connection Connectionless	Trailer
Header	Data Link 802.2 802.3 802.4 802.5 HDLC X.25 ATM AAL Media Access Control	Trailer
Header	Physical RS422A RS232D RS449 X.21 V.35 V.42 DS-1 DS-3 SONET	Trailer

Figure 3.8 OSI application layer

▲ Reporting the status of an operation (printer out of paper, cannot print)

▲ Aborting an operation

▲ Error and flow control

Some application layer specifications include:

- NFT (Network File Transfer)
- RFA (Remote File Access)
- NTP (Network Time Protocol)
- TFTP (Trivial File Transfer Protocol)
- NFS (Network File System)
- SNA/FS File Services
- FTAM (File Transfer and Access Management)
- VT (Virtual Terminal)
- PostScript

Protocol Bits and Pieces

There are data communications protocols that exist to provide the orderly exchange of information in a network. One such protocol is Transmission Control Protocol/Internet Protocol (TCP/IP). TCP/IP was originally developed by the Department of Defense to connect or network Department of Defense computers with university computers. TCP/IP is a set of rules used by software programmers who write networking code. There are other network protocols, usually proprietary.

Every protocol must specify how the network components will identify data and control information. A fundamental component of network protocols is the grouping of data and control information into clearly defined and therefore manageable buckets called *frames*. The most basic component of a frame is the simple binary bit. Bits are grouped into bytes, which consist of eight bits. The bytes are then grouped together into frames. Frames are grouped together to form packets.

The position of the bits in a byte and the position of the bytes in the frame determine if the network components will interpret the bits as data or as control information. The bits are transmitted serially, that is, one after the other. Depending upon the network software, the first bit in a byte is either interpreted as the most significant bit (big endian) or as the least significant bit (little endian). And the network software also must interpret each transmitted or received byte as either big endian or little endian. The choice of big endian or little endian is not significant as long as all the network components interpret the bits and bytes in the same fashion.

Why do we care about upper layer protocols when TCP/IP is itself a lower layer (layers 2 and 3) protocol? Because TCP/IP may interwork with all protocol layers.

Frames

One of the key components of a network protocol is the ability to group electrical signals into precise, meaningful units. Meaningful for whom or what? Well, eventually, meaningful to the end user, which may or may not be a human (how about automatic feeders for livestock?), and certainly meaningful to the hardware and software that acts upon or reacts to the individual signals. Electrical signals that are without a precise, known ordering based upon some defined relationship are not much more useful than noise. To facilitate the precise, known order necessary for intelligent communication, electrical signals called bits are grouped into ordered units. The typical bit arrangement of modern networks is called a frame. Each protocol must define the bit framing relationships used to pass information from source to destination. The following is a more in-depth look at bit framing.

The objective of a communications network is to reliably transfer information from source to destination within some specified performance criteria, such as speed and bandwidth utilization. In order to accomplish the purpose of communications networks, communications protocols specify how a system will segment and package the data, called a Protocol Data Unit (PDU). Segmentation and packaging of the user data is necessary to maximize the use of the available bandwidth due to the bursty nature of data communications. Each data package, or PDU, is called a frame. Contained within the PDU is not only the user data but also routing and frame control information. The routing and frame control data is called the PDU header. The data is called, interestingly enough, the data unit. In terms of the OSI communications model, a frame is a group of data at the data link layer while a group of frames forms a packet at the network layer.

PVCs/SVCs

A LAN connecting several computers together in an office setting represents a communications network that does not need to be switched to perform its intended function. Each computer is hard-wired to the server. However, a server connected to another computer through the public switched telephone network in a dial-up mode is switched. An example of such a network is an office LAN whose server provides Internet access to the office client computers by dialing up the Internet.

Communications networks may or may not be switched between source and destination, depending upon the application and the geographical location of the system elements. WANs, GANs, and the Internet are examples of networks that must pass data through switched intermediate networks. Also, any particular user may have the ability to connect to more than one other user. If a network connection is not switched, it is referred to as a *permanent virtual circuit* (PVC). When a network connection is switched, it is referred to as a *switched virtual circuit* (SVC).

PDUs

In order to route data from the source to the proper destination, whether the network is switched or not, the PDU contains the address of the sender and the address of the receiver of the data. Regardless of the network topology—token ring, Ethernet, or some other topology—including the address of both the sender and intended receiver in the PDU provides some measure of confidence that the data will reach its correct destination. And the correct destination will recognize who sent the data.

The use of sender and receiver addresses in the PDU gives a network the freedom to route PDUs through the network in the most efficient manner possible, allowing the network to maximize bandwidth usage. The result is one PDU may follow a specific path through the network while the next PDU may follow a different path. Also, PDUs may be buffered, or held temporarily, by network elements due to the network link status (busy), the intended receiver not ready to receive, or supercession by higher priority traffic. Yes, Uncle Sam can preempt your Internet session and so can companies that have paid telecommunications companies for a higher class of service. The result? Not all PDUs arrive at the destination in order of transmission, and the delay between each PDU's arrival at the destination can vary significantly. Such routing of the data is anathema to audio- and video-based applications.

CRC

To determine if the PDU is corrupted when received, the PDU contains an eight-bit byte (octet) that represents a magical number called a CRC (cyclic redundancy check). The CRC is calculated by the sender using a polynomial and the number of ones (or zeroes) bits then stuffed into the PDU. Upon receipt, the receiver calculates the CRC based upon the number of ones (or zeroes) bits received and compares the number calculated to the CRC received. If the two numbers are equal, the receiver can assume, with a high degree of accuracy (better than 1 in 10^{12}), that the data received was actually the data sent.

However, if the CRC calculation by the receiver does not match the number transmitted, the receiver can perform some sleight of hand and may be able to reconstruct the correct data, using the transmitted CRC. But sometimes the tricks do not work and the receiver must ask the sender to retransmit the corrupted PDU. Such retransmission of the data is anathema to audio and video-based applications.

System Performance

So we are shipping PDUs all around the countryside and we do not have good control over when they reach their destination and in what order. This situation is okay for data communications applications that do not have an intimate relationship with time. But if the data is time sensitive, such as video and multimedia, then data processing issues such as time lapses and delays result in unacceptable system performance.

To provide the throughput necessary to support process-sensitive communication applications a better method is needed. Fortunately, just when we were beginning to need it most, ATM was discovered! Actually, the real story is our transmission systems (SONET) have become sufficiently reliable that we can now do away with much of the header overhead, giving us a speedy PDU.

Frame Structures

To really appreciate the benefits of ATM, and to understand why ATM is much faster than legacy systems, a look at the framing used by some legacy systems is worthwhile. When one understands where one has been, it is much clearer to see where one is going.

Header Type	Field	Size
802.3	destination address	6 bytes
802.3	source address	6 bytes
802.3	length	2 bytes
802.2	destination SAP	I byte
802.2	source SAP	I byte
802.2	control data	I byte

Table 3.2 IEEE 802.3 framing with 802.2 headers

Table 3.2 shows the framing organization for Ethernet IEEE 802.3 with IEEE 802.2 headers. Novell Netware networks use this type of framing by default. It is the framing type automatically selected when the network software for a Novell Netware adapter driver is installed. Novell sets the Service Advertising Protocol (SAP) field to 0xe0, specifying that the upper layer protocol is IPX.

Header Type	Field	Size
802.3	destination address	6 bytes
802.3	source address	6 bytes
802.3	length	2 bytes
802.3	0xffff	2 bytes
	data	x

Table 3.3 IEEE 802.3 framing

IEEE 802.3 framing, shown in Table 3.3, is used most often in Novell networks that use Netware 2.x/3.x servers. Since Novell developed this framing while IEEE 802.3 was still being developed, it is not 100 percent IEEE 802.3 compliant. The data size is unlimited as indicated by the "x."

Header Type	Field	Size
Ethernet II	destination address	6 bytes
Ethernet II	source address	6 bytes
Ethernet II	type	2 bytes
	data	x

Table 3.4 Ethernet II framing

Ethernet II framing is an attempt to simplify framing and header overhead.

Header Type	Field	Size
802.3	destination address	6 bytes
802.3	source address	6 bytes
802.3	length	2 bytes
802.2	0xaa	I byte
802.2	0xaa	I byte
802.2	UI	I byte
SNAP	protocol ID	I byte
SNAP	type	I byte
	data	x

Table 3.5 Ethernet SNAP framing

Ethernet SNAP framing, shown in Table 3.5, allows networks to use Ethernet II frames on IEEE-compliant networks without any modification to the network. Notice the use of three protocol headers in the frame: IEEEE 802.2, IEEE 802.3, and SNAP.

Header Type	Field	Size
802.5	AC	I byte
802.5	FC	I byte
802.5	destination address	6 bytes
802.5	source address	6 bytes
802.5	routing data	0-I8 bytes
802.2	destination SAP	I byte
802.2	source SAP	I byte
802.2	control	I byte
	data	x

Table 3.6 Token Ring framing

As shown in Table 3.6, Token Ring framing includes the SAP field which Novell sets to 0xe0 to indicate that the upper layer protocol is IPX. Token Ring framing is specified by IEEE 802.5 and IEEE 802.2.

Header Type	Field	Size
802.5	AC	1 byte
802.5	FC	1 byte
802.5	destination address	6 bytes
802.5	source address	6 bytes
802.5	routing data	0-18 bytes
802.2	0xaa	1 byte
802.2	0xaa	1 byte
802.2	UI	1 byte
SNAP	protocol ID	1 byte
SNAP	type	1 byte
	data	x

Table 3.7 Token Ring SNAP framing

Token Ring SNAP framing, illustrated in Table 3.7, allows networks to use Ethernet II frames on IEEE-compliant networks without any modification to the network. Notice the use of three protocol headers in the frame: IEEE 802.2, IEEE 802.5, and SNAP.

But What Does It All Mean?

Framing is really a TCP issue and not an IP issue. The OSI model features and constraints of the first three layers are well represented in the features offered by TCP/IP as a transmission and data link switching technology working with a protocol such as Ethernet or Token Ring.

Summary

ISO is moving forward with new Internet protocols that are compliant with the OSI model. These protocols are found in Europe, which is to be expected since ISO is primarily a European agency. As the percentage of businesses connected to a network on the continent increases, the desire to interconnect to TCP/IP-based protocols will increase. The IETF will need to support interoperation of OSI protocols and TCP/IP protocols with appropriate emulation of the OSI protocols. One such circumstance already exists. RFC 1006 specifies the particulars for a TCP/IP-based host to emulate TP0, necessary for TCP/IP to support OSI applications. Some industry analysts think the Internet will eventually support both TCP/IP and OSI protocols in tandem. Then, OSI applications can run using the full OSI stack on the Internet.

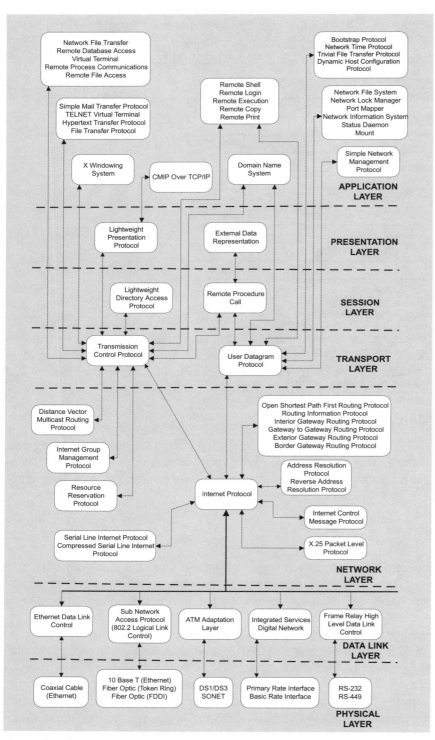

Figure 3.9 depicts the various relationships between the TCP/IP protocols and where they fit on the OSI model. It now becomes easy to see how the different protocols relate to one another. Observe that IP and TCP/UDP form toll gates that all lines to and from other protocols must pass through. TCP/IP clearly runs the networking show.

Figure 3.9 The total picture

Chapter 4

Transmission Control Protocol

Questions answered in this chapter:

What are ports?

What are sockets?

What is the format of a TCP segment?

What information does a TCP segment contain?

How does TCP manage a reliable connection?

Introduction

Two transmission protocols are covered in this chapter. One is the already somewhat familiar TCP and the other is User Datagram Protocol (UDP). UDP actually forms the foundation of TCP, so it is fitting that UDP be covered in this chapter. Basically, TCP is UDP with a more reliable personality. Unless otherwise specified, whenever the discussion refers to TCP, it is assumed the information is also applicable to UDP. The discussion will point out the differences between the two protocols when it is appropriate.

TCP is actually the protocol that directs datagrams to the correct application layer services while providing some degree of reliability for the successful transmission of the datagrams. Transmission Control Protocol is specified in RFC 793. It is a transmission level protocol. TCP is designed to take datagrams from the appropriate application layer service, include error control and management information to the datagram, and send the datagram on down the pike to the network level. In a reverse process, TCP receives the datagram from the network layer and sends it on to the appropriate application layer service. UDP performs the same functions sans the error control.

The formal declaration of the intent of TCP is covered quite well in the Internet documentation. RFC 793 states "the Transmission Control Protocol

(TCP) is intended for use as a highly reliable host-to-host protocol between hosts in packet-switched computer communication networks, and in interconnected systems of such networks." TCP is a connection-oriented, source-to-destination, and (the flip side) destination-to-source (also known as end-to-end) reliable transmission protocol intended to perform in a layered hierarchy (IP below and application services such as Telnet above) of protocols that support internetwork applications.

TCP is software modules that require an operating system platform to function. Typical operating systems include UNIX and Windows. Some might argue the classification of Windows as an operating system but the assertion is sufficient to illustrate the need for UDP and TCP to work with other software modules that provide basic computing functionality such as keyboard, input/output, and file management. The details regarding the need for Windows to utilize the functionality of a disk operating system (MS-DOS) to provide its own functionality may be lost on the networking neophyte and is not the focus of this text. Anyway, TCP operates within the confines of other software modules and calls upon those functions necessary to help get its job done. As an example, TCP may call upon low-level device drivers to assist with such mundane activities as managing data structures.

Windows users may view or set up their TCP "properties" by clicking on Start|Settings|Control Panel and then double-clicking on Network and TCP/IP. Then the user is presented with various TCP/IP "properties" or variables that can be modified. However, it still takes an application program, such as one provided by an Internet service provider to dial-up users, to initiate the TCP/IP module. Remember the OSI protocol model and where TCP fit in? As a gentle reminder, a portion of the OSI model is replicated in Figure 4.1.

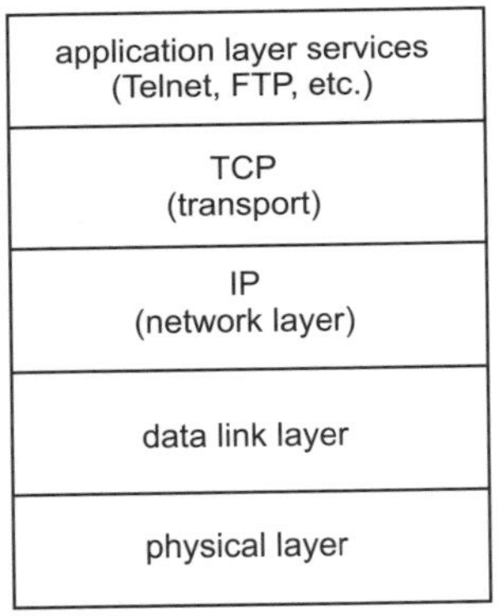

application layer services (Telnet, FTP, etc.)
TCP (transport)
IP (network layer)
data link layer
physical layer

Figure 4.1 TCP and the OSI model

For consumers, a compatible application program provided by an ISP is necessary to connect to the Internet. This ISP-provided application program is represented by the topmost layer in Figure 4.1. Actually, the consumer can use a free version of Telnet to connect to any Internet site. However, that is not the same as connecting to THE Internet (e-mail, Usenet, etc.). The ISP-provided application program is just another software "module" that plugs into and works with other software modules, of which TCP and IP are just two more. In any case, the point is there are many software modules interworking to bring the glorious features of the World Wide Web and its offspring, the Internet, into your home or office with TCP and IP the central figures in a cast of many software modules.

TCP Interfaces

TCP interfaces on the higher level side to application layer services and on the lower side to an Internet protocol (IP). TCP is a software program itself and calls upon software routines and programs whenever the need arises. In the actual TCP software, there are no obvious distinctions between "upper level" or "lower level" protocol routines. Just like the recruit who spends all day fruitlessly wandering around the airbase looking for five gallons of prop wash, so too is the novice programmer searching through the code looking for "upper level" routines. There are just software routines and programs to call and pass parameters to and from. It is in the documentation that a great distinction is made between "upper" and "lower," that we might more easily visualize the relationships among all the various software routines and programs.

The software interface between an application service, such as FTP, and TCP consists of a set of software routines similar to the routines an operating system provides to an application service for manipulating files. Routines to open connections, close connections, transmit data on the established connections, and receive data on established connections are part of the routines.

Two processes accomplish the exchange of data by making software calls to the TCP, then passing buffers of data as arguments. On the transmit side, TCP partitions the buffered data into groups of bits called segments, adds the TCP header information to the data segments which are now called datagrams, then calls on the IP to transmit the datagrams to the destination process, usually IP. The receive side of the connection removes the header information from the datagram, places the resulting data segment into a buffer, then notifies the receive process of the reception of data.

The TCP software does have readily identifiable routines to accomplish establishing the connection, receiving, and passing the data. The routines are OPEN, CLOSE, SEND, RECEIVE, ABORT, and STATUS. These routines operate in much the same manner as operating system calls such as open a file or close a file. OPEN will open a TCP connection for communication; CLOSE will close a TCP connection; SEND will prepare TCP to send data; RECEIVE will prepare TCP to receive data; ABORT will cancel the current SEND or RECEIVE; and STATUS will return to the application program the current status of the connection. Each of these routines is covered in some detail in later paragraphs and chapters.

In the TCP interfaces, provision is made for identifying the sender of the data and the intended recipient. TCP would not be of much use to anyone if the TCP datagrams did not include such addressing information.

When the TCP requires the attention of the user process, it signals a user process/program that it has data for processing and certain information is passed to the user process. The information passed may be an error message or information relating to the completion of processing a RECEIVE, a SEND, or some other user call. The TCP provides the user process the following information every time it signals the user process:

Local Connection Name: TCP always passes the local connection name to the user process

Response String: TCP always passes a response string to the user process. The response string may be one of several different types. In the case of a SEND call, the response string will be a status string informing the user process if the data was acknowledged by the recipient. If the recipient does not acknowledge the data within the allowable time, the user process must decide if the data should be resent.

Send & Receive Buffer Address: TCP will pass the send or receive buffer address if appropriate. Status messages do not require the buffer addresses. The user process must know the buffer addresses so that it will know where to fetch or send data bits and bytes that form a part of the bit stream involved in the flow of information between the two parties of the connection.

Received Byte Count: TCP will pass the receive byte count if it is passing receive data to the user process.

Received Push Flag: If the receive push flag is set, the TCP will notify the user process.

Received Urgent Flag: If the receive urgent flag is set, the TCP will notify the user process.

The TCP depends upon a Lower Level Interface (LLI) software module to actually send and receive information over the network. In our case, the LLI module is the Internet Protocol. But other LLIs exist and some are designed to work with TCP. If the LLI is IP (or any other protocol that provides IP-like features) and source routing is used, the LLI must allow the route information to be communicated from the source TCP to the destination TCP. Inclusion of the source and destination addresses in the IP datagram is especially important so that the correct checksum values are calculated using the originating source and the ultimate destination. Also, the return route must be preserved to be able to answer connection requests. The source TCP will have to provide the source address, destination address, protocol fields, and the TCP length to the LLI. If the LLI is IP, TCP provides arguments for Type of Service and time-to-live parameters. TCP uses the following values for these parameters:

Type of Service =
precedence:routine,
delay:normal,
throughput:normal,
reliability:normal; or 00000000.

time-to-live =
one minute; or 00111100.

The time-to-live parameter determines how long an IP datagram/IP segment, called a packet now, can bounce around a network before the network routers will drop, or "kill," it as undeliverable. The time-to-live value of one minute assumes a maximum segment lifetime of two minutes. That is, a time-to-live of one minute means the packet has one minute to get from source to destination and then there is one minute for the original source to receive a received-packet acknowledgment from the original destination. In other words, the maximum value for the round trip from source to destination back to source will be twice the time-to-live value.

Ports

Port is the name given to the logical connection between the IP and a higher level process such as Telnet or FTP. Each host can bind ports to processes independently of any other host. Also, every host is capable of determining the port number and process assignments of every computer they connect to by querying the other computer's port mapper. The port mapper is a dynamic process that assigns or allocates the next available port number to a process. However, there are certain useful "community" ports that are commonly used by many hosts. To expedite service between hosts, it is useful to assign these community processes fixed port numbers and call them "well-known port numbers." There are several well-known ports of particular interest to us. Table 4.1 lists several of the well-known ports and their associated service.

Name	Port	Service
qotd	17	Quote of the Day
chargen	19	Character Generator
ftp-data	20	File Transfer [Default Data]
ftp	21	File Transfer [Control]
telnet	23	Telnet
	24	Any private mail system
smtp	25	Simple Mail Transfer
	35	Any private printer server
time	37	Time

Name	Port	Service
rap	38	Route Access Protocol
rlp	39	Resource Location Protocol
graphics	41	Graphics
nameserver	42	Host Name Server
nicname	43	Who Is
nicname	44	MPM FLAGS Protocol
login	49	Login Host Protocol
domain	53	Domain Name Server
bootps	67	Bootstrap Protocol Server
bootpc	68	Bootstrap Protocol Client
tftp	69	Trivial File Transfer
gopher	70	Gopher
www-http	80	World Wide Web HTTP
hostname	101	NIC Host Name Server
pop3	110	Post Office Protocol - Version 3

Table 4.1 A few "well-known" port numbers

Figure 4.2
No sweat

Perhaps the most significant idea to get out of this discussion is the idea that the port identifies for the data stream which application it is supposed to go to. If there is only one application running at a time, there is really no need to associate the data with the application. The data can only go to one application, as in Figure 4.2.

However, with a client/server computing model, concurrent processing allows multiple applications to exist simultaneously. Additionally, multiple copies of the same application can exist simultaneously. Now, where does the data go?

With port addressing, there is never any doubt. There is one application incarnation, and only one application incarnation, associated with the connection and the users of that connection. Port addressing is fundamentally a component of traffic management. Similar to the traffic cop standing in the intersection, port addressing ensures the data goes in the right direction.

Figure 4.3 Which way to data

Figure 4.4 Port addressing

Does it make any difference which port is used for a particular application? In the great scheme of life, no, it doesn't. In the long ago days of yesteryear, port number assignments were fixed and listed in files. Port numbers below 1024 were reserved by the original internetwork design team for common applications. Port numbers 1024 and above were available for use by the networking community for use with any applications desirable. Now, dynamic port mappers negotiate between hosts to establish the port used for that particular communication link. Some dynamic mappers ignore the reserved well-known numbers and assign port numbers based upon their own unique numbering scheme. Generally, these dynamic mappers just assign the next unused port number. But, most TCP varieties do recognize the well-known port numbers as reserved for the specified processes.

To prevent a conflict between a system that reserves well-known port numbers and one that dynamically allocates all port numbers, the network manager should start the system services in a certain order. The first services to start are those well-known port number services that are available continuously. Besides the obvious choices in this category, such as FTP at port 21 and Telnet at port 23, the network manager should include rpcbind at port 111. rpcbind is the port mapper! Next, start inetd. inetd automatically creates sockets for the application services with reserved port numbers but which run only when demanded. An example of this service is chargen on port 19. Finally, start any platform-unique services that dynamically allocate port numbers, such as Sun's RPC services.

The operating system kernel actually makes the port number assignment while the port mapper is a file list of the currently active port numbers as they are assigned. However, the port mapper discussed above is the software routine that must still prod the kernel to make the assignment.

Sockets

A *socket* identifies the unique source or destination to or from which information is transmitted in the network. A socket is also identified by the host in which the sending or receiving process is located. The socket is specified as a 32-bit number where even-numbered sockets identify receiving sockets and odd-numbered sockets identify sending sockets.

Figure 4.5 illustrates the idea of sockets quite well. Some "device" plugs into the receptacle of a host computer. The receptacle is connected to a specific application on that host and is identified by the connection socket number. In reality, the figure should also include a receptacle on the other end of the cord to illustrate that the other host

Figure 4.5 A socket connection

participating in the connection is also "plugged" into a socket on its end of the transmission.

Sockets assigned to each host must be uniquely associated with a known process running on that host or be undefined. The names of some sockets must be universally known (well-known ports) and associated with a known process operating with a specified protocol (i.e., FTP). The names of other sockets might not be well known, but are given in a transmission over a well-known socket.

Typically, server processes are in demand from several to many clients simultaneously. The ability for one server to provide services to many clients at the same time is the heart of the client/server computing model. To accommodate the traffic demands, a server must be able to "plug in" as many clients as possible at the same time. Sockets are a way of providing the "plug-in" capability needed to fulfill the needs of the client/server computing model. By adding more sockets, the server can accommodate more clients, until system resources reach their maximum ability to deal with clients.

A socket is just a way of identifying a connection between two hosts, which may be a server and a client, or perhaps just two computers connected to exchange files. Communication over the network is from one socket to another socket with each socket being identified with a user process running at a known host.

The socket is formed when the internet protocol concatenates the port number with the network and host addresses. So, a pair of sockets (one socket on each end of the connection) uniquely specifies a connection (the network and host addresses) and a process (the port number).

If we take the next step in this line of reasoning we will discover that any socket can be used simultaneously in multiple connections. That is, the server running a process on a particular port number, such as time on port 37, may connect to multiple clients demanding to know the time of day simultaneously. A client wanting to know the time of day can query multiple servers on port 37. This facet of TCP/IP communications, using sockets for multiple connections, is called *multiplexing*. Also, the connection identified by the socket can carry on communications in both directions (send and receive).

The use of this method of identifying TCP connections has become ever more important as newer implementations of TCP have begun to assign port numbers without regard to the use of the well-known port number assignments. The binding (possession of or ownership) of the process to the port number is a local host programming issue addressed in the higher level processes. The higher level processes must maintain sufficient information about port assignments to ensure each connection remains unique.

The higher level processes that maintain port assignment information are called network control programs. Network control programs log each socket connection made and record the time the connection was opened, the time the connection was closed, the number of messages and bits transmitted over the connection, the sending and receiving hosts, and the socket identifiers at the sending host and receiving host that participated in the connection. Sockets are identifiable by the user, account number, and process name that is associated with each socket. A major economic benefit of sockets is the ability of user processes to determine and assess network charges for usage, if appropriate.

Transmission Control Protocol Reliability

When packets carom around networks, bouncing from router to router, possibly in various digital incarnations and perhaps undergoing reincarnation as various types of electrical signals, it is imaginable that some packets will become damaged due to transformations of the signal, disruption of service, imposition of interfering signals with the original signal, or any one of many other ways packets may be damaged.

Packets may take any one of several possible routes from node A to node B in most networks. Packets may also be delivered out of order and some packets may even get lost, never to arrive at their intended destination.

A road rally is a good analogy of the life of packets. They start in a given order, but by taking diverse routes they may arrive in no particular order and may even "crash" along the way, never to arrive at the intended destination.

To provide some measure of reliable communications between a source and a destination, TCP includes provisions for sequencing, error checking, and flow control. Sequencing is achieved by assigning each packet a sequence number and having the destination return an acknowledgment (ACK) that the correct sequence was received. If the ACK is not received by the source TCP within a defined time-out limit, the packet is automatically retransmitted by the source. The destination uses the packet sequence numbers to correctly reassemble the data stream and toss out duplicate packets. Error checking is accomplished by calculating a checksum on the datagram and including the value in the TCP header by the source. The destination recalculates the checksum, then compares it to the value transmitted by the source. If the two values are equal, the destination assumes the data is good. Checksum routines typically provide an

Figure 4.6 Road rally—A realistic perspective of packet-switched networks

accuracy of 1 in 10^{-6} parts per million or better. Flow control is established by the destination when it transmits to the source its receive buffer size when the initial connection is established. Flow control is maintained by the destination when it sends its current receive buffer size to the source with each ACK.

We have discussed TCP until now while usually ignoring UDP. Now it is time to state that TCP is UDP with error checking, sequencing, and flow control. Remove these three components from TCP and the remainder is UDP. The rest of the chapter focuses on TCP. Everything that is applicable to TCP is also applicable to UDP except for the reliability functions of TCP.

Basic TCP Operation

TCP must dutifully complete three basic chores in order when performing its intended function. The first is the connection setup. The connection setup establishes a communication link with the remote host. Next comes data transmission which is, of course, the actual transmission of whatever data is deemed necessary by the parties involved in the communication link. Finally, upon completion of the data transfer or the intentional act of one of the two connecting parties, the connection is torn down. The following discussion of basic data transfer provides the necessary information to understand these three fundamental TCP jobs.

TCP Events

The TCP connection progresses from one state to the next state in response to TCP events. *Events* are user software calls and certain other circumstances that trigger special processing. The user software calls are a result of the upper layer process managing the TCP connection to accomplish some intended purpose. The basic TCP events are OPEN, SEND, RECEIVE, CLOSE, ABORT, and STATUS. Also, incoming segments can be considered events as those segments containing the SYN, ACK, RST and FIN flags are circumstances that trigger special processing. Finally, time-outs are considered events as they trigger special processing, too.

Connection States

TCP has ten basic connection states listed in Table 4.2. The connection states are ordered from top to bottom in the sequence a connection progresses from beginning to end of its life. CLOSED is sometimes called the fictional state in the TCP literature. CLOSED represents the lack of a transmission control block (TCB) and therefore can be considered no state at all as far as TCP is concerned.

LISTEN
SYN SENT
SYN RECEIVED
ESTABLISHED
FIN WAIT 1
FIN WAIT 2
CLOSE WAIT
CLOSING
LAST ACK
TIME WAIT
CLOSED

Table 4.2 Connection states

The definition of the connection states are:

LISTEN is the state of waiting for a connection request from another remote TCP.

SYN SENT is the state of waiting for a matching (returning or echo) connection request from a remote TCP after sending the initial connection request.

SYN RECEIVED is the state of waiting for a connection request confirmation and acknowledgment from a remote TCP after having received and subsequently sent a connection request.

ESTABLISHED is the state of a working connection between two TCPs. In this state, data received will be transported to the application process.

FIN WAIT 1 is the state of waiting (we sure do an awful lot of waiting) for a request to terminate the connection from the remote TCP or the acknowledgment from the remote TCP of a connection termination request previously transmitted by the local TCP.

FIN WAIT 2 is the state of waiting (again?) for a request to terminate the connection from the remote TCP.

CLOSE WAIT is the state of waiting for a request to terminate the connection from the local TCP.

CLOSING is the state of waiting (!) for an acknowledgment of a request to terminate the connection from the remote TCP.

LAST ACK is the state of waiting (too much waiting) for the acknowledgment of the request to terminate the connection previously sent to the remote TCP.

TIME WAIT is the state of waiting for a sufficient amount of time to ensure the remote TCP has received the acknowledgment of its connection termination request.

CLOSED is the state of no TCP connection. Each state, except CLOSED, is characterized by the existence of a transmission control block (TCB) that includes all the pertinent information regarding the remote user of the connection. The CLOSED state is really the state of no TCB.

CLOSED, LISTEN, SYN SENT, and SYN RECEIVED are considered non-synchronized states because any host in one of these states does not have an established connection with another host. *Synchronization* refers to the exchange of sequence numbers between two hosts, called the connection handshake, so that each host can acknowledge the receipt of each other's segments. Without an established connection, sequence numbers cannot be synchronized.

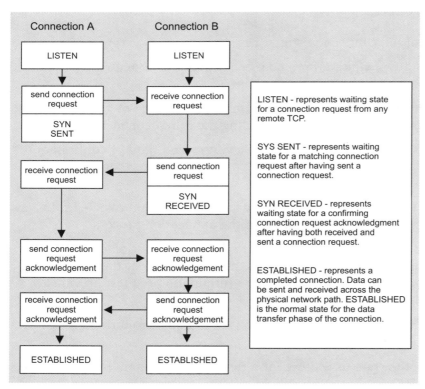

A connection progresses through the series of states illustrated here in an ordered fashion during its lifetime. The usual progression of the state of the connection is: LISTEN, SYN SENT, SYN RECEIVED, ESTABLISHED, FIN WAIT 1, FIN WAIT 2, CLOSE WAIT, CLOSING, LAST ACK, TIME WAIT, and CLOSED.

Figure 4.7 Getting the connection established

Reliability

When two users are connected and data is flowing back and forth, the casual observer may think that everything is going smoothly. Appearances can be deceiving. During transport across the physical medium (the stuff the telephone company has from your place to mine), packets may be lost, damaged, duplicated, or delivered out of sequence.

A discussion of routing is necessary to demonstrate the necessity of imposing some degree of reliability on TCP. Routing is the process of getting packets from source to destination through a multitude of interconnecting information byways and highways. For the uninitiated, a discussion of telephone switching may help to understand network routers.

When just two homes in the world had telephones (probably only the first week Bell invented the wonderful little machine) and formed only one telephone network, there was no need for a switchboard. If either party picked up the phone, there was only one choice for the destination of the call. Additional possible destination choices became available as soon as a third telephone was added to the network. Now, there was a need for switching. *Switching* determines how to route a call placed by the source to the intended destination. The mechanism used by the telephone companies to determine the intended destination is the telephone number. You dial in the number and you get connected to the destination. Now, telephone circuits are "connection" oriented. "Connection" oriented means there is a hard-wired physical path set up by the telephone company between the source and destination and each portion of the communication goes along the identical path. Since the path is hard-wired and there is only one possible recipient of the call, your destination does not need to know your telephone number to be able to communicate in a reciprocal fashion with you.

Routing works very similar to telephone switching. The "telephone number" in this instance is the destination internetwork address. Some significant differences do exist between public switched telephone networks (PSTNs), though. The connection between the source and destination most often is a connectionless-oriented connection. The "connectionless" term is used to differentiate this type of connection from a PSTN type connection. The connectionless is hard-wired, but each time the source and destination send packets, the packets may travel a different byway or highway. In other words, connectionless means the path is not dedicated to the service of a specific set of sources and destinations. An additional significant difference is that at the destination of a telephone call there is only one (disregard conference calling situations) location or telephone with a unique number assigned. However, with data networks, the destination can have a multitude of computing devices connected to a common medium, such as the case of a token ring network. Which is the intended computing device? The destination address identifies one, and only one, device as the intended recipient. Since the path is not dedicated from source to destination, the destination must have a means for reciprocating the communication. So, the source must also include its address in the communication, as the destination must have the source address to know where to send any return packets.

Every packet does not necessarily travel the exact same physical path from source to destination. Routers and/or switches are responsible for routing the packets. In the good ol' days, routers used hard-coded routing tables and there was no deviating from the paths defined in the routing tables. That was okay as long as the network was small and there was little or no traffic on the network. As networks grew and became networked themselves, routers became a toll gate that could not deal with the volume of diversified traffic. Network congestion became a daily nightmare for the commuters of the network highways and byways.

So, a new way of routing was necessary. Just in time to save the day, Open Shortest Path First (OSPF) routing was implemented. OSPF routers are capable of searching the network and determining the optimum path from one node to another on the network. Optimum usually means the shortest path that is "open," or free from congestion. However, optimum could mean the lowest-cost path, or the fastest known path, or the most secure path.

OSPF routers can also detect and identify a new node when it is connected to the network. So, now we have "intelligent" routers that can choose, from moment to moment, which path to use to send any packet from node A to node Z. One packet might go directly from node A to node Z while another packet might be transported through every intervening node, B through Y. Now, it becomes obvious that all packets will not be received in the order sent. One packet may take the high (long) road while another may take the low (short) road.

Convinced that packets will not always arrive in the sequence sent? Good. Now there must be a mechanism for reassembling the data packets into the original data stream. TCP does that by numbering the packets with the sequence number and using a reassembly procedure to place the packet data segments into the correct order before sending the data on to the upper layer process. However, there is a time limit imposed by IP (time-to-live parameter) on the life of a packet. Imposing a time limit becomes necessary, otherwise lost packets could wander around the labyrinth of networks, theoretically, forever. This situation is unacceptable because at some point all the networks would become totally congested with lost packets.

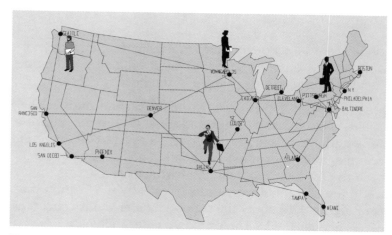

Figure 4.8 A "packet-man" in Dallas looking for San Francisco

Routers are programmed to check this time-to-live value and decrement the value as appropriate, before sending the packet on down the road. As Figure 4.8 depicts, a packet, represented by the "packet-man," in Dallas that is bound for San Francisco must find its way there while its time-to-live value is still greater than zero. There is a multitude of route choices for "packet-man" to get to San Francisco and he must choose wisely. Actually, the router in Dallas must choose wisely for "packet-man." If the time-to-live value has zeroed out, the router is supposed to discard or "drop" the packet.

The receiving TCP will acknowledge the reception of the data segment in the packet by sending a return segment with the ACK set to the SEQ number of the segment received.

If the transmitting TCP receives this ACK before the time-out has occurred, it will recognize the segment was received. If the ACK does not return before the time-out, the sending TCP will resend the segment.

If the packet is dropped by the router, the sending TCP will recognize (by not receiving the ACK from the receiving host) that a packet was dropped and transmit the packet again.

Figure 4.9 A dropped packet

The time-to-live parameter and the management of dropped packet detection and packet retransmission works very well to give TCP a very reliable end-to-end (user-to-user, also known as source-to-destination) transmission process. Well, there is opportunity for missteps in this process, which may result in a host receiving duplicate packets. TCP will recognize when a duplicate packet is received and discard one.

As stated previously, UDP does not concern itself with reliability issues. UDP has no sense of dropped packets.

TCP Header Format

The TCP header length is always a whole number multiple of 32 bits. Even if the header includes options, the length is always divided evenly by 32. Figure 4.10 shows the TCP header format and the names of the header fields.

There is also a TCP pseudo header that is used by the checksum routine. The pseudo header is 96 bits and contains the source address, destination address, protocol type, and TCP length. The pseudo header provides the TCP datagram some degree of protection against misrouted segments. The pseudo header information is present in the Internet Protocol and is transposed across the TCP/network interface in the arguments or results of calls by the TCP on the IP. The top three rows of Figure 4.10 show the pseudo header fields conceptually in relation to the TCP header fields. The pseudo header fields are discussed in the IP chapter.

	1	2	3
0 1 2 3 4 5 6 7 8 9	0 1 2 3 4 5 6 7 8 9	0 1 2 3 4 5 6 7 8 9	0 1

source IP address (32 bits)
destination IP address (32 bits)

zero (8 bits)	protocol (8 bits)	TCP length (16 bits)
source port (16 bits)		destination port (16 bits)

sequence number (32 bits)
acknowledgment number (32 bits)

data offset (4 bits)	reserved (6 bits)	control flags (6 bits)	window (16 bits)
checksum (16 bits)			urgent pointer (16 bits)
options (variable bit size)			padding

data begins

Figure 4.10 TCP header format

The TCP header fields are of a specified length and are necessary to perform specific tasks. The field lengths in bits and definitions follow:

The TCP length field contains the sum of the TCP header length plus the data length in octets. The length field does not count the pseudo header octets (quantity 12).

The source port field is 16 bits. The source port number identifies the port number used by the host that is originating this datagram. The source port number identifies the source process, such as Telnet, FTP, etc.

The destination port field is 16 bits. The destination port number identifies the port number used by the host to receive this datagram. This is the port number the destination will use to receive and accept the datagram which identifies the specific process (Telnet, FTP, etc.) this datagram should be transferred to at the destination.

The sequence field is 32 bits. The sequence number identifies where this datagram fits into the overall data stream. Remember, not all packets may arrive at the same time at the destination, so the sequence number identifies the correct order for reassembling the datagram in the correct order. The sequence number applies to the first data octet in this segment except when SYN is present. When SYN is present, the sequence number is the initial sequence number (ISN) and the first data octet is ISN + 1.

The acknowledgment field is 32 bits. When the ACK control bit is set, the acknowledgment field is the value of the next sequence number the sender of the segment is expecting to receive. In other words, the destination sends to the source the next sequence number it is expecting to receive and the source sends to the destination the next sequence number it is expecting to receive. The acknowledgment number is always sent as soon as a connection is established.

The data offset field is 4 bits. The data offset field contains the number of 32-bit words in the TCP header. If the field contains all ones, then the number of 32-bit words possible is 1111, or 15, which is 480 bits. The data offset points to the location in the bit stream where the data begins.

The reserved field is 6 bits. This field is reserved for future use and must be zero to ensure compatibility at some later date. In the meantime, it is available for use if there is a need for 6 extra bits.

The control/flag field is 6 bits. Each bit represents the state of a particular feature used by TCP. The features and their associated flag bit are listed in Table 4.3. If the bit is set, the feature is enabled. If the flag is reset, the feature is disabled.

From left to right the meaning of the control/flags bits are:		
Bit	**Acronym**	**Meaning**
1st bit	(URG)	urgent pointer field significant
2nd bit	(ACK)	acknowledgment field significant
3rd bit	(PSH)	push function
4th bit	(RST)	reset the connection
5th bit	(SYN)	synchronize sequence numbers
6th bit	(FIN)	no more data from sender

Table 4.3 Control/flags bit values

The window field is 16 bits. The number specified in the window is the number of data octets beginning with the octet identified in the acknowledgment field that the sender of this segment can accept. In other words, the sender of this window field is telling the recipient the size of the sender's receive buffer. Hopefully the other end of the connection will not transmit any packets that exceed the buffer size.

The checksum field is 16 bits. The checksum value is the one's complement of the one's complement sum of all the 16-bit words in the TCP pseudo header, header, and data. If a segment contains an odd number of octets (segment includes both header and data octets) to be summed, the last octet is padded on the right with zeroes to form a 16-bit word for checksum purposes. The checksum pad is not transmitted as part of the segment. When the checksum is computed, the checksum field itself is replaced with all zeroes.

The urgent pointer field is 16 bits. If the URG flag bit is set, this field points to the octet that follows the end of urgent data in the data segment.

Figure 4.11 Urgent pointers to urgent data

As its name implies, urgent data receives priority processing before any other data that is not identified as urgent. Seems to make sense. The urgent field and the corresponding data segment can be used to force data through the network and to interrupt normal processes. The use of this field is probably mostly limited to military applications. Hey, boss!...da planes...da planes are coming! (Sorry, could not resist that urgent "urge.")

The options field is not a fixed number of octets. Depending upon the option desired for use, the number of octets can vary from one to *n*. TCP options are specified at the end of the TCP header and can be padded to complete a full 32-bit word. All options are included in the checksum calculation. An option may begin on any octet boundary.

The TCP options field can have one of two possible formats. There can be a single octet that defines the option kind. Or there can be an octet of option kind, an octet of option length, and lastly the option data octets. The option-length counts the two octets of option-kind and option-length as well as the option-data octets.

TCP must implement all options.

Option Type (Kind)	Length	Meaning
00000000	1 octet	end of option list [see RFC 793]
00000001	1 octet	no operation [see RFC 793]

Option Type (Kind)	Length	Meaning
00000010 [00000100] [MSS 1st octet] [MSS 2nd octet]	4 octets	maximum segment size (MSS) [see RFC 793]
00000011	3	WSOPT – Window Scale [see RFC 1323]
00000100	2	SACK Permitted [see RFC 1072]
00000101	N	SACK [see RFC 1072]
00000110	6	Echo (obsoleted by option 8) [see RFC 1072]
00000111	6	Echo Reply (obsoleted by option 8) [see RFC 1072]
00001001	10	TSOPT – Time Stamp Option [see RFC 1323]
00001010	2	Partial Order Connection Permitted [see RFC 1693]
00001011	3	Partial Order Service Profile [see RFC 1693]
00001100	CC	experimental
00001101	CC	experimental
00001110		TCP Alternate Checksum Request [see RFC 1146]
00001111	N	TCP Alternate Checksum Data [see RFC 1146]
00010001		experimental
00010010		experimental
00010011	3	Trailer Checksum Option
00010100	18	MD5 Signature Option [see RFC 2385]

Table 4.4 Option field values

The options that are currently defined are given in Table 4.4. The binary value under the "option type" column is the value that specifies the type, or kind, of option. It is the octet that is first encountered in the options field of the TCP header. For "end of option list" and "no operation" there is but one octet in the TCP header option field.

However, for the MSS option there are four octets in the TCP option header field. The first octet is 00000010 and the second octet is 00000100. The third and fourth octets represent the physical size of the segment which includes both the TCP header and the included data.

The end of option list field marks the end of the option list. The end of the option list might not coincide with the end of the TCP header according to the data offset field. The end of option list field is used at the end of all options. It is used if the end of the options does not coincide with the end of the TCP header.

The no operation option field may be used between options. An example of its usage is to align the beginning of a subsequent option on a word (16-bit) boundary. There is no guarantee that sending TCPs will use this option, so receiving TCPs must be prepared to process options that do not necessarily begin on a word boundary. Oh, joy!

The maximum segment size option field specifies the maximum receive segment size the TCP can process. The TCP that sends this segment is telling the other TCP how large a chunk of data it can handle without choking. The option field is only sent in the initial connection request (which are the segments with the SYN control bit set). When this option field is not used, any segment size is allowed.

The padding field is a variable bit size. This field is used to make sure the TCP header ends and the data field begins on a 32-bit boundary. The padding field value is always all zeroes.

Flow Control Via a Window

TCP provides a mechanism for the receiving host to control the amount of data sent by the transmitting host. The flow control mechanism is the use of a "window" in the acknowledgment segment that specifies the range of sequence numbers beyond the last successfully received segment the TCP can accept. The window indicates the current available space in the receive buffer in units of octets. Of course, by the time the TCP receives this window and transmits data to fit (assuming there is sufficient data to fill the window, which is not always the case), the receiving host's buffer may have emptied. So some inefficiency does exist in the use of this method of flow control, but the trade-off is a very reliable connection with just a minimum of effort.

The Window

To provide a reliable flow control between TCPs, each TCP communicates the number of bytes it can receive without "overflowing." Overflowing means the receive buffer has reached its limit and cannot accept any more data without overwriting already received but unprocessed data. The typical receive buffer configuration is a ring buffer, so when the buffer gets full, it starts writing data into the beginning of the buffer, overwriting whatever data was present. As long as the TCP has processed the data being written over, all is well. So, to keep the receive buffers from overflowing, each TCP communicates the current buffer size so the transmitting TCP does not send too much data at one time. Figure 4.12 shows how the TCP communicates the buffer, also called the receive, window size.

Actually, the window size sent in each transmitted segment identifies the range of sequence numbers the sender of the window, who is also a data receiver, is currently able to accept. The window size must be the same size, or smaller, as the available buffer space assigned to this connection. A window identified as too large can result in data discards (giving rise to unnecessary retransmissions while network efficiency goes down the tubes), overwriting buffer contents, or system hang-ups, depending upon the robustness of the user program design, as the remote TCP can send data segments as large as the identified window. A window that is too small also creates network inefficiency as an artificial round trip delay time. When a segment arrives at a TCP with a zero window size, the receiving TCP must still return an acknowledgment showing the next expected sequence number and current zero window size.

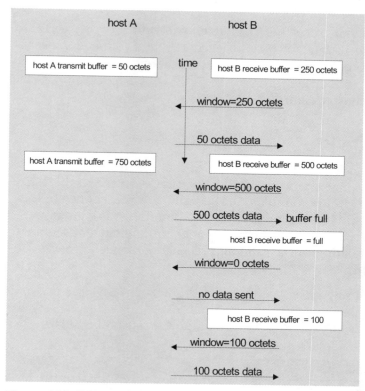

Figure 4.12 TCP Receive buffer window

TCP Alternate Checksum Routines

Number	Description
0	TCP Checksum
1	8-bit Fletchers' algorithm
2	16-bit Fletchers' algorithm
3	Redundant Checksum Avoidance

Table 4.5 Alternate checksum routines

The TCP alternate checksum field is used to identify alternate checksum routines, as shown in Table 4.5. A discussion of checksum routines is beyond the scope of this book. Suffice it to say that the transmitting end calculates the checksum and places the value calculated in the TCP header. The receiving

TCP calculates a checksum on the data it receives and compares the two values. If the two values are equal, the receiving TCP assumes the data received is identical to the data transmitted.

The sending TCP informs the receiving TCP which checksum routine was used to calculate the checksum. Obviously, if each TCP in a connection uses a different checksum routine, then each would get a different answer. The alternate checksum routine number identifies for the TCP which checksum routine was used to calculate the checksum.

Transmission Control Blocks

A *transmission control block* (TCB) is a TCP record that stores connection-related information. The connection-related variables stored in the TCB are the local and remote socket numbers, the security and precedence of the connection, pointers to the user's send and receive buffers, and pointers to the holding buffer (the retransmit queue and timer) and the current segment. Additionally, variables relating to the send and receive sequence numbers are stored in the TCB record.

SEND Sequence Space

SEND sequence variables are stored in the TCB. Table 4.6 lists the SEND sequence variables.

Variable Name	Meaning
SND.UNA	send unacknowledged
SND.NXT	send next
SND.WND	send window
SND.UP	send urgent pointer
SND.WLI	segment sequence number used for last window update
SND.WL2	segment acknowledgment number used for last window update
ISS	initial send sequence number

Table 4.6 SEND sequence variables

SEND UNACKNOWLEDGED — SND.UNA are sequence numbers that either have been acknowledged or are allowed for new data transmission.

SEND NEXT — SND.NXT are sequence numbers of unacknowledged data.

SEND WINDOW — SND.WND are future sequence numbers that are not yet allowed.

SEND URGENT POINTER — SND.UP is the send urgent pointer and indicates if the urgent pointer has been sent.

SEND LAST WINDOW 1 — SND.WL1 is the segment sequence number used for last window update.

SEND LAST WINDOW 2 — SND.WL2 is the segment acknowledgment number used for last window update.

INITIAL SEND SEQUENCE — ISS is the initial send sequence number. If the first sequence number transmitted does not equal this number, the attempt to communicate will fail.

The use of sequence numbers is crucial to the reliability of TCP. There is an ordered "SEND sequence space" that contains the appropriate sequence numbers. Individuals writing code for TCP/IP programming must recognize the importance of SEND sequence space.

SND.UNA [1]	SND.NXT	SND.UNA [2]	SND.WND

Table 4.7 SEND Sequence Space

Table 4.7 shows the ordered SEND sequence space. The meaning of each SEND sequence space component is given:

SND.UNA [1] are old sequence numbers that have been acknowledged.

SND.NXT are sequence numbers of unacknowledged data.

SND.UNA [2] are sequence numbers allowed for new data transmission.

SND.WND are future sequence numbers that are not yet allowed.

RECEIVE Sequence Space

Variable Name	Meaning
RCV.NXT	receive next
RCV.WND	receive window
RCV.UP	receive urgent pointer
IRS	initial receive sequence number

Table 4.8 RECEIVE sequence variables

RECEIVE NEXT — RCV.NXT are either old sequence numbers that have been acknowledged or sequence numbers allowed for new reception.

RECEIVE WINDOW — RCV.WND are future sequence numbers that are not yet allowed.

RECEIVE URGENT POINTER — RCV.UP is the receive urgent pointer and indicates if the urgent pointer has been received.

INITIAL RECEIVE SEQUENCE NUMBER — IRS is the initial receive sequence number. If the initial receive sequence number does not match this number, the attempt to communicate will fail.

The RECEIVE function has an ordered RECEIVE sequence space similar to the SEND function's. This is given in Table 4.9.

RCV.NXT	RCV.NXT	RCV.WND

Table 4.9 RECEIVE sequence space

The definition of each RECEIVE sequence space follows:

RCV.NXT [1] are old sequence numbers that have been acknowledged.

RCV.NXT [2] are sequence numbers allowed for new reception.

RECEIVE WINDOW — RCV.WND are future sequence numbers that are not yet allowed.

Segment Variables

The current segment contains variables that specify several important values used by TCP to determine issues such as precedence and urgency of the data associated with the segment. These are shown below:

Variable Name	Meaning
SEG.SEQ	segment sequence number
SEG.ACK	segment acknowledgment number
SEG.LEN	segment length
SEG.WND	segment window
SEG.UP	segment urgent pointer
SEG.PRC	segment precedence value

Table 4.10 Current segment variables

The current segment variables are stored in the TCB. These variables are used in a number of comparisons to resolve data link issues:

SEG.SEQ specifies the segment sequence number.

SEG.ACK specifies the segment acknowledgment number.

SEG.LEN specifies the segment length.

SEG.WND specifies the segment window.

SEG.UP specifies the segment urgent pointer.

SEG.PRC specifies the segment precedence value.

Sequence Numbers

The original internetworking designers decided every segment transported across a connection should have its own unique sequence number. That way, the reception of each segment could be acknowledged by the receiving host. By combining segment tracking and acknowledgment with retransmission capability, a reliable host-to-host data link can be established.

Sequence numbers are based on the number of data octets included in the segment. The data octet closest to the header is the octet with the lowest sequence number and the octet farthest from the header is the octet represented by the highest sequence number. For every octet of data there is a sequence number identifying that octet. Now if TCP transmitted all the sequence numbers, the resultant cost in overhead would slow the TCP transmission rate to the point of a crawl. For every data octet, TCP would have to transmit a sequence number, doubling the amount of information required for transport. However, only the highest sequence number in each segment is transmitted. This is the sequence number that is found in the sequence number field of the TCP header.

Let us assume the last sequence number transmitted was 100. In the current segment there are 20 data octets. Then the sequence number for this segment of data is $100 + 20 = 120$. In this manner, each and every octet of data is identified with a unique sequence number. But only the highest sequence number is included in the TCP header. So, if a router decides to split a segment, the resulting two segments can still have unique (to the two hosts that are connected) sequence numbers. Let's say the router decides to split the segment into two equal parts. Then the segment containing the lowest ten data octets, which would be those ten octets closest to the original TCP header, would have a sequence number of 110. The other segment containing the ten octets farthest from the TCP header would have a sequence number of 120. If additional routers broke the segment into smaller pieces until finally there were 20 segments, and resultant packets, the receiving host would be able to identify each data octet individually and reconstruct the entire original data segment in the correct order.

The acknowledgment capability is designed so that the acknowledgment of any segment implies that all previous segments are acknowledged except for the current segment. The acknowledgment of sequence number D tells the remote host that all segments up to, but not including D, have been received. In other words, the acknowledgment number identifies the next sequence number the host expects to receive.

The numbering of segments using sequence numbers continues in numerical order until the host runs out of numbers; then it just ratchets back to zero. A

32-bit machine will continue numbering until it reaches $2^{\wedge}32-1$, then roll over to 0 and continue on.

TCP must perform certain comparisons on the sequence space variables to determine the status of the data link. TCP must be able to:

▲ Determine if an acknowledgment received refers to a sequence number sent but not yet acknowledged.

▲ Determine if all sequence numbers occupied by a segment have been acknowledged. This is necessary to determine if the segment should be removed from the retransmission queue.

▲ Determine if an incoming segment contains sequence numbers which are expected. This is necessary to determine if the received data is within the current receive window and to determine if any data is duplicated.

After sending data to the remote host, the sending TCP will receive acknowledgments from the remote host's TCP. The sending TCP must perform the following assignments and comparisons to determine the link status:

SND.NXT = next sequence number to be sent

SND.UNA = oldest unacknowledged sequence number

SEG.SEQ = first sequence number of a segment

SEG.SEQ + SEG.LEN – 1 = last sequence number of a segment

SEG.LEN = number of data octets in the segment including SYN and FIN octets

SEG.ACK = acknowledgment from the receiving TCP which is the next sequence number expected by the receiving TCP

SND.UNA < SEG.ACK =< SND.NXT (a new acknowledgment)

All data octets in a segment in the retransmission queue are completely acknowledged if the sum of its sequence number and length is equal to or less than the acknowledgment value in the incoming segment. If the sum of its sequence number and length is greater than the acknowledgment value, then the segment may be partially acknowledged. The receiving TCP must perform the following assignments and comparisons to determine the link status:

RCV.NXT = next sequence number expected in a segment from transmitting host. It is the lower edge of the receive window.

RCV.NXT + RCV.WND – 1 = last sequence number expected in a segment from transmitting. It is the upper edge of the receive window.

SEG.SEQ = first sequence number of an incoming segment

SEG.SEQ + SEG.LEN – 1 = last sequence number of an incoming segment

RCV.NXT =< SEG.SEQ < RCV.NXT + RCV.WND (checks to see if segment beginning occupies valid receive sequence space)

RCV.NXT =< SEG.SEQ + SEG.LEN – 1 < RCV.NXT + RCV.WND (checks to see if segment ending occupies valid receive sequence space)

There exist four sets of conditions the receiving TCP should test for when a segment is received. Each condition concerns the length of the segment and the size of the receive window.

Condition 1 Receive ACK segments only
segment length = 0; window size = 0
SEG.SEQ = RCV.NXT

When the receive window size is zero, no segments are acceptable except ACK segments. It is possible for a sending TCP to maintain a zero receive window size while transmitting data and receiving ACKs. This condition replicates a simplex type communication link where one side transmits while the other side listens. Simplex is useful if one side has a lot of urgent data to send. When might this occur? Possibly when it is time to shoot the missiles! Even when the receive window size is zero, a receiving TCP must still process the RST and URG fields of all incoming segments.

Condition 2 Okay to receive data
segment length = 0; window size > 0
RCV.NXT =< SEG.SEQ < RCV.NXT+RCV.WND

The window size is greater than or equal to the segment length. This condition is okay for data reception.

Condition 3 Unacceptable receive condition
segment length > 0; window size = 0

This is an unacceptable condition. With a zero window size, the receiving TCP cannot accept any data.

Condition 4 Unknown condition
segment length > 0; window size > 0

This condition requires a test to determine if the segment length is less than or equal to the window size. The following tests are performed to determine if the segment fits into the window:

RCV.NXT =< SEG.SEQ < RCV.NXT + RCV.WND
RCV.NXT =< SEG.SEQ + SEG.LEN – 1 < RCV.NXT + RCV.WND

Initial Segment Number Selection

TCP has no restriction to prevent a particular connection from being used over and over again. Remember, a connection is defined by a pair of sockets. So, a connection that is being opened then closed in rapid order or a connection that is closed then restarted with loss of memory of any previous connection can duplicate segment numbers from previous instances of the connection unless measures are used to prevent such duplication. Either TCP must be able to identify duplicate segments from previous connection incarnations, or there must be assurance that previous segments do not exist.

Maintaining a current list of segment numbers in use in real time on some permanent media such as a hard drive is an option to prevent duplication of segment numbers. But it is not the best option. New segment number sequences are determined when a connection is created. The new segment sequence starts with an Initial Segment Number (ISN) that is selected by a 32-bit ISN generator. The 32-bit ISN generator is a recycling clock that returns to zero every 4.55 hours, assuming a 2 Mbps clock rate, giving a 4 microsecond period between value changes. Of course, a faster clock rate will yield a shorter period. For example, a 100 Mbps (Ethernet, anyone?) gives an 80-nanosecond period and a clock cycle time of 5.4 minutes. The clock cycle time, regardless of length, can be used to give a high degree of confidence that ISN numbers will be unique, without resorting to reading/writing data to storage media.

The Maximum Segment Lifetime (MSL) is something less than 4.55 hours. The Internet community originally set the MSL as two minutes. This means all segments will remain in the network no longer than two minutes. Any segments lasting two minutes in a network will be dropped by the next router it encounters. So, if there is a wait of two minutes every time a connection is created before the assignment of an ISN, we are guaranteed there will be no datagrams passing between the connection with duplicate sequence numbers. But who wants to wait two minutes to reconnect every time an ISP bumps you off due to connection inactivity? (Gosh, I just cannot read those e-mails fast enough!) However, it is sufficient to wait only a few fractions of a second for a high degree of assurance the ISN will be unique for the connection. Of course, the longer the wait, the higher the degree of confidence in the connection not having duplicate segment numbers floating about.

Each host is free to set the wait time as they determine appropriate. Perhaps Uncle Sam and Auntie Martha will wait the MSL time period because they want to make darn sure the missile does not launch except under the most proper circumstances. But my ISP will soon be out of business if I, and every other consumer, must wait two minutes to check e-mail every time I connect.

Finally, a well-behaved TCP will not lock up if it receives datagrams with duplicate sequence numbers. The proper course of action in this circumstance is to request the sending host to retransmit the data identified by the duplicate sequence number. Then, the receiving TCP does not have to make any judgment concerning the validity of the data received with the duplicate sequence numbers. By default, the incorrect data will be trashed by the reception of the re-sent data.

Summary

The Internet community originally identified two transmission protocols, TCP and UDP. TCP differs from UDP only in that TCP provides for a more reliable connection. UDP rips off the data with the underlying assumption that someone, somewhere will concern themselves with reliability.

TCP forms a reliable point-to-point transmission protocol by using several flow control and reliability mechanisms including retransmission and error checking.

The concept of numbered sequence space is fundamental to TCP. Every segment transmitted occupies some portion of the sequence space. When a sequence number is assigned to a segment, it is considered in use and cannot be used again until the sequence space clock recycles. The sequence space clock may recycle anywhere from five minutes to five hours, depending upon the clock rate.

Chapter 5

Internet Protocol

Questions answered in this chapter:

What is an IP datagram?

What is an IP header?

What are the IP header fields?

How does IP encapsulate data?

How does IP transmit data?

How does IP receive data?

Introduction

The Internet Protocol (IP) comes to us from the United States Department of Defense via ARPA and the Request for Comments (RFC) specifications. RFC 791 details the requirements for a class-based internet protocol used to connect distinct and separate networks regardless of their physical location into a mesh of interconnected networks. The specification governs data communications via the familiar Internet and its associated World Wide Web (WWW). There are six earlier revisions of RFC 791.

A note concerning the usage of the term internet. The term "internet" is a short form of internetwork. "Internetwork" and "internet" mean the same thing. Generally speaking, any two networks, public or private, connected together form an internet. The general public may or may not have some access to any particular internet. In fact, there are many internets that exist for the sole use of their owners and only individuals who are employees or members of the owning entity (corporation, government agency, etc.) are authorized access. However, the term "Internet" (note the capitalization) has recently come into popular usage and denotes the networks (public and private) that are connected together through the public switched telephone networks, providing more general access to various networks and network services to members of the global community. The World Wide Web is the most familiar service of the Internet. The Internet is a special case of an internet. For the remainder of this chapter, the term "internet" is used to denote the more general form of the term, that is, any two or more networks connected together to form an internet.

Internet Protocol

Now that we have filtered the water a little, let's peer into the pool and see if we can identify any fish. We begin by defining the internet protocol. The internet protocol is a software module intended for use in interconnected systems of packet-switched computer-based data communications networks. Figure 5.1 shows just such a data communications network, at a nebulous level, of course. Else, why the (cumulus) clouds?

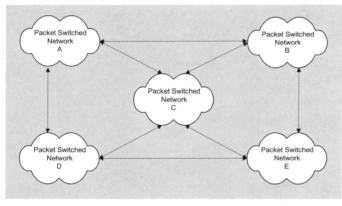

Figure 5.1 A packet-switched data communications network

So much for filtered water. That definition was comparable to dumping a truckload of dirt into the pool. Let's look at each clause of the internet protocol definition and see if we can get beyond the muddy water.

"The internet protocol is a software module" seems simple enough, providing we know what a software module is. A computer program is a set of step-by-step instructions called computer code, written by humans called programmers and/or nerds, that instruct a computer what to do. A healthy computer cannot legally deviate from the set of instructions that is its program. That is, it does not have the innate ability to determine if it should (there are no computers yet with the ability to reason, regardless of how many times you have watched *2001: A Space Odyssey*). Sick and rebellious computers are another matter.

Have you ever put together a complicated Christmas toy for a child? Did you follow the step-by-step instructions? What happened when you deviated from the instructions? It likely didn't quite fit together properly, or you had to disassemble some portion and start over. When computers deviate from their step-by-step instructions, usually unpredictable things happen. So, humans write step-by-step instructions which the computer must follow without deviation. Well-written software programs include provisions for error trapping, so the computer does not "lock up," but provides the human user the opportunity to make informed decisions regarding the status of the program.

When software programs are very large, it becomes cumbersome or impossible for humans to follow the program step by step and determine the impact of code additions and changes on the overall operation of the computer. In the interest of efficiency, humans divide the computer program into blocks of code called modules. Each module, which may be tens of thousands of code lines itself, contains all the software code necessary for it to instruct the computer to accomplish some specific set of tasks.

Now, let us continue with the remaining portion of the internet protocol definition. "intended for use in interconnected systems of packet-switched computer-based data communications networks" seems very daunting, but it really is not. "interconnected systems of... networks" means, of course, an internet. "packet-switched" means that the data is sent down the transmission path from point A to point B via units called packets. These packets contain the information (address of destination) necessary for the path switching elements (routers, bridges, gateways, and switches) the packet will encounter to route the packet to the proper destination.

Now, we are left with little else in the definition of an internet protocol. Just "computer-based data communications networks" which is pretty much self-explanatory. "computer-based" means the data sent over these packet-switched networks originates in the bowels of computers and is in the form that a computer can interpret. "computer-based" encompasses all types of computers including, but not limited to personal computers, mini-computers, mainframe computers, supercomputers, and many other "intelligent" or "computing" devices. These computers connected to the internetwork use diverse operating systems such as MS-DOS and BSD.

"Data communications" means we are working with information in the form of digital (binary) data rather than, say, analog (voice or video) data. But, analog data can easily be converted to digital data for transmission over data communications networks. More narrowly, data communications is usually taken to mean information of a digital nature.

IP Datagrams

The internet protocol processes blocks of data called *datagrams* and prepares them for transmission from the source to some destination. Each source and destination are hosts that are identified by fixed length addresses. The host may be either a computer or a gateway or some other "intelligent" device connected to the internet. The source internet protocol may fragment the data, if necessary, for transmission through networks that cannot accommodate larger packet/datagram sizes. Such a network is known as a "small packet" network. The destination internet protocol can reassemble the fragmented data in the correct order. Figure 5.2 illustrates a simple internetwork.

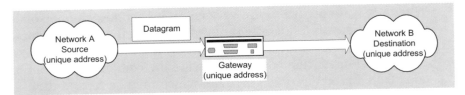

Figure 5.2 A simple internetwork

The internet protocol capabilities are intentionally limited to only those functions necessary to transmit a datagram from the source to the destination over interconnected systems of networks (LANs/MANs/WANs/GANs). The internet protocol does not concern itself with host-to-host network services such as data reliability, sequencing, and flow control.

The internet protocol could busy itself with all manner of network services if the original network architects and IP programmers deemed such functions useful in the IP module. However, in the interest of

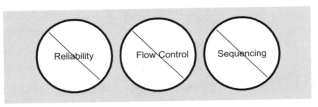

Figure 5.3 Hear no evil, speak no evil, see no evil

top-down, distributed programming, such functions were placed elsewhere. IP is part of a larger whole that includes TCP and other protocols which form a data communications service. IP, taken by itself, is not useful for much of anything. Through the network services of all the related protocols forming the data communications service, various types and qualities of services are provided the user.

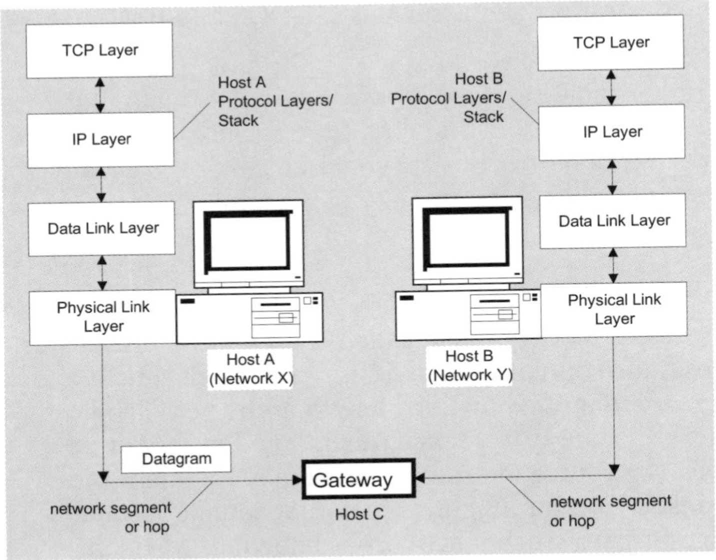

The internet protocol is used by host-to-host protocols such as the TCP protocol in an internetwork communications environment. The internet protocol uses local network protocols such as media access control (MAC) to send the datagram to the next internetwork gateway or to the destination host. The physical connection between any two nodes, such as a host connected to a gateway, is called a *segment* or a *hop.* Any two

Figure 5.4 IP and the internetwork

networks may be physically connected by just one segment, a few segments, or many segments.

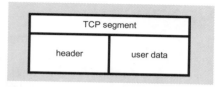

Figure 5.5 A TCP segment

As an example, the host TCP module passes the IP module the TCP header and user data (called a TCP segment; see Figure 5.5) as the transport layer portion of an internetwork datagram. The TCP module provides, as arguments to the IP, the address and other parameters in the internetwork header to the IP module when the TCP module invokes the IP module. Upon invocation by the TCP module, the IP module creates an internet datagram. Then the IP module invokes the local network interface to transmit the datagram onto the internetwork physical link. The local network interface interprets the network datagram address, packages the datagram into a packet that includes the local network destination address (which may be a local host or a gateway to another network), and routes the datagram accordingly to the appropriate, possibly intermediate, destination. This is shown in Figure 5.6.

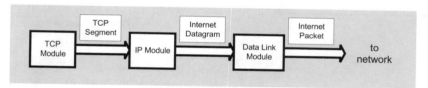

Figure 5.6 Beating packets out of segments

To illustrate the process, let us see what happens if a Network A host desires to transmit to another Network A host. The source Network A's host internet protocol module calls a local network module. The local network module adds the local addressing information, called the IP header, to the datagram. Now we have a bona fide internet message, called a packet, for transmission. When the datagram arrives at the next host, which might be a gateway to other networks or a client/server, the new host's local network module reads the IP header and determines if this host is the destination. If this host is the destination host, then the local network module calls the internet module and passes the datagram to it. If this host is an intermediate host, the local network IP module repackages a new IP header and (old) TCP segment into a new packet, then causes the physical medium to transmit the packet on to the next host in the chain.

Operation

There are two important functions the internet protocol is required to perform: addressing and data fragmentation. *Addressing* involves the identification of the source node and the destination node in the appropriate IP header field. *Fragmentation* involves the division of the datagram into smaller size packets for traversing small packet networks and the subsequent reassembly of the datagram into its original size.

Node source and destination addresses are located in the internet header field of the datagram. The host internet module, either server or gateway, utilizes the addresses to transmit internet datagrams toward their destinations by selecting an appropriate transmission path through the network. The selection of a transmission path is called *routing*; routing decisions are an important software element in internetworking, especially for gateways.

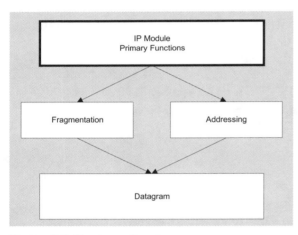

Figure 5.7 IP primary functions

Figure 5.7 shows the primary functions of IP. The output of the IP module is called a datagram or a packet. Because these packets are switched from source to destination, TCP/IP networks are usually called packet-switched networks.

Sometimes, a datagram may encounter a gateway to a network that cannot accommodate the size of the datagram. To successfully traverse the gateway and the network, the datagram must be divided into smaller packets. The IP header includes fields for fragmenting and reassembling datagrams when necessary.

The operational model used by the original IP designers included an internet protocol module resident in each host responsible for internet communications and in each interconnecting network gateway. Figure 5.8 illustrates the fact that an IP module is just a software routine resident within the innards of a computer. Each module interprets address fields in the same manner. Additionally, each module fragments and reassembles data following the same rules.

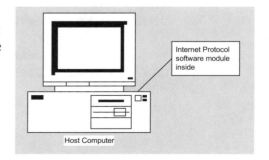

Figure 5.8 Where's the IP module?

Each datagram is unique to every IP module encountered while it travels from source to destination. The IP module processes each datagram without regard to the datagram's relationship to any other datagram. That is, there are no permanent or switched virtual connections or any other logical circuits involved in getting a datagram from source to destination. This means each datagram may be routed from source to destination via a different path. The path used depends upon the decisions made by IP routers along the way.

IP Addressing

Addressing is required to ensure the datagram successfully transits the maze of interconnected and geographically diverse gateways from source to destination. Without addressing, only two networks at a time could be interconnected. Why? Well, if your telephone is connected directly to your next door neighbor's house, you always know who you are talking to whenever you pick up the phone. There is never any doubt about the connection and who is there, and there is no need to provide switching. But what if your telephone is connected directly to all the phones in a large city? Not only do you not know everyone who may be on the line, but now there is no control over who gets on the line and when. Not so long ago, similar situations occurred in rural areas, where people had party lines that connected up to eight homes simultaneously. When you picked up the phone in such a circumstance, you most likely would encounter numerous people attempting to connect with another party simultaneously. The line could become a jumble of voices with no one succeeding in reaching their destination. Now, if we connect all of those phone lines together through a common switching element, there is control over who connects to whom, providing some coherent addressing scheme is used to identify sources and destinations. For telephones, the addressing scheme used to route calls from source to destination is the telephone number. For networks, the addressing scheme is the network address.

With just two networks connected together, each datagram transiting the interconnecting medium would have only one choice for a destination. However, if three or more networks are interconnected, each network must have a unique address so datagrams might find their way in the dark. The destination address becomes the datagram's flashlight in the dark.

Data Fragmentation

The second important function that an internet protocol must perform is fragmentation. The protocol layer above the IP layer does not concern itself with the length of the data to be transmitted, as long as the data segment fits into the intended receiving TCP's window. The IP layer is charged with the responsibility of fragmenting the data into transportable units. Data fragmentation is normally required when a datagram originates in a network that allows large size datagrams and it must transit another network with a smaller datagram size limit.

Additional IP Functions

The IP module includes four additional functions in addition to addressing and fragmentation. While internetworking could exist in some fashion without these four functions, their inclusion in the IP header makes life easier for someone. The four functions are: Type of Service, Time-to-Live, Options, and Header Checksum. These are covered below in the IP Header Format section.

IP Header Format

The IP header format, illustrated in Figure 5.9, consists of a minimum of five 32-bit double words with 14 fields of various lengths comprising the header. There are five 32-bit double words if the options field and its associated padding field are empty. Otherwise, there can be more than five double words, depending upon the number of options selected.

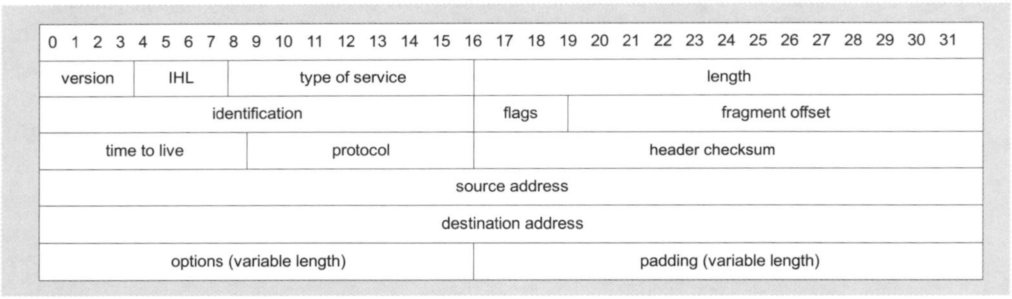

0 1 2 3 4 5 6 7 8 9 10 11 12 13 14 15 16 17 18 19 20 21 22 23 24 25 26 27 28 29 30 31
version	IHL	type of service	length
identification	flags	fragment offset
time to live	protocol	header checksum
source address
destination address
options (variable length)	padding (variable length)

Figure 5.9 IP header format

The largest IP header is 60 octets. The minimum IP header is 5 octets. A typical IP header is 20 octets.

Version Field

The Version field is 4 bits. It indicates the format of the internet header. The IP version we are interested in is version 4 (0100). See Table 5.1 for the assigned version numbers.

Bit Value	Protocol Version
0000	reserved
0001	unassigned
0010	unassigned

Bit Value	Protocol Version
0011	unassigned
0100	Internet Protocol (IP)
0101	ST datagram mode (ST)
0110	simple internet protocol (SIP)
0111	TP/IX (the next internet) (TP/IX)
1000	P internet protocol (PIP)
1001	TUBA
1010	unassigned
1011	unassigned
1100	unassigned
1101	unassigned
1110	unassigned
1111	reserved

Table 5.1 Assigned IP version numbers

IHL Field

The Internet Header Length field is 4 bits. The value of this field is the length of the internet header in 32-bit increments called words. The IHL points to the end of the header. By adding one to the number, the beginning of the data is found. The minimum value for a correct header is 5.

Type of Service Field

The Type of Service (TOS) field is 8 bits. TOS is a quality of service metric set by the user to specify which of several network parameters the routing devices, typically gateways, should select when deciding which route is optimal from source to destination. The destination could be the same network the gateway is part of, an intervening network that is the next hop, or a distant network that is the final destination. There may be any number of routes possible from source to destination. Then again, there may be only one. Not all routes from source to destination are necessarily equal. One route may be over private lines (no cost), while another might be over the public switched telephone network (some cost). One route may be physically short while another might be some great distance. One route might consist of many network segments while another might consist of just a few network segments. (Do not confuse network segments, or pieces of the physical network, with TCP segments, which are data pieces.)

The Type of Service network parameters are minimize delay, maximize throughput, maximize reliability, minimize monetary cost, and normal service. The user can choose one and only one type of service. As you can tell from the five choices available, each choice, except normal service, requires the user to sacrifice the other parameters for the sake of the chosen one. That is, maximum reliability may yield maximum cost, maximum delay, and minimum throughput. Sometime in the dim, distant past (July 1992) an internet user could set multiple bits in the TOS byte and choose multiple network parameters such as maximize reliability and minimize cost. But the Network Working Group decided for some strange reason (probably because such things as maximize reliability and minimize cost is an oxymoron) to eliminate the multiple bit settings. RFC 1349 provides the logic used to justify changing how the TOS field is interpreted. Now, only one choice is recognized by hosts and routers that can recognize the TOS value.

The TOS functionality has been largely ignored in the past by developers and equipment manufacturers. Without an infrastructure platform to work on, TOS was not much use outside intranetworks. Routing protocols were recently developed that can make routing decisions based upon the TOS. Open Shortest Path First (OSPF) is one such router protocol that attempts to make routing decisions based on some acquired knowledge of its network. OSPF routers compute separate routes for each TOS.

The hope of the IP designers was that TOS usage would not decrease user performance on the network. That is, usage of the TOS functionality would not yield any worse performance than not using it at all and possibly better routing decisions could be accomplished using the functionality. So, if a router cannot provide the requested TOS it should not drop the packet, either selecting a reasonable alternative, choosing a default route, or picking a route at random, if necessary.

Figure 5.10 The Type of Service octet

The Type of Service octet consists of three fields. These are precedence, TOS, and unused. The first field (bits 0 - 2) in the TOS octet is the precedence field. The precedence bits denote the attention this datagram should receive from all routers while en route from source to destination. This field identifies the priority the user has established for this datagram.

The TOS field (bits 3 - 6) identifies the criteria the router should use when making routing decisions for this datagram. The TOS criteria are delay, cost, reliability, and throughput.

The last field (bit 7) is not currently used in normal network operations. It is normally set to zero. The usage of this bit is confined to internet experimentation.

TOS Field

The four bits of the TOS field represent binary integer values, rather than individual bits that are set or reset to indicate a particular TOS parameter.

Value	Meaning
0000	normal service
0001	minimize cost
0010	maximize reliability
0011	not used
0100	maximize throughput
0101	not used
0110	not used
0111	not used
1000	minimize delay
1001	not used
1010	not used
1011	not used
1100	not used
1101	not used
1110	not used
1111	not used

Table 5.2 TOS values

Table 5.2 lists the TOS values and their meaning. The TOS value of 0000 is the default and should be used unless there is compelling reason to use another value. The unused values are legal TOS values and may be assigned a particular meaning in the future.

Minimize and maximize in the TOS meanings are not concrete terms but are relative to the ability of any individual router to make decisions concerning the appropriate path based upon the TOS value. Routers most often do not have full and complete knowledge of the interconnecting networks. Additionally, routers do not have real-time knowledge of the status of the networks known to the router. So, while the TOS values have a meaning, the meaning is relative only with respect to the current knowledge the router has of the known networks. Minimize cost means the router, at the moment it makes its routing decision, will attempt to send the packet along the route it has knowledge of that is of minimum cost. In fact, the route might not be the lowest cost route available at all. Routers attempt to choose paths based upon their often imperfect knowledge of the paths available to them.

There are no laws governing when and for what purpose each TOS value is used. However, there are some rules of thumb concerning the assignment of TOS values that should provide the network manager with a little better network performance. Applications that deal with network management including diagnostics should use the maximize reliability TOS value. Obviously, the network will not function as smoothly if its management is problematic. Applications that ship around huge amounts of data should choose a maximize throughput TOS unless cost is of significant concern. If cost is the primary consideration, then, of course, minimize cost should be the TOS selected. If the application involves direct human participation, such as a text echo mode, the TOS value of interest is minimize delay.

Protocol	TOS Value	Meaning
BOOTP	0000	default
DNS UDP Query	1000	minimize delay
DNS TCP Query	0000	default
EGP	0000	default
FTP Control	1000	minimize delay
FTP Data	0100	maximize throughput
ICMP Errors	0000	default
ICMP Requests	0000	default
ICMP Responses	0000	default
NNTP	0001	minimize monetary cost
SMTP Command	1000	minimize delay
SMTP Data	0100	maximize throughput
SNMP	0010	maximize reliability
TELNET	1000	minimize delay
TFTP	1000	minimize delay
Zone Transfer	0100	maximize throughput
Any IGP	0010	maximize reliability

Table 5.3 TOS values for specific protocols

IP RFC 791 recommends the TOS values for the services identified in Table 5.3. The bottom line is each network manager must set the values to get the best performance out of the network. Most likely, the settings will require some trial and error if the network is to perform at its optimum efficiency.

Precedence Field

The precedence field of the TOS octet consists of three bits. As previously explained, the three bits comprise a binary integer value. Each value has a unique meaning. Table 5.4 lists the meaning of each precedence value. The default value is 000 (routine) and should be used most often.

Bits	Meaning
000	routine
001	priority
010	immediate
011	flash
100	flash override
101	CRITIC/ECP
110	internetwork control
111	network control

Table 5.4 Precedence values

The precedence values are more or less self-explanatory. As the numerical value of the precedence value increases from 000, so does the import of the datagram. The datagram with the highest precedence is 111. There are all kinds of scenarios that make use of precedence ranging from the military wanting its data to pass before any others to businesses that demand priority for their traffic. There is much room for abuse here and the network manager who sends all of his traffic "routine" can probably be assured his data sits and waits at the gateways. Policing the use of the precedence functionality by limiting how many datagrams per minute/hour/day/week/month a user can send at any particular precedence level will become a necessity before too many moons pass.

The Old Way

Figure 5.11 shows the values and meanings of the old TOS octet. RFC 791 changed the definition of the TOS octet. Previous to RFC 791, each individual bit of the TOS octet could assume a unique value and meaning. RFC 791 changed the interpretation of the octet to discrete binary integer values with

Value	0	1	2	3	4	5	6	7
0		precedence		normal delay	normal throughput	normal reliability	reserved (always low)	
1				low delay	high throughput	normal reliability		

Figure 5.11 The old TOS octet

defined meaning for each value. Before, a user could test the TOS octet by determining if a bit was set or reset for a specified meaning. Now, the user must interpret each group of bits (Precedence or TOS fields) as numerical values. While the interpretation of each bit as a unique meaning is history, the information is provided here because routers installed in networks prior to the issuance of RFC 791 will use the old interpretation of the Precedence and TOS fields.

Choosing the TOS

The user process requests the transport protocol (TCP in this case) to utilize a specific TOS. Neither TCP nor IP require both ends of the connection to use the same TOS value. A transport protocol might be designed to discover the sending IP's TOS value and utilize the same value in its TOS field. Or a protocol might be designed to change TOS values as appropriate while the socket is still hot (connected). A user process that transmits large amounts of data periodically interrupted by small housekeeping packets might go for a maximize throughput with the bulk data packets and minimize delay for the housekeeping packets. Of course, switching TOS values in this manner will most likely invalidate the round trip time estimates used to determine the time-to-live value.

The Assigned Numbers document (RFC 2000) lists the TOS values that are used by a number of common applications. For any other applications, user processes are responsible for choosing the desired TOS values for any traffic originated by the user process. The designer of the user application should assign suitable values based upon the network design criteria reflecting application, system, and business objectives. A desired application feature is the ability to override the default TOS and assign any other TOS as the need may arise. Network traffic diagnostic programs especially must have the ability to assign TOS values on the fly (while the socket is connected, or "hot") to be able to perform appropriate diagnostic functions. If the ability to change the TOS value while the socket is connected is not a feature of the application, then only the default TOS should be used by the application.

Length Field

The Length field is 16 bits. It is the total length of the datagram, measured in octets (8-bit increments), including the IP header and the TCP header and data. This field provides for datagrams to be up to 65,535 octets long. Aspiring network managers will not make use of the maximum total length! Imagine the blockage of the internetwork intestines if network managers made use of the maximum length! A practical length that yields good efficiency is something in the neighborhood of 1,200 octets of data for bulk data transfers. The network manager can use a little trial and error in adjusting the Length field to fine-tune the network's performance. The IP RFC recommends all hosts be prepared to receive 576 (512 data octets and 64 header octets) octets, which implies the preferred transmit size is 576 octets.

Identification Field

The Identification bit field is 16 bits. Identification is a value assigned by the sending IP to assist in assembling the fragments of a datagram. Each fragment that contains the same Identification field value will be reassembled in the correct order.

Flags Field

value	0	1	2
0	reserved	may fragment	last fragment
1	not allowed	cannot fragment	more fragments

Figure 5.12 Flags bit field

The Flags bit field is three bits and identifies the control flags status.

Bit zero is reserved for future use.

Bit 1 is used to identify when fragmentation of data is allowed. Fragmentation may be necessary to pass through a gateway and travel through the next hop. However, fragmentation is not always a good thing. In real-time audio and video applications, fragmentation most likely will destroy the timing relationship of the original signal, resulting in incoherent audio and distorted video.

Bit 2 is used to identify the last fragment if the original datagram was fragmented anywhere along the road to its destination. The flag determines when an IP should cease looking for more fragments of the original datagram and start reassembling the pieces into the original.

Fragment Offset Field

The Fragment Offset bit field is 13 bits. The Fragment Offset indicates where in the original datagram this fragment belongs. It is measured in units of 8 octets (64 bits). If the datagram is not fragmented, the Fragment Offset is always equal to zero. Also, the first fragment always has a Fragment Offset equal to zero.

Time-to-Live Field

The Time-to-Live bit field is 8 bits. This field specifies the maximum time the datagram is allowed to remain in transit in the internetwork. If the time-to-live value is zero, then the datagram must be destroyed. The IP header processing performed by every network router and gateway recalculates this value and modifies it as appropriate. However, if the value decreases to zero (or below), the router or gateway will immediately destroy the datagram. The time-to-live value represents time measured in units of seconds. There is a requirement imposed on routers and gateways to decrement this value by a minimum of one when the header is processed. What if the transit time from the source to this gateway was only 250 milliseconds? It still must be decremented by one full second. So the value really represents a limitation that is loosely associated with time. If the datagram passes through 63 gateways (not conceivable just a year or two ago but very possible today) in less than 64 seconds, the datagram will still be dropped by the 64th gateway as it will zero out the value. So, the field really represents a limitation on the life of a datagram imposed by the combination of time and number of gateways the datagram is allowed to pass through. This limitation on the life of a datagram generates some interesting network analysis and design issues rendered pressing as networks continue to grow exponentially. The upper bound on the life of datagrams may become a stumbling block to TCP/IP usage.

Every network manager should be aware of the number of dropped packets occurring on the network links. The number of dropped packets is an excellent measurement of the real-time health of the network. The IP RFC currently recommends a default time-to-live of 64. The savvy network manager will use the faithful trial and error method to determine the optimum value for his network.

Protocol Field

The Protocol bit field is 8 bits. The Protocol field identifies the next level protocol (transport layer) used in the data segment portion of the IP datagram. The Protocol field can identify 256 ($2^8 = 256$) different protocols. There are not, however, 256 protocols used. Most of the values are unassigned, such as the block of values from 101 to 254. Table 5.5 is a partial listing of the protocol numbers.

Bit Value	Internetwork Protocol Acronym	Internetwork Transport Layer Protocol
0		Reserved
I	ICMP	Internet Control Message
2	IGMP	Internet Group Management
3	GGP	Gateway-to-Gateway
4	IP	IP in IP (encapsulation)
5	ST	Stream
6	TCP	Transmission Control
7	UCL	UCL

Bit Value	Internetwork Protocol Acronym	Internetwork Transport Layer Protocol
8	EGP	Exterior Gateway Protocol
9	IGP	any private interior gateway
10	BBN-RCC-MON	BBN RCC Monitoring
11	NVP-II	Network Voice Protocol
12	PUP	PUP
13	ARGUS	ARGUS
14	EMCON	EMCON
15	XNET	Cross Net Debugger
16	CHAOS	Chaos
17	UDP	User Datagram

Table 5.5 Assigned transport layer numbers for IP header

Header Checksum Field

The Header Checksum bit field is 16 bits. This checksum is calculated on the IP header only. Since some header fields change at each point that the internet header is processed, the header checksum is recomputed and verified at each processing point.

The IP RFC recommends the following algorithm be employed by all devices (hosts, routers, gateways, etc.) to calculate the header checksum:

> The checksum field is the 16-bit one's complement of the one's complement sum of all 16-bit words in the header. For purposes of computing the checksum, the value of the checksum field is zero.

> This is a simple-to-compute checksum and experimental evidence indicates it is adequate, but it is provisional and may be replaced by a CRC procedure, depending on further experience.

The following example demonstrates the header checksum calculation in action. The example, intended only to illustrate the process, is representative of the way the procedure works and does not actually use IP header values.

Bit	0	1	2	3	4	5	6	7	8	9	10	11	12	13	14	15
1st value	1	1	1	1	1	0	0	1	1	0	0	1	1	0	0	0
one's comp	0	0	0	0	0	1	1	0	0	1	1	0	0	1	1	1

Table 5.6 The first value and its one's complement

Table 5.6 shows the first 16-bit value to be complemented. To complement a bit, just take the inverse value. Replace ones with zeroes and replace zeroes with ones.

Bit	0	1	2	3	4	5	6	7	8	9	10	11	12	13	14	15
2nd value	1	0	0	1	1	1	0	0	0	1	1	0	0	1	0	0
one's comp	0	1	1	0	0	0	1	1	1	0	0	1	1	0	1	1

Table 5.7 The second value and its one's complement

Table 5.7 shows the second 16-bit value to be complemented and its one's complement.

Bit	0	1	2	3	4	5	6	7	8	9	10	11	12	13	14	15
one's comp	0	0	0	0	0	1	1	0	0	1	1	0	0	1	1	1
one's comp	0	1	1	0	0	0	1	1	1	0	0	1	1	0	1	1
add	0	1	1	0	1	0	1	0	0	0	0	0	0	0	1	0

Table 5.8 The sum of the one's complement

Now, we add the one's complement of the two data values. The result is shown in Table 5.8.

Bit	0	1	2	3	4	5	6	7	8	9	10	11	12	13	14	15
sum of one's	0	1	1	0	1	0	1	0	0	0	0	0	0	0	1	0
one's comp	1	0	0	1	0	1	0	1	1	1	1	1	1	1	0	1

Table 5.9 The one's complement of the one's complement sum

The last step is to take the one's complement of the one's complement sum calculated in Table 5.9. See how easy it is? Even a Macintosh computer can do it!

Source Address Field

The Source Address bit field length is 32 bits. The source address identifies the internet address of the data source.

Destination Address Field

The Destination Address bit field length is 32 bits. The destination address identifies the internet address of the intended destination of the data.

Options Field

The Options bit field is either one octet or four octets in length. It may or may not be present in a datagram. If the Options field is used, it must be used by all hosts and gateways in the network. The transmission of options in any particular datagram may be optional itself. In some networks the transmission of options in every datagram may be mandatory. For example, in military environments, the transmission of the security option may be mandatory.

However, the implementation of options is not optional; if they are present, they must be utilized.

An option may be formatted in one of two ways: a single octet of option-type or four octets consisting of an option-type octet, an option-length octet, and two option-data octets. For the latter case, the option-length octet count includes the option-type octet, option-length octet, and the number of option-data octets.

Bit	0	1	2	3	4	5	6	7
Meaning	copy	option class		option number				

Figure 5.13 Options bit fields

The option-type octet has three bit fields. Figure 5.13 shows the arrangement of the Options bit field. Bit 0 is the Copy bit flag, bits 1 - 2 are the Option Class bits, and bits 3 - 7 are the Option Number bits.

The Copy bit, also called the Copy flag, specifies if this option must be copied onto all fragments when the datagram is fragmented. Table 5.10 shows the possible states and the meaning of the Copy bit.

Bit Value	Meaning
0	do not copy
1	copy

Table 5.10 Options for the Copy bit field

The Option Class bit field states and meanings are shown in Table 5.11. The control class (00) is used by network management applications. The debug and measurement class (10) is used by diagnostic programs to troubleshoot and verify network status. Classes 1 and 3 are reserved for future use.

Field Value	Decimal Value	Meaning
00	0	control
01	1	reserved
10	2	debug and measurement
11	3	reserved

Table 5.11 Option Class bit field

The Option Number field describes the option carried in the IP header. Of particular interest are the LSR, SSR, RR, and TS options. The LSR option, option field = 3, requires all routing devices along the route to choose what it believes to be the optimum path to the destination. The SSR option, option field = 9, requires all routing devices along the route to route the packet to the next address specified in the packet. SSR may result in packets being dropped because the specified route is not achievable. RR requires each routing device to record its address in the packet. TS requires each routing device to include the time the packet transited the device in the packet. These options are useful if a user wishes to select a specific route from source to destination, to discover an unknown route, or to discover the transit times from source to destination. They are very valuable network management tools.

Copy Field no=0 yes=1	Option Class Field	Option Number Field	Decimal Option Number	Name
0	0	0	0	EOOL—End of Option List
0	0	1	1	NOP—No Operation
1	0	2	130	SEC—Security
1	0	3	131	LSR—Loose Source Route
0	2	4	68	TS—Time Stamp
1	0	5	133	E-SEC—Extended Security
1	0	6	134	CIPSO—Commercial Security
0	0	7	7	RR—Record Route
1	0	8	136	SID—Stream ID
1	0	9	137	SSR—Strict Source Route
0	0	10	10	ZSU—Experimental Measurement
0	0	11	11	MTUP—MTU Probe
0	0	12	12	MTUR—MTU Reply
1	2	13	205	FINN—Experimental Flow Control
1	0	14	142	VISA—Experimental Access Control
0	0	15	15	ENCODE
1	0	16	144	IMITD—IMI Traffic Descriptor
1	0	17	145	EIP
0	2	18	82	TR—Traceroute
1	0	19	147	ADDEXT—Address Extension

Table 5.12 Option Number field values

End of Option List

End of Option List (EOOL) is a Class 0 option with no length value. It is only 1 octet long. End of Option List specifies this is the end of the option list! The end of the option list does not necessarily coincide with the end of the IP header as specified in the IP header length. The EOOL is used at the end of all options and is used only if the end of the options does not coincide with the end of the IP header. The EOOL may be copied, added, or deleted upon datagram fragmentation or for any other reason.

No Operation

No Operation (NOP) option is a Class 0 option with no length value. It is only 1 octet long and specifies this option does not perform any operation. The NOP may be used between options to align the beginning of a subsequent option on a 32-bit boundary. The NOP may be copied, added, or deleted upon datagram fragmentation or for any other reason.

Security

The Security option is a Class 0 option with an 11-octet field length. Security identifies the Compartment, Closed User Group (transmission control code, or TCC), and Handling Restriction Code compatible with Department of Defense security requirements. The format for this option is shown in Figure 5.14.

8 bits	8 bits	16 bits	16 bits	16 bits	24 bits
10000010	00001011	security	compartment	handling restrictions	transmission control code

Figure 5.14 Security bit field

The Security subfield of the Security option, shown in Table 5.13, specifies one of 16 levels of security. Eight of these security levels are reserved for future use.

Bit Value	Meaning
0000000000000000	Unclassified
1111000100110101	Confidential
0111100010011010	EFTO
1011110001001101	MMMM
0101111000100110	PROG
1010111100010011	Restricted
1101011110001000	Secret
0110101111000101	Top Secret
0011010111100010	Reserved for future use
1001101011110001	Reserved for future use

Bit Value	Meaning
0100110101111000	Reserved for future use
0010010010111101	Reserved for future use
0001001101011110	Reserved for future use
1000100110101111	Reserved for future use
1100010011010110	Reserved for future use
1110001001101011	Reserved for future use

Table 5.13 Security bit field

The Compartment field is 16 bits. It is zero when the data is not compartmented. The values used for compartment data may be obtained from the Defense Intelligence Agency, Israeli intelligence agencies, or by hacking.

The Handling Restrictions field is 16 bits. The values for handling restrictions may be obtained from the Defense Intelligence Agency, Israeli intelligence agencies, or by hacking.

The Transmission Control Code (TCC) field is 24 bits. The TCC is used to segregate users into groups with common interests.

The values for TCC may be obtained from the Defense Intelligence Agency, Israeli intelligence agencies, or by hacking. The TCC cannot be copied upon datagram fragmentation. This option appears at most once in a datagram.

Loose Source and Record Route

The Loose Source and Record Route option (LSRR) is a Class 0 option with a variable length value. It is used to route the IP datagram based on information supplied by the source. Loose routing allows routers to decide the path the datagram should take through the network to reach the intended destination.

1st octet	2nd octet	3rd octet	4th – 6th octets
10000011	length	pointer	route info

Table 5.14 LSRR bit field

The LSRR option provides a way for the source of an internet datagram to supply routing information to be used by the gateways in forwarding the datagram to the destination, and to record information about the actual route taken.

The first octet of the LSRR option is the LSRR option type code. The second octet is the option length which includes the option type code and the length octet, the pointer octet, and three octets of route information. The third octet is the pointer into the route information indicating the octet which begins the next source address to be processed. The pointer origin is the beginning of the LSRR, giving the smallest valid value of 4.

The procedure for recording the route consists of replacing the source route addresses with the recorded route addresses at the appropriate points along the route. Route information is composed of a series of IP addresses. Each internet address is 32 bits (four octets). If the pointer is greater than the length, the source route is empty, the recorded route is full, and any additional routing is to be based on the destination address field.

Here is how the IP records the route addresses along the way when the packet reaches the destination address: If the pointer value is not greater than the length value, the IP replaces the IP header destination address with the next address in the source route field. The source route address just moved to the IP destination address field is replaced by this destination's address and the pointer value is incremented by four.

The recorded route address is the IP module's own local internet address as known in the LAN/WAN environment into which the datagram is being transported. The LSSR option must be copied upon IP datagram fragmentation.

Internet Time-stamp

The Internet Time-stamp is a Class 2 option with a variable length field. When the Time-stamp option is used, the host generating the option must create a sufficiently large time-stamp data area to hold all of the expected time-stamps since the data area is fixed when it is created and does not get any larger when additions are made. The user may have to do a little guesstimating to determine the right size for the specific connection of interest. When the time-stamp data area is created, the originating host must set all time-stamp values to zero.

The Time-stamp bit field is right-justified, meaning the least significant bit is on the right. The 32-bit time-stamp value is measured in milliseconds since midnight Greenwich Meridian Time (GMT), also known as Universal Time (UT). Any time value can be used for the time-stamp if the time is not available in milliseconds or from GMT. If a time value other than GMT in milliseconds after midnight is used, the most significant bit (the high-order bit) of the time-stamp field is set to 1 to indicate the use of a non-standard time value.

When the time-stamp pointer exceeds the length value, the data area is full. If the data area is full, the datagram must be forwarded to the next router without inserting a time-stamp. In this case, the overflow count is incremented by one. If the available time-stamp area is more than zero octets but less than four, the datagram is considered corrupted and the router will discard it. The time-stamp option is not copied whenever the datagram is fragmented.

1st octet	2nd octet	3rd octet	4th octet	5th octet	6th octet
01000100	length	pointer	overflow (4 bits) flag (4 bits)	internet address	time-stamp

Table 5.15 Internet Time-stamp bit field

The internet Address and Time-stamp bit areas are shown, for simplicity, as single octet quantities in Table 7.15. However, the originating host can increase the size of the two bit fields to any size necessary to include all addresses and time-stamps expected between source and destination. The two bit fields should always be the same size—if there is a time-stamp, there should be an address; if there is an address, there should be a time-stamp.

The Time-stamp option Length bit field value is the number of octets in the time-stamp option counting the type, length, pointer, and overflow/flag octets. The Time-stamp option length is a maximum of 40 octets.

The Time-stamp Pointer is the number of octets from the beginning of the current Time-stamp option to the end of the last time-stamp octet plus one more. The Time-stamp Pointer points to the beginning octet of the next Time-stamp option. The smallest valid value is 5 octets. The Time-stamp space is full when the Time-stamp pointer is greater than the length.

The Time-stamp Overflow (4 bits) bit field represents the number of IP modules that cannot register time-stamps due to lack of space.

The Time-stamp Flag (4 bits) values are defined as:

Flag Value	Meaning
0	Time-stamps only are stored in consecutive 32-bit words
1	Each time-stamp is preceded with the internet address of the host registering the time-stamp
3	Internet address fields are prescribed and packet must follow prescribed route

Table 5.16 Time-stamp Flag bit field

If the Time-stamp flag value is 0, the time stamp bit field contains only time-stamps. Time-stamps are stored in consecutive 32-bit words.

If the Time-stamp Flag value is 1, then each time-stamp value is preceded by the IP address, in the fourth octet, of the module adding the time-stamp, in the fifth octet.

If the Time-stamp Flag value is 3, the IP address fields are prescribed in the fourth octet. An IP module will register its time-stamp if it matches its address with the next listed IP address (fourth octet) the pointer (third octet) is pointing to.

Record Route

Record Route (RR) option is a Class 0 option with a variable length value. The RR is used to trace and record the route an IP datagram takes from source to destination. The RR is identical to the LSRR and SSRR except no routing specifics are provided to guide the datagram through the network. The RR just records wherever the datagram goes.

1st octet	2nd octet	3rd octet	4th – 6th octets
00000111	length	pointer	route info

Table 5.17 Record Route bit field

The source host must compose this option with a sufficiently large enough route address header area to hold all the anticipated addresses. The size of the option does not change due to adding addresses. The initial contents of the area reserved for the route addresses must be zero. When any IP module routes a datagram, the IP module tests for the presence of the Record Route option. If this option is present, the IP module inserts its own internet address into the header area reserved for recording route addresses. The address the IP module inserts is the address of the IP module in the LAN/WAN environment into which this datagram is routed. The IP module inserts the address into the reserved route address area beginning at the octet specified by the pointer, and then increments the pointer by four.

If the route address area is full, the IP datagram is forwarded to the next hop in the network without inserting the address of the current router. The IP module tests for a full address area by determining if the pointer exceeds the length. If the pointer value is less than the length value, the route address area is not yet full.

If there is some room but not enough for a full address to be inserted, the original datagram is considered to be in error and is discarded. In either case, an ICMP parameter problem message may be sent to the source host.

The Record Route option is not copied if the datagram is fragmented. Upon datagram fragmentation, the route will be recorded in the first fragment and no others.

Stream Identifier

The Stream ID option is a Class 0 option with a length of 8 bits as illustrated in Table 5.18. The Stream ID is used to carry the stream identifier.

1st octet	2nd octet	3rd octet
10001000	00000010	Stream ID

Table 5.18 Stream ID bit field

The Stream ID option is specifically included in the IP datagram to accommodate the SATNET stream identifier. The Stream ID must be copied upon IP datagram fragmentation.

Strict Source and Record Route

Strict Source and Record Route (SSRR) option is a Class 0 option with a variable length value. It is used to route the IP datagram based on information supplied by the source. Strict routing requires routers to follow the path as specified in the datagram without deviation. The SSRR provides for the datagram to record the route taken. The structure of the SSRR option, shown in Table 5.19, is identical to the LSRR option structure. The process of recording the route taken is the same as described in the LSRR option.

1st octet	2nd octet	3rd octet	4th – 6th octets
10001001	length	pointer	route info

Table 5.19 SSRR bit field

The SSRR option must be copied upon IP datagram fragmentation.

Padding Field

The IP header Padding field is a variable length bit field always set to 0. The Padding length is set to ensure the IP header ends on a 32-bit boundary.

Relation to Other Protocols

Figure 5.15 illustrates the place of the internet protocol in the networking protocol hierarchy:

Internet protocol interfaces on the higher level to a transport layer protocol. The transport layer protocol of interest to us is TCP. On the lower side of the protocol hierarchy, IP interfaces to the data link layer. Data link layers are not covered in this book. Of course, the data link layers are intimately connected to a local network or WAN gateway.

Theory of Operation

The purpose of the internet protocol is to transport datagrams through an interconnected set of networks, whether they are LANs, MANs, WANs, or GANs. IP accomplishes this task by passing the IP datagrams, called packets when transiting the physical medium in between IP modules, from one IP module to another IP module until the destination is reached. The IP modules reside in local hosts and network gateways in the system of interconnected networks. The IP datagrams, now called packets, are routed from one IP module to another through individual and disparate networks based on the local interpretation of the destination internet address. Addressing is therefore of critical importance to the success of the IP protocol. Addressing is covered in detail in the next section.

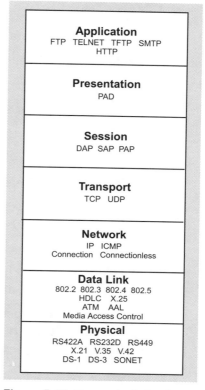

Figure 5.15 Protocol relationships

Now is a good time to illustrate the process of getting data from one application on a local host to another application running on a remote host. Obviously, if two applications are running on the same host, there is no need for TCP/IP to communicate the data from application to application. The theory of operation for transmitting a TCP data segment from one application program to another is illustrated in the following steps:

Step 1   The application program prepares the data to be transported.

Step 2   The application program calls the TCP module and passes the data and destination address.

Step 3   TCP prepares data segment.

Step 4   TCP prepares header.

Step 5   TCP attaches TCP header, creating TCP segment.

Step 6   TCP calls IP and passes destination address and parameters.

Step 7   IP prepares header.

Step 8   IP attaches header to TCP segment, creating IP datagram.

Step 9   IP determines the local network address from destination address.

Step 10 IP calls data link layer which is the local network interface.

Step 11 Local network interface creates a local network header.

Step 12 Local network interface attaches IP datagram to header, creating the network packet.

Step 13 Local network interface physically transmits packet onto network physical medium.

Step 14 Packet arrives at local network interface destination.

Step 15 Local network interface compares destination address to its address to verify it is intended destination.

Step 16 Local network interface removes local network header.

Step 17 Local network interface calls IP module and passes IP datagram to it.

Step 18 IP module receives datagram.

Step 19 IP checks to see if the destination address is this IP module.

Step 20 IP module decrements time-to-live value, discards the datagram if less than zero, and continues processing if the time-to-live is greater than zero.

Step 21 IP module calculates checksum and compares to IP header checksum.

Step 22 If calculated checksum is equal to header checksum, datagram continues processing.

Step 23 If calculated checksum does not equal header checksum, datagram is dropped.

Step 24 If this IP module is the final destination, IP module calls the transport layer protocol (TCP in our case), passes the datagram to the TCP, and skips to step 26. If this IP module is not the final destination, go to step 25.

Step 25 Return to step 7.

Step 26 If this is the final destination, IP removes its header.

Step 27 IP calls the TCP module and passes the data segment.

Step 28 TCP module checks for such things as authorized access, valid sequence numbers, valid acknowledgment numbers, etc.

Step 29 If the data segment fails any TCP tests, it is dropped.

Step 30 TCP verifies all fragmented segments are available and reassembles the data into original segment. If any fragmented segments are missing, TCP sends the data fragments to a buffer to await the arrival of any additional fragments.

Step 31 If the data segment passes all TCP tests, TCP calls its application program and passes the data segment to it.

Addressing

Anyone with an Internet account is probably somewhat familiar with the use of Internet names and may be aware of the conventions used. To inform the rest of us, we will conduct a short discussion of the topic. Names are easier for humans to remember than long lists of lengthy numbers. How many names do you know and how many telephone numbers have you memorized? If you are like the majority of us, you may have hundreds, even thousands of names memorized, but pitifully few telephone numbers, say maybe less than 25. Why? I don't know, other than to say it is easier for me to remember Jane Doe than it is to remember 888-591-7284 (Jane Doe's phone number).

The Internet consists of hundreds of thousands of hosts, each identified by an 11-digit number. Does anyone want to try to remember all the 11-digit numbers necessary to conduct their affairs over the Internet? Probably not many are willing to memorize such large quantities of numbers. So, to make it easier for us humans to use the Internet, the Internet provides for the use of domain names. What is a domain name? Well, my e-mail address is **mbusby@airmail.net**. "airmail.net" is a domain name. That is a lot easier to remember than **mbusby@206.138.231.13**. Names are used at the application/user interface to make it easier for us humans to understand who we are trying to conduct some type of discourse with.

While names are important in the machine-human interface, the machine-machine interface works much more efficiently when dealing with numbers. Numbers are the machines' native tongue. So, the Internet deals primarily with numbered addresses. The "206.138.231.13" portion of my e-mail address is the actual Internet address of my ISP provider. The "mbusby" portion of my address just identifies me to my ISP. The "airmail.net" is the name of my Internet ISP. To summarize, a name specifies who (or what) is sought while an address specifies where the sought-after thing is located.

Now to get from source to destination, the packet must traverse a route. A route specifies how to get from one location to another. Routers are physical electronic devices connecting network elements that maintain routing tables. There are two basic types of routers. One type of (older) router requires a human to determine the routes through the networks and to build and maintain routing tables in files accessible by the router. A newer type of router can dynamically and on the fly determine the valid routes it is connected to by broadcasting messages onto the network seeking other connected routers, receiving responses, and building/maintaining routing tables. Whether the router tables are maintained automatically or by human hands, specific routes to all known points must be identifed.

So, we have a diverse set of addressing tools to get data from one (local) application to another (remote) application. The tools are names, Internet addresses, local network addresses, and routes. User applications must map names to Internet addresses. The Domain Name Server (DNS) helps applications accomplish the name conversion activity. The IP module maps internet addresses to local network addresses. Local network routers or network gateways map local network addresses to routes. Figure 5.16 illustrates the steps in the process from name to route.

The internet address bit field is fixed at 32 bits. An internet address begins with a variable length network number, followed by local address.

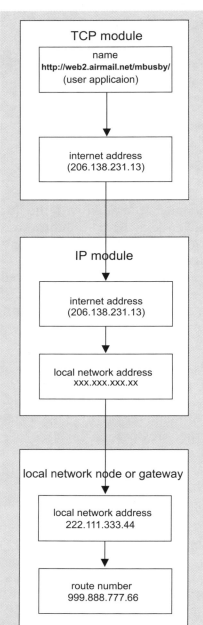

Figure 5.16 IP address translation from name to route

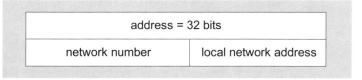

Figure 5.17 Internet address bit field

There are two internet addressing schemes in place today. One is a class-based scheme and the other is classless. The class-based scheme is the original internet addressing scheme. Class-based addressing lumps all internet addresses into one of five different classes. These classes are Class A, B, C, D, and E. Classes A, B, and C addresses are used for unicast (single recipient) addresses. Class D addresses are used for multicast (multiple recipients) addresses. Class E addresses are reserved for future use.

The class-based method of assigning internet addresses has three formats of internet addresses as shown in Figure 5.18. For class A, the left-most (high-order) bit is set to zero, the next 7 bits identify the network, and the last 24 bits identify the local address. In the class B format, the two left-most bits are one and zero respectively, the next 14 bits identify the network, and the last 16 bits identify the local address. For the class C format, the three left-most bits are one, one, and zero respectively, the next 21 bits identify the network, and the last 8 bits identify the local address.

bit	0 1 2 3 4 5 6 7 8 9 0 1 2 3 4 5 6 7 8 9 0 1 2 3 4 5 6 7 8 9 0 1	
class A	0 network address	local address
class B	1 0 network address	local address
class C	1 1 0 network address	local address
no class	1 1 1 classless addressing	

Figure 5.18 Internet address classes

Some hosts may have several physical interfaces, usually identified by the number of network cards plugged into the host. Each physical interface will have at least one internet address and could possibly have several.

The explosive growth of the Internet over the last five years has made obsolete some of the original TCP/IP design features. One such obsolete feature is class-based addressing. Due to the sheer volume of addresses in demand by users, the 32-bit class-based addressing quickly became too restrictive. A means of addressing was needed that could work with the class-based addressing method and still allow for the assignment of any number of internet addresses. The solution was a classless addressing scheme that allows the network portion of the address to be any length necessary. For now, the classless addressing scheme is undefined.

The following three reasons are given by the internet community for the need for classless addressing. These are quoted directly from RFC 1519.

> 1. Exhaustion of the class B network address space. One fundamental cause of this problem is the lack of a network class of a size which is appropriate for mid-sized organization; class C, with a maximum of 254 host addresses, is too small, while class B, which allows up to 65,534 addresses, is too large for most organizations.

2. Growth of routing tables in Internet routers beyond the ability of current software, hardware, and people to effectively manage.

3. Eventual exhaustion of the 32-bit IP address space.

The class-based addressing scheme is still very much in use. At least eight companies producing networking products announced new IP-based "network tuners" in 1998. These "network tuners" can perform all the functions of a classic router and they can prioritize traffic based upon the network address class. So, while the old class-based addressing scheme will likely be around for another few years, the trend is to move away from classing the address.

As always, there are special cases that require special attention. Internet addressing is no exception. The following tables list the special network addressing cases.

Network Number	Host Number
0000000000000000	0000000000000000

Table 5.20 "this host on this network"

Table 5.20 shows the address for "this host on this network." This address may only be used as a source address.

Network Number	Host Number
0000000000000000	xxxxxxxxxxxxxxx

Table 5.21 "specified host on this network"

Table 5.21 shows the address for the "specified host on this network." This address may only be used as a source address.

Network Number	Host Number
IIIIIIIIIIIIIIII	IIIIIIIIIIIIIIII

Table 5.22 Limited broadcast

Table 5.22 shows the address indicating limited broadcast. This address may only be used as a destination address, and a datagram with this address must never be forwarded outside the network of the source.

Network Number	Host Number
xxxxxxxxxxxxxxx	IIIIIIIIIIIIIIII

Table 5.23 Directed broadcast to the specified network

Table 5.23 shows the address for a directed broadcast to the specified network, as identified by the network number. This address may only be used as a destination address.

Network Number	Subnet Number	Host Number
xxxxxxxxxxxxxxx	xxxxxxx	I I I I I I I I

Table 5.24 Directed broadcast to the specified subnet

Table 5.24 shows the address for a directed broadcast to the specified subnet, as identified by the subnet number. This address may only be used as a destination address.

Network Number	Subnet Number	Host Number
xxxxxxxxxxxxxxx	I I I I I I I I	I I I I I I I I

Table 5.25 Directed broadcast to all subnets

Table 5.25 shows the address for a directed broadcast to all subnets of the specified network, as specified by the network number. This address may only be used as a destination address.

Network Number	Host Number
000000001 I I I I I I I	xxxxxxxxxxxxxxx

Table 5.26 Host internal loopback address

Table 5.26 shows the address for a host internal loopback address. This addressing mode is useful for testing and troubleshooting the host and should never be transported outside a host.

Fragmentation

IP datagram fragmentation is necessary when it originates in a local net that allows a large packet size and must traverse a local net that limits packets to a smaller size to reach its destination. The IP module acting as the gateway into the network requiring small packets is responsible for fragmenting the datagram. However, the originating host can specify in the IP header whether or not to allow fragmentation. If the "don't fragment" flag is set (bit 2 of the IP header Flags bit field) in an IP datagram and it encounters a gateway that requires a smaller size datagram, the gateway will drop the packet.

Fragmentation and reassembly that occurs outside of the internet protocol, such as the fragmentation and reassembly that may occur in a local intranetwork, does not necessarily conform to any of the requirements for this internet protocol fragmentation and reassembly. The internet fragmentation and reassembly process must be able to fragment a datagram into any arbitrary number of datagrams, keeping in mind that certain minimum datagram sizes (1 octet of data minimum) are required. These datagram fragments must be capable of being reassembled when all the pieces arrive at the intended destination.

The destination IP module uses the fragment identification field to ensure that fragments of different datagrams are not mixed. The fragment offset field tells the destination IP module the position a fragment held in the original datagram. The fragment's position in the original datagram is determined by the offset and length values in the datagram containing the fragment. The IP module can determine whether or not any one fragmented datagram is the last one by testing the last fragment flag. If it is set, there are more fragments to come. This explanation assumes that all fragments travel through the internetwork along the exact same route and in order. Actually, since packets may take diverse routes through the internet to their intended destination, it is possible for the last fragment of a fragmented datagram to arrive at the destination before any other fragments. The "last fragment" flag just tells the IP module that the fragment carrying that flag goes on the end of the reconstructed datagram. The IP module identifies the original datagram fragments by the use of the identification, destination, source, and protocol fields of the IP header. The IP module can reconstruct the original datagram as soon as all the pieces are on hand (in the receive buffer) using the IP header fragment offset values.

Remember from the earlier fragmentation discussion that the fragment offset bit field is 13 bits and the fragment offset indicates where in the original datagram this fragment belongs. If the datagram is not fragmented, the fragment offset is always equal to zero and the first fragment always has a fragment offset equal to zero. With this information in hand, it is a reasonably simple matter to program a computer to keep track of fragments and where they belong in the original data bit stream.

The IP header identification field is used to distinguish the fragments of different datagrams. The source IP module of a datagram sets the identification field to a value that must be unique for the intended source-destination pair for the length of time the packet is a live packet in the internetwork.

Fragmentation of a large IP datagram by any IP module (for example, in a gateway) creates at least two new IP datagrams. Fragmentation cannot occur unless there are at least 9 octets of data, as the datagram is divided at 8-octet boundaries. So, the first fragment must have any multiple of 8 octets of data for fragmentation to be enabled. Additional fragments must have at least 8 octets of data and must have integer multiples of 8 octets if they have more than 8, except for the last fragment which can have less than 8 octets of data. When a datagram is fragmented, the contents of the IP header fields are copied from the original datagram into each of the fragments.

When fragmentation occurs, the first set of data octets (any integer multiple of 8) from the original data bit field is inserted into the first new IP datagram, and the total length field is set to the length of this datagram. The "more fragments" flag is set to one to indicate at least one more datagram contains fragmented data. The fragment offset is set to the number of 8-octet groups of data in this fragment. Since there must be at least 8 octets of data in the first fragment, the fragment offset will always be at least one, if fragmentation occurred.

The next set of data octets from the original datagram are inserted into the second IP datagram and the "total length" field is set to the length of this second datagram. If this is the last of the data octets, the "more fragments" flag is set to false; otherwise it is set to true. The fragment offset field of the second IP datagram is set to the value of the fragment offset in the first fragment plus the number of octets in this datagram. And on and on and on, for however many fragments the data is divided into. The IP header fields which may be affected by fragmentation include: internet header length field; total length field; header checksum; options field; "more fragments" flag; and fragment offset.

The fragments of an IP datagram are assembled at the destination host by the IP module. The IP module combines the IP datagrams having the same value for identification, source, destination, and protocol header fields. The reassembly of the original datagram is accomplished by placing the data portion of each fragment in its correct position in the original datagram. The correct position is specified by the fragment offset in the fragment's IP header. The first fragment has a fragment offset of zero, and the last fragment has the "more fragments" flag set to false.

Gateways

Gateways are network routers that connect two or more networks together. Gateways utilize internet protocol to transport datagrams between networks. Gateways also utilize the Gateway to Gateway Protocol (GGP) to coordinate routing and other internet control information. Gateways do not utilize higher level protocols above IP so the GGP functions are added to the IP module.

Summary

IP is a software-based process for interfacing higher level protocols to the physical resources of a network-based system of interconnected computing devices for the purpose of transporting data from a source to a destination. IP is a robust software program that works very well for its intended purpose. IP has the ability to adapt to a changing purpose as the well-known Internet blossoms, placing an ever-increasing burden on its ability to meet our evolving communications needs.

Chapter 6

TCP User Process Commands

Questions answered in this chapter:

What are the basic user process commands?

What is the format of the basic user process commands?

What functionality do the basic user process commands provide?

Basic Commands

TCP must provide a minimum set of commands necessary to provide for a basic connection management functionality. The TCP command set provides the basic functionality needed to carry on an interprocess communication between two or more TCPs. The TCP command set may be further refined by including additional commands and/or command functionality, as any particular vendor so desires, but the minimum command set must be functional on any TCP implementation.

There are several cases where the TCP must communicate with higher and lower processes. The TCP must be capable of signaling, through the local operating system, the user process/program, then passing appropriate information about the connection to the user process. The information passed to the user process includes connection status messages and response strings. These are the basic TCP user process commands:

OPEN call
SEND call
RECEIVE call
CLOSE call
ABORT call
STATUS call

As you may observe from the set of basic commands, they are really very basic. Do not confuse the commands with the status of a connection. That is, do not confuse SEND call with the SEND Status. SEND call is a software function that requires the operating system to place the TCP connection in the SEND Status, assuming the SEND call was successful. Some implementations of TCP/IP provide for additional functionality that is not included in the above basic set of commands. Since the IETF lists the above commands as the minimum required for a compliant TCP, that is all we will discuss in the following sections.

The basic command set provides for communication in both directions—up to the user process and down to the Lower-level Interface. In our case, the LLI is IP. It is always beneficial to know the status of a connection when receiving and transmitting data. For instance, when the user process is ready to transmit data, it is useful to know that the connection is still valid. Otherwise, what is the point of attempting to transmit? And when data is received, it is useful to know the data was transmitted from an authorized node. Hence, the STATUS call is necessary for both transmit and receive functions. The other commands are useful for either receiving data, sending data, or ending a connection.

Commands used to communicate up the (software) chain to the user process include RECEIVE call and STATUS call. These are the minimum commands necessary to determine the status of the connection and receive data from a valid network node.

Commands used to communicate to the LLI include OPEN call, SEND call, CLOSE call, ABORT call, and STATUS call. These are the minimum commands required to determine the status of the connection and transport data across the network from the source node to the destination node.

The remainder of this chapter is devoted to mapping out the commands and their format. Flow charts are used to graphically illustrate the relationships of the various states of the connection to the TCP commands, and the typical response of TCP/IP to the commands. The format for the commands is given as:

COMMAND (mandatory arguments, [optional arguments]) : return arguments

COMMAND represents the command of interest such as OPEN or CLOSE. Mandatory arguments are those parameters that must be present when the function is called, or else an error is returned to the calling process. Optional arguments are those arguments that may be present. Return arguments are those arguments (values) that the routine returns to the user process.

OPEN Call

The format for the OPEN call is:

> OPEN (local port number, foreign socket number, active/passive [time-out], [precedence], [security/compartment], [options]) : local connection name

An OPEN call is a command for the local TCP/IP to open a connection to a remote TCP/IP. The OPEN call can occur under two different circumstances. First, if the local user process wishes to establish a connection to a remote TCP/IP, the user process will issue an OPEN call to its TCP/IP module. If a remote TCP/IP is attempting to establish a connection with a local TCP/IP, the local TCP/IP will notify its user process of the attempted connection and wait for the user process to decide what to do. In either case, the TCP may be in the LISTEN state or the CLOSED state. Figure 6.1 on the following page shows the sequence of events the TCP follows to go from the CLOSED state to the SYN SENT state when the OPEN call is made.

When the user process determines that a network connection is desired, the user process must initiate opening the connection by making an OPEN call to the TCP. When the user process initiates an OPEN call, the user process must pass to the TCP the local port number, foreign socket number, and whether the connection is active or passive. Additionally, the user process may pass the connection time-out value, precedence, and security parameters. Lastly, the user process may include other options in the OPEN call to the TCP.

In Figure 6.1, the use of the term "return" means the TCP will return the text message to the process that called the TCP. Usually, but not always, especially in the world of UNIX, the return will prompt the process to display a meaningful message to the user concerning the status of the connection. Such a meaningful message occurs when a user dials into the Internet and receives status messages from the dialer process concerning the progress of the connection. Typical user process messages are "dialing," "connecting," and "verifying user name and password." TCP returns the status of the connection for a defined set of status conditions. The software that implements the user process can vary in the manner of using and/or ignoring the TCP.

Figure 6.2 shows the sequence of events the TCP follows to go from the LISTEN state to the SYN SENT state when an OPEN call is made.

A connection is specified in the OPEN call by the remote host socket and local host port arguments of the OPEN call routine. Typically, the process initiating the OPEN call will use a short name, which is usually a "pointer" to the TCB data structure, to identify the service associated with the OPEN call. Such an example would be the use of "telnet" to identify an OPEN call to establish Telnet service.

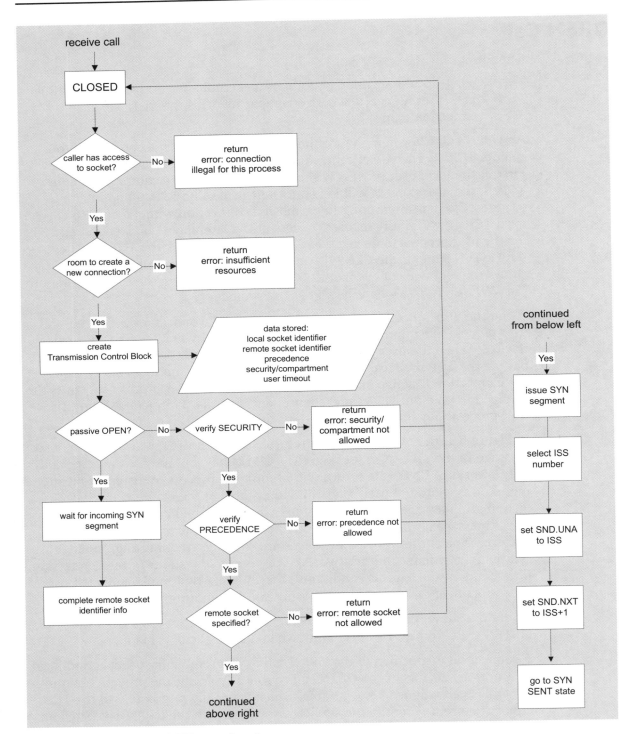

Figure 6.1 OPEN call/CLOSED state flowchart

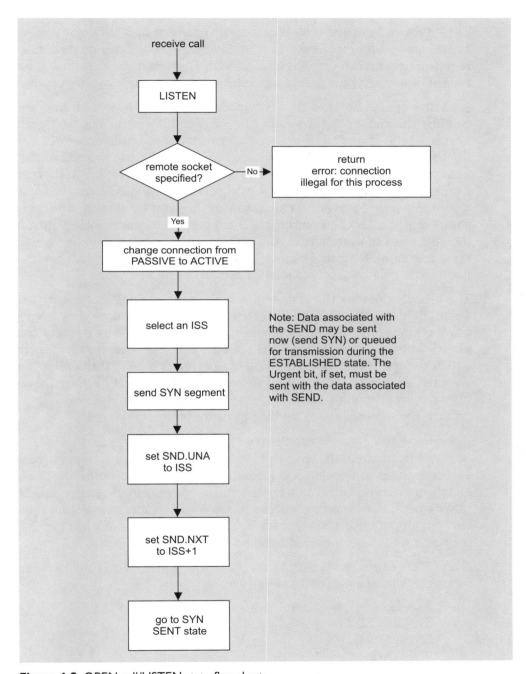

Figure 6.2 OPEN call/LISTEN state flowchart

The OPEN call must specify whether the connection is active or passive. An active connection means the host initiating the OPEN call sends connection requests to establish communication with another host. This host behavior is typical of a client host seeking to establish a connection with a server.

A passive connection means a connection where the host initiating the OPEN call just sits and waits for another host to send it a connection request. This host behavior is typical of a server host running multiple processes and waiting for a client to establish communication. Usually, the process initiating a passive OPEN call will accept a connection request from any authorized caller. Examples of such processes are a mail server and a file server. To be able to meet the need of server processes to wait for connection requests and still be compliant to the TCP requirement that every connection socket must include the addresses of both parties, the remote socket is identified as all zeroes in the passive OPEN state. Only the passive OPEN state allows all zeroes to denote the existence of unspecified remote hosts.

The process opening the connection in the passive OPEN state with an unspecified remote socket will then accept a connection request from any other remote process. If the remote process adheres to the conventional use of well-known port numbers, it is then easy for the local host to determine which service the remote host wishes to connect to. But if the remote host does not adhere to the standard use of well-known port numbers, then hopefully the programming team has made some provision for identifying which process the remote host is seeking to connect to.

If the local host has several passive OPENs, and a connection request is received from a remote host, the local host will attempt to match the remote socket number to a local socket number first. If the attempt fails, it will then match the remote OPEN to a socket with an unspecified remote socket. In other words, the local host checks to see if the remote connection request fits with an already open connection (a TCB with the remote socket exists) before connecting to an unspecified local socket.

If an OPEN call is made during the following states, the TCP will return the message: "error: connection already exists":

SYN SENT
SYN RECEIVED
ESTABLISHED
FIN WAIT 1
FIN WAIT 2
CLOSE WAIT
CLOSING
LAST ACK
TIME WAIT

It is assumed the local TCP is aware of the identity of the processes it serves and will check the authority, including precedence, security, and compartment, of the remote process to use the intended connection. If authorized to use the connection, then permission is granted to establish the connection; otherwise an error message is returned. If the precedence, security, or compartment parameters are left out, the default values are used.

If the active/passive flag in the OPEN call is set to passive, the state of the connection is LISTEN for an incoming connection request. A passive OPEN may include either a fully specified foreign socket required to wait for a particular connection request or an unspecified foreign socket required to wait for any connection request. A fully specified passive OPEN call may be made active by executing a SEND. The time-out parameter, if present, overrides the default value of 1 minute.

Upon determining the remote user has authority and there is room to establish a connection, the TCP creates the transmission control block (TCB) and partially fills it with data from the OPEN command parameters. If the OPEN is an active OPEN command, the TCP will begin the process of synchronizing the connection at once by use of the three-way handshake.

A local connection name is returned by the TCP to the user process. The local connection name is used to identify the connection defined by the [local socket, foreign socket] pair.

SEND Call

The format for the SEND call is:

> SEND (local connection name, buffer address, byte count, Push flag, Urgent flag, [timeout])

A SEND call is a command for the local TCP/IP to send, or transmit, data to a remote TCP/IP. The SEND call must identify for the TCP the local connection name, the SEND buffer address (of the data to be sent), the number of bytes to send (includes the byte occupying the buffer address), whether or not to push (hurry) the data, and whether or not the data is urgent.

If the local TCP receives a SEND call from the user process and the

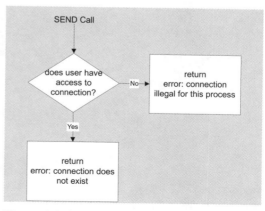

Figure 6.3 SEND call/CLOSED state

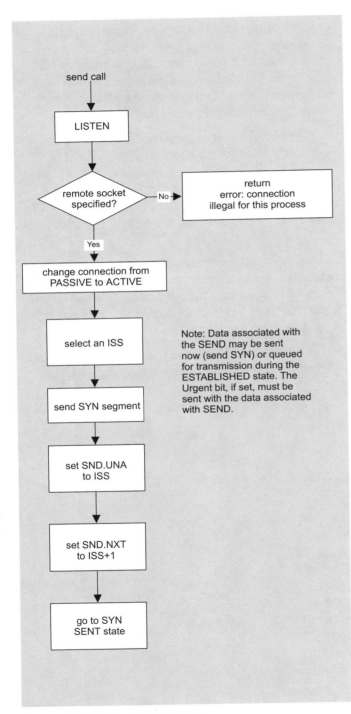

Note: Data associated with the SEND may be sent now (send SYN) or queued for transmission during the ESTABLISHED state. The Urgent bit, if set, must be sent with the data associated with SEND.

Figure 6.4 SEND call/LISTEN state

connection is not already established, then the TCP returns an error. See Figure 6.3.

The normal state for the TCP to receive a SEND call from the user process is the LISTEN state. The LISTEN state exists after a connection is established. From Figure 6.4 it can be seen that the TCP state progression is from LISTEN to SYN SENT states after the TCP receives the SEND call.

A SEND call during the CLOSE WAIT state causes the TCP state to progress to the FIN WAIT 1 state. See Figure 6.5. This situation occurs when a connection is in the process of closing.

A SEND call is not valid during the following states:

SYN SENT
ESTABLISHED
FIN WAIT 1
FIN WAIT 2
CLOSING
LAST ACK

The SEND call causes the data contained in the specified user buffer to be sent to the specified connection. For most TCP implementations, if the connection is not open, the SEND generates appropriate error messages. However, some proprietary TCP implementations may allow users to use SEND without establishing a connection first. In the latter case, an automatic OPEN must be performed before the SEND call is initiated. If the calling user process is not authorized to use this connection, an error message is returned.

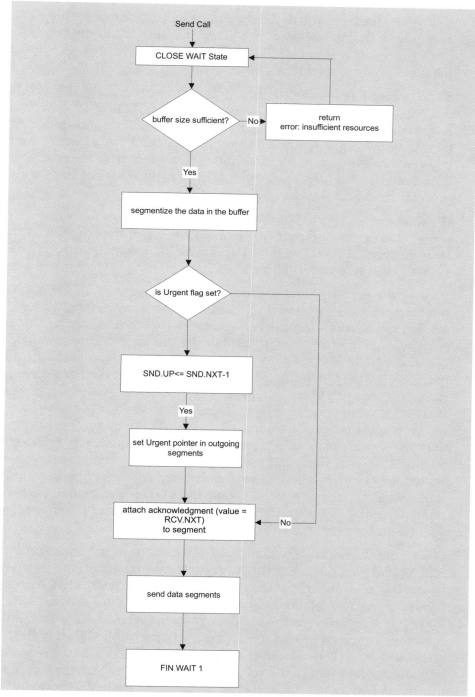

Figure 6.5 SEND call/CLOSE WAIT state

If the Push flag is enabled, the data must be transmitted by the local host promptly to the remote host. The Push bit will be set in the last TCP segment. If the Push flag is not enabled, the data may be combined with data from subsequent SENDs in the interest of efficiency.

If the Urgent flag is enabled, segments sent to the remote TCP will have the urgent pointer set. The remote, or receiving, TCP will signal the urgent condition to the receiving process if the urgent pointer indicates that data preceding the urgent pointer has not already been processed by the receiving process. The purpose of the Urgent flag is to identify to the receiving TCP data deemed of an urgent, or priority, nature and to stimulate the receiver to process the urgent data as soon as possible.

If a time-out is specified in the SEND call, the current user time-out for this connection is changed to the new one. Remember, the time-out specifies how long the local TCP will wait for the remote TCP to send an acknowledgment before it will retransmit the segment.

There are two possible scenarios for sending data from a local host to a remote host. One scenario is for the local host to send data, then wait the maximum segment lifetimes (MSL) time period for the remote TCP to acknowledge the reception of the data. This is an asynchronous mode of operation and it is very inefficient. The TCP sending the data would spend much of its time just waiting for the acknowledgments. If our data networks were plagued with unreliable physical mediums and switching equipment, such as found in underdeveloped areas of the world, then networking would not be worth the time or trouble due to the TCP requirement to retransmit unreceived/unacknowledged packets. However, due to very reliable physical mediums, such as fiber, and fast, reliable switching equipment, very few packets require retransmission. Since hundreds of trillions of packets are transported about every day, a couple of billion retransmitted packets is still a small percentage. Anyway, asynchronous transmission is inefficient, even with a no-loss transmission medium, and should be avoided.

The second scenario is for the local TCP to continue sending data for the first MSL period which yields a window of transmitted data the TCP must manage by storing in an "unacknowledged data" buffer. If the local TCP does not receive an acknowledgment from the remote TCP after the first MSL, then the local TCP must requeue the old data and send it again. However, if the remote host acknowledges the data packets transmitted during the first MSL, the local host only need move its "unacknowledged data" window down and include the data sent in the second MSL period. The TCP must continue moving the "unacknowledged data" window for each MSL period. If the connection is a good connection, the TCP will spend little time retransmitting packets. And the TCP will require little processing overhead by stuffing the "unacknowledged data" packets into the buffer, yielding a very lean and mean transmission protocol. What happens now if a packet is not acknowledged at the expiration of 2 times the MSL? The connection will close, as stated in a previous chapter. Your ISP does not want you tying up its resources (phone line, modem, etc.) while you peruse your e-mail.

RECEIVE Call

The format for the RECEIVE call is:

RECEIVE (local connection name, buffer address, byte count) : byte count, urgent flag, push flag

The different states are illustrated in Figures 6.6, 6.7, and 6.8.

The TCP may receive calls from a remote TCP only when it is prepared to process the received data. Not all TCP states can receive data. If a RECEIVE call is attempted while the TCP is in one of these states, an error message is created and returned to the remote TCP as an ICMP error message. Table 6.1 shows the states the TCP may and may not receive calls in.

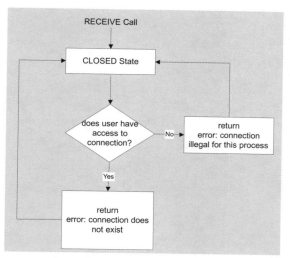

Figure 6.6 RECEIVE call/CLOSED state

State	Return Response
LISTEN	none
SYN SENT	none
ESTABLISHED	none
FIN WAIT 1	none
FIN WAIT 2	none
CLOSING	error: connection closing
LAST ACK	error: connection closing
TIME WAIT state	error: connection closing

Table 6.1 RECEIVE call received from remote TCP return response

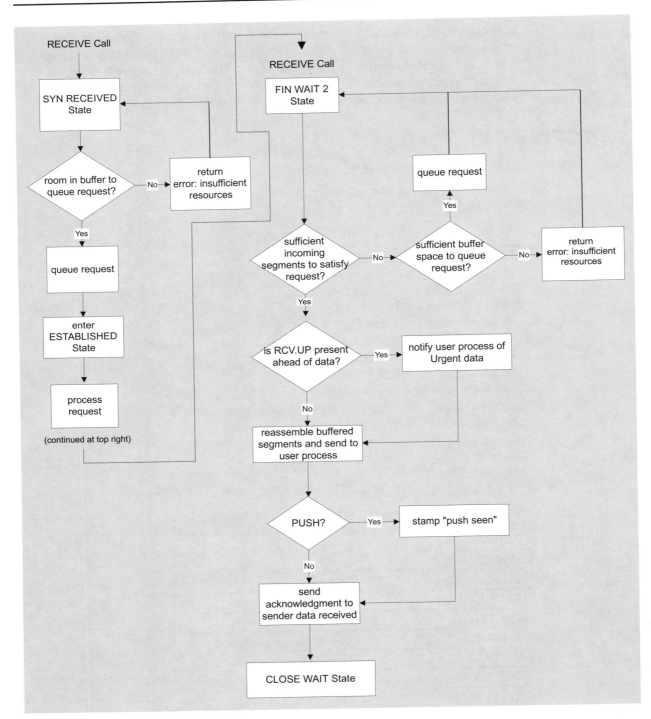

Figure 6.7 RECEIVE call/SYN RECEIVED state

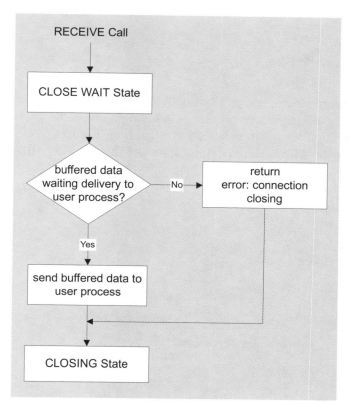

RECEIVE Call

CLOSE WAIT State

buffered data waiting delivery to user process? —No→ return error: connection closing

Yes

send buffered data to user process

CLOSING State

Figure 6.8 RECEIVE call/CLOSE WAIT state

The RECEIVE call allocates a receive data buffer that is assigned specifically to the connection identified in the RECEIVE call. If the connection is not open when the RECEIVE call is made, the TCP returns an error. Also, if the user process making the RECEIVE call is not authorized to use the connection identified in the RECEIVE call, an error is returned.

In the interest of efficiency, the TCP (or the user process in some implementations) will set up multiple receive (data) buffers allowing several or many RECEIVEs for each connection to be in process simultaneously. Most, if not all, implementations allow the user to set up the number and size of buffers allowed. Too few buffers and your computer idly waits for data to arrive. Too many buffers and your system resources cannot support all the tasks required. The TCP will send the data on to the user process when a buffer becomes full or when the TCP receives a PUSH associated with a RECEIVE call-buffer pair.

If a segment arrives containing urgent data (Urgent flag is enabled) the user process is notified immediately via a TCP-to-user process signal. The receiving user process is then placed in "urgent" mode. Additional urgent data remains if the Urgent flag is enabled (on or set) in following segments. If the Urgent flag is disabled (off or reset), this call to RECEIVE has returned all the urgent data, and the user may now leave "urgent" mode. The buffer containing the urgent data is pushed to the user process. In robust implementations, TCPs do not mix urgent and non-urgent data in receive data buffers.

The format of the RECEIVE call includes the pointer (address) to the data buffer and the byte count of the data received. The RECEIVE call passes the buffer pointer and number of bytes received to the user process, allowing the user process to determine the success or failure of individual SEND calls. The buffer pointer identifies for the user process the particular connection (and therefore the particular remote user process) the data is associated with and the number of bytes received, so far.

CLOSE Call

The format for the CLOSE calls is:

CLOSE (local connection name)

Upon completion of a communication, each TCP must close the connection in order to free the resources for use by other processes. Closing a connection involves the exchange of segments carrying the FIN control flag. Figures 6.9, 6.10, 6.11, 6.12, 6.13, and 6.14 shows the different states of the CLOSE call.

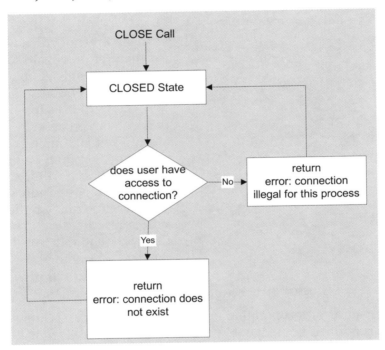

Figure 6.9 CLOSE call/CLOSED state

CLOSE (local connection name) will cause the connection identified by the local connection name to be closed. If the user process calling this command is unauthorized to use the connection identified as the local connection name or the connection is not open, the call will return an error. The initiation of a CLOSE requires that all outstanding SENDs be serviced in the normal manner (send data, receive acknowledgment, etc.). Since a TCP will continue sending the last of its queued data after

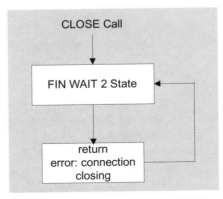

Figure 6.10 CLOSE call/FIN WAIT 2 state

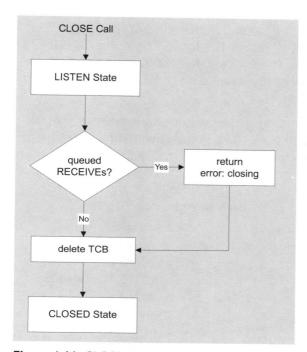

Figure 6.11 CLOSE call/LISTEN state

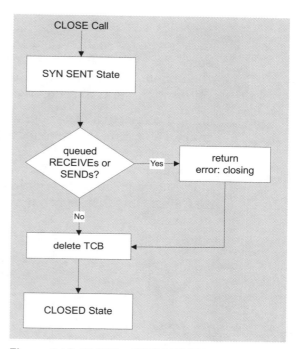

Figure 6.12 CLOSE call/SYN SENT state

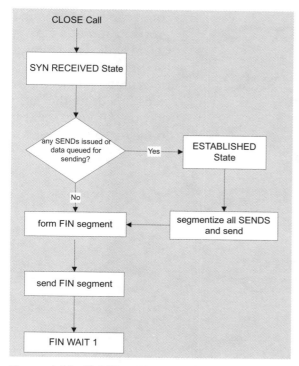

Figure 6.13 CLOSE call/SYN RECEIVED state

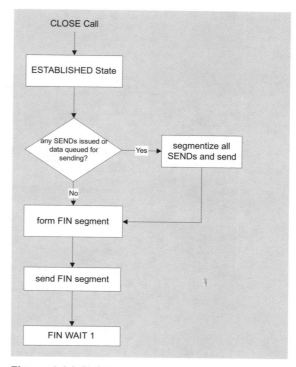

Figure 6.14 CLOSE call/ESTABLISHED state

initiating a CLOSE call, the call itself is actually queued until the last of the data is sent. Even after the CLOSE call places the local TCP in the CLOSING state, the local TCP must still expect to receive data from the remote TCP, as the remote TCP has the same opportunity to send all of its queued data upon notification the connection is closing.

A local connection may close at any time as the result of a local user process initiative or in response to local TCP flow control initiatives, such as time-out exceeded or a remote TCP CLOSE connection initiative. Logically, once a connection moves to the CLOSING state, neither TCP may reopen the connection until the connection incarnation in the CLOSING state has progressed to CLOSED. Only then may one of the TCPs attempt to re-establish the connection.

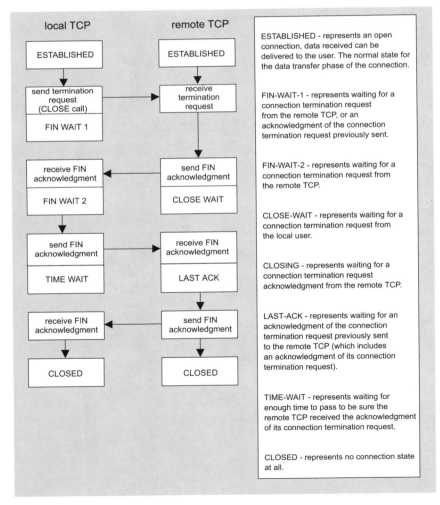

Note that when a TCP receives a CLOSE call, the TCP will push the data out to the IP for transmission.

Figure 6.15 shows the steps the two TCPs follow to gracefully close a connection. Either user process can initiate a CLOSE call. The block at the right of the flowchart explains the steps in closing the connection with due regard for civilized behavior.

Figure 6.15 Closing the connection

ABORT Call

The format for the ABORT command is:

ABORT (local connection name)

Figures 6.16, 6.17, and 6.18 illustrate the different states of the ABORT call.

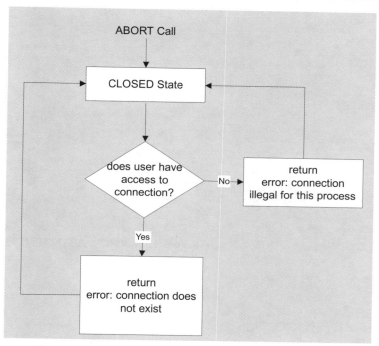

Figure 6.16 ABORT call/CLOSED state

State	Return Response
SYN RECEIVED	error: connection reset
ESTABLISHED	error: connection reset
FIN WAIT 1	error: connection reset
FIN WAIT 2	error: connection reset
CLOSE WAIT	error: connection reset

Table 6.2 ABORT call received from remote host

The ABORT command causes all locally pending SENDs and RECEIVEs to be aborted and the TCB to be discarded, and triggers the transmission of a special reset message to the remote TCP. Depending on the particular TCP implementation, a local user process may receive abort acknowledgments for each outstanding SEND or RECEIVE from its local TCP, or the user process may receive a single ABORT acknowledgment for all SENDs and RECEIVEs.

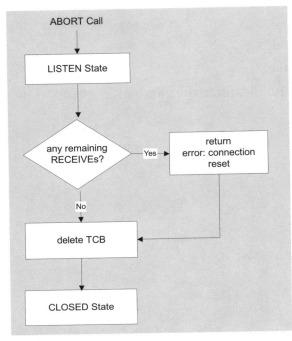

Figure 6.17 ABORT call/LISTEN state

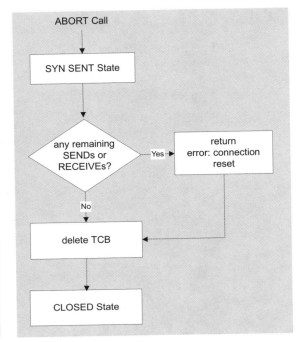

Figure 6.18 ABORT call/SYN SENT state

STATUS Call

The format for the STATUS command is:

STATUS (local connection name) : status data

The following figures show the 11 states of the STATUS command.

If the calling user process is not authorized to use this connection, an error is returned.

This command returns a data block from the TCB containing the following information: local socket, foreign socket, local connection name, receive window, send window, connection state, number of buffers awaiting acknowledgment, number of buffers pending receipt, urgent state, precedence, security/compartment, and transmission timeout. The data is not necessarily in the order given or even present. The order is immaterial and dependent upon each individual implementation.

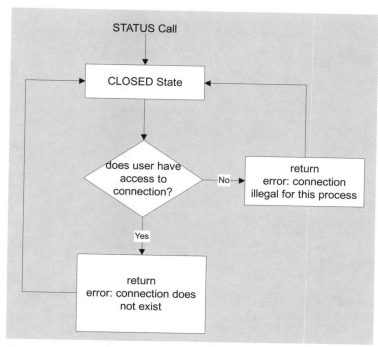

Figure 6.19 STATUS call/CLOSED state

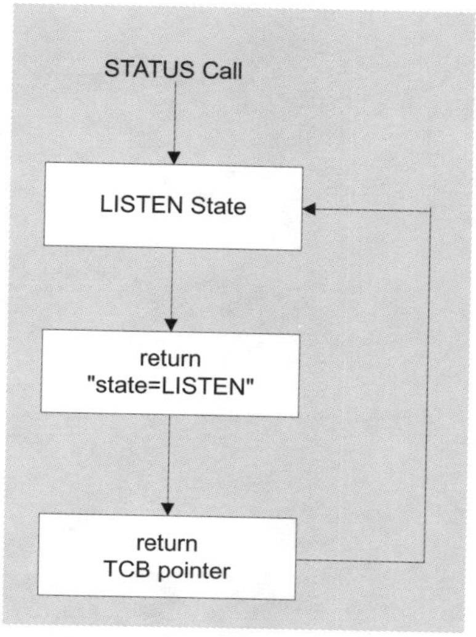

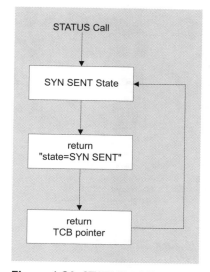

Figure 6.21 STATUS call/SYN SENT state

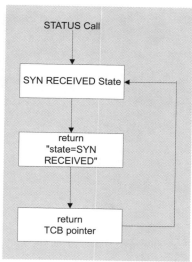

Figure 6.22 STATUS call/SYN RECEIVED state

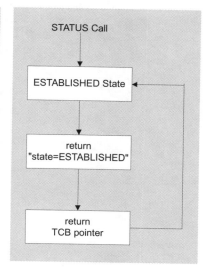

Figure 6.23 STATUS call/ESTABLISHED state

Figure 6.20 STATUS call/LISTEN state

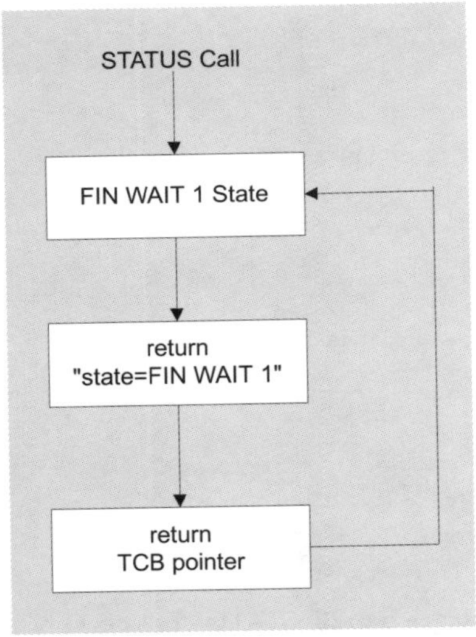

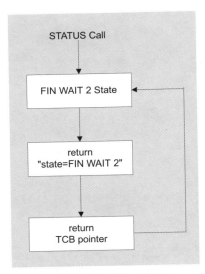

Figure 6.24 STATUS call/FIN WAIT 1 state

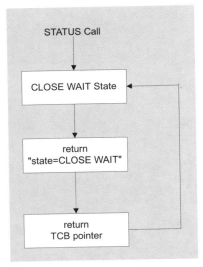

Figure 6.25 STATUS call/FIN WAIT 2 state

Figure 6.26 STATUS call/CLOSE WAIT state

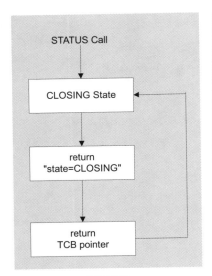

Figure 6.27 STATUS call/CLOSING state

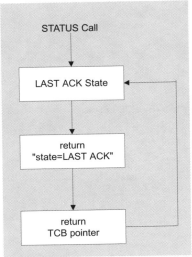

Figure 6.28 STATUS call/LAST ACK state

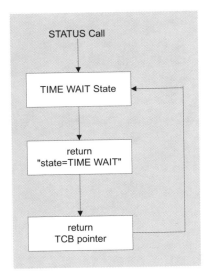

Figure 6.29 STATUS call/TIME WAIT state

Summary

TCP uses several user process commands to manage the TCP/IP connection. These user process commands correspond to actions that a user program must perform to open a network connection, send data, receive data, and close the network connection. In some user programs, such as an e-mail program, these actions may occur automatically without any human action or intervention. When I click on my e-mail icon, it will automatically call my ISP and download all my e-mail without any other action on my part. In other programs, such as an FTP program, some or all of these commands are executed only on the specific command of a human operator. Regardless of the manner in which a program uses the commands, they are the minimum set of commands necessary to manage the TCP/IP connection.

Chapter 7

Establishing and Closing the Connection

Questions answered in this chapter:

How is a TCP connection established?

What is the TCP handshake?

How does the TCP transmit the data?

How does the TCP receive the data?

How does the TCP close the connection?

Establishing the Connection or Socket

Reliability (error checking) and flow control (sequencing) mechanisms need to know certain status information regarding each connection and its associated data stream. To meet this need, TCP must initialize and maintain the status information. The status information includes local host address, remote host address, and port number combined with the connection socket number, sequence number, and window size. This status information is maintained in the transmission control block (TCB) and is the actual "connection" between the two hosts. The remote host socket number and the local host socket number pair uniquely specify the connection, the TCB, between the two hosts.

For any two processes to successfully communicate, the TCP of each host must establish the connection. The connection is established when each TCP initializes its TCB data structure containing the appropriate information concerning the connection. Connections are attempted, established, and torn down over a multitude of networks of varying distances using a variety of computing and transmission equipment. To ensure a reliable connection to an acceptable host, TCP uses a handshake mechanism to verify the connection request and to ensure the attempted connection is authorized. The handshake mechanism includes the use of sequence numbers that are time-based and the SYN (synchronize) control flag. TCP uses the handshake to garner information about the connection that is stored in the TCB. After completing the handshake, each TCP has a completed TCB structure.

A connection attempt occurs when one host transmits an active OPEN call to another host. When the datagram containing the SYN flag in the set condition is received by a host, it creates a TCB to record pertinent information about the connection. The receiving host then matches the local and remote sockets, thus initiating the connection. After the two hosts exchange sequence information and synchronize the sequence numbers, the connection is "established."

The Handshake

The method of establishing the TCP connection is usually called the handshake. It is known as a three-way handshake due to the number of times the two TCPs communicate during the handshake process. A three-way handshake is slightly more elaborate than a plain two-way handshake, but the three-way provides greater protection against the possibility of a false connection. While false connections may seem a rather mundane issue, it is a serious problem for servers connecting to hundreds or even thousands of users per day.

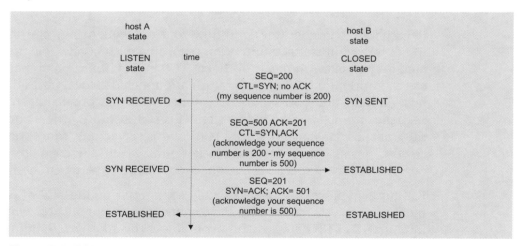

Figure 7.1 TCP connection setup—the three-way handshake

Figure 7.1 illustrates the simple three-way handshake. The TCP of host B is in the CLOSED state. Upon prompting from the higher-level process, it opens communication with TCP A, which is in the LISTEN state, by sending a segment with the CTL bit set to SYN (synchronize the sequence numbers). Host

B is now in the SYN SENT state. Host A receives the request to connect (CTL=SYN) and immediately goes from the LISTEN state to the SYN RECEIVED state. Host A returns an acknowledgment of the request to connect segment received by setting the ACK value to the sequence number (201) received and by including its own sequence number (500) in the segment. When host B receives the return acknowledgment from host A, it immediately goes into the ESTABLISHED state and returns an acknowledgment (ACK=201) of host A's acknowledgment. As soon as host A receives host B's acknowledgment, host A changes to the ESTABLISHED state. Each host is aware of the other host's sequence numbering and can determine when a segment is received or not received, providing a fundamental cornerstone of the TCP reliability pyramid.

A note concerning the ESTABLISHED state. ESTABLISHED is the state where data communications may occur. When the connection is ESTABLISHED, all valid segments must contain an acceptable acknowledgment of the reception of the previous data segment.

A send sequence number and a receive sequence number occupying the send sequence number space and the receive sequence number space, respectively, exist for every connection. The Initial Send Sequence number (ISS) is determined by the TCP initiating the connection. The Initial Receive Sequence number (IRS) is determined by the TCP receiving the connection request. Put another way, when you dial up your ISP, your computer generates the ISS while the ISP computer generates the IRS. For the connection request to succeed, the two TCPs must synchronize on the ISS and the IRS. If only it were this easy in the dating game!

This description of the way the connection is set up does not include such TCP features as windowing (flow control). Also, the above connection description assumes the connection will be completed without any problems such as might occur if one of the segments were lost in the maze of internets.

Post-handshake

After the two TCPs have completed the handshake, they are ready to transport data across the network. Figure 7.2 shows the inclusion of the next segment after the handshake, which is the first data segment going from host B to host A. Notice that the sequence and acknowledgment numbers are the same as the last sequence and acknowledgments of the handshake. This is a crucial idea concerning TCP. The software is written so that each host knows the sequence number of the first data segment is the same as the sequence number of the last handshake acknowledgment segment. The duplicated sequence and acknowledgment numbers are necessary to prevent the TCP from going into an infinite loop acknowledging ACKs. For those who want to speed their TCP up, you can actually send data with the last acknowledgment of the handshake, since the connection/socket with the receiving TCP is established.

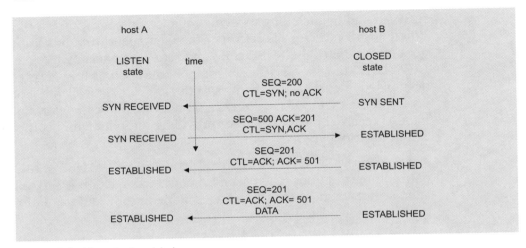

Figure 7.2 After the handshake

A common programming ploy dating from the 1960s is to send the text string "Hello World!" when initially checking a new computer program and/or data link. Don't ask: It's just one of those '60s things. In Figure 7.3, the transmission of the string "Hello World" from host B to Host A is illustrated. For instructional purposes only, we assume the string is divided into two text words that are transported sequentially. In reality, if echo character mode is on, each character is transported individually from host B to host A. If echo character mode is off, then perhaps all of the text string is transmitted at

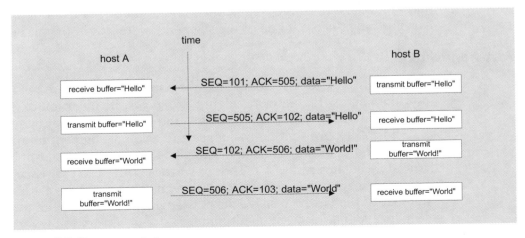

Figure 7.3 Data transmission

once, or maybe just a few characters. The number of characters transmitted in each packet depends upon the state of each host's receive and transmit buffers and is in the (good) hands of the TCP software.

The figure does show host A echoing the data transmitted by host B. Data echoing may or may not occur, depending upon the desires of the users.

Reset

All manner of things can go wrong during the attempt to communicate over unreliable networks. Equipment can fail in any number of ways and places between a source and a destination. Acts of nature (mice eating wires/cables), acts of humans (uh-oh, shouldn't have pushed THAT button), and acts of God (lightning, hurricanes) work to give us communication links that can be very unreliable. Transporting data from point A to point B can be rife with uncertainty. TCP provides a means to cope with a lot of that uncertainty by using a Reset function designed to make sure two hosts are reading from the same page, same paragraph, and same sentence of the same book.

Every connection request should be prefaced with a request to Reset by the initiating TCP before the initiating TCP sends the request to connect. The purpose of the Reset request is to avoid confusion with old or duplicate connections. How could this occur? Well, if you are on the Internet and you get bounced off due to a physical medium failure somewhere in the network and you immediately attempt to reconnect, the server may still have an active TCB for your host and the particular service you are using. So, Reset clears the receiving host's TCB, allowing the sender to try again.

When a host receives a Reset, the receiving TCP returns to the LISTEN state if it is in the SYN SENT or SYN RECEIVED state. If the TCP is in ESTABLISHED, FIN WAIT 1, FIN WAIT 2, CLOSE WAIT, CLOSING, LAST ACK, or TIME WAIT state, the TCP aborts the connection (deletes the TCB) and informs its user process.

Reset should be used sparingly and only when it is clear from the state of the connection that it is necessary. Typically, a Reset should be returned to a remote host when a host receives a segment that does not fit in with the current state of the host.

Sending a Reset

Besides sending a Reset prior to requesting a connection, there are also times when a local TCP should return a Reset to a remote TCP. The three situations that always require a Reset to be returned to a remote TCP are:

Situation 1

> If the connection is CLOSED (does not exist—TCB is not present for the connection), the host sends a Reset in response to any incoming segment except another Reset. SYNs addressed to a nonexistent connection are rejected in this manner.
>
> If the incoming segment has an ACK field, the Reset segment sequence number is taken from the ACK field of the segment. If the incoming segment does not have an ACK field, the Reset segment takes a sequence number of zero and the ACK field is set to the sum of the incoming segment sequence number and segment length. The local host keeps the connection in the CLOSED state.

Situation 2

> If the connection is in LISTEN, SYN SENT, or SYN RECEIVED state and the incoming segment ACK field acknowledges a segment not yet transmitted, the local host issues a Reset.
>
> The situation of one TCP sending a segment containing an acknowledgment of a segment never received is a critical situation. This situation occurs when two TCPs are no longer synchronized. Continued normal operation in this situation is impossible and the two TCPs must become synchronized again through the use of the Reset command.
>
> The Reset takes its sequence number from the ACK field of the incoming segment with an incorrect ACK number. The connection remains in the same state it was in before the receipt of the incoming segment.

Situation 3

> If the connection is in LISTEN, SYN SENT, or SYN RECEIVED state and the incoming segment has a security level, compartment, or precedence which does not match the security level, compartment, and precedence originally requested for the connection, a Reset is returned by the local host to the remote host. The connection reverts to the CLOSED state. The Reset segment sequence number is taken from the ACK field of the incoming segment.

Receiving a Reset

The receiving host of a Reset segment must first validate the Reset before changing state. In every state except SYN SENT, a Reset segment is validated by checking its SEQ field. A reset is valid if its sequence number is in the window of the receiving host. In the SYN SENT state, a Reset is received in response to an initial SYN that was sent. In this case, the Reset is valid if the ACK field acknowledges the SYN.

If the receiving TCP is in the LISTEN state, it ignores the Reset. If the receiving TCP is in the SYN RECEIVED state, the receiving TCP returns to the LISTEN state. If the receiving TCP was in any other state, the connection is aborted, the TCP advises the user process, and the TCP returns to the CLOSED state.

Data Transmission

After establishing a connection between two TCPs, data can be transmitted across that connection. Data transport, or communication, is accomplished by the two TCPs exchanging segments. When a TCP receives a data segment, it performs certain tests on the segment to determine its acceptability. Validating the segment as uncorrupted by its journey across the medium is the first order of business. The TCP will validate the segment by calculating and comparing the checksum. Checking the segment for a valid sequence number is the second important test. Next, the TCP must determine if the data segment will fit into its receive buffer window. Afterwards, the TCP checks the acknowledgment number to determine if the other TCP received its last transmission.

The sending TCP tracks the next sequence number to use in the variable SND.NXT. The receiving TCP tracks the next sequence number to expect in the variable RCV.NXT.

The sending TCP tracks the oldest unacknowledged sequence number in the variable SND.UNA. If the connection becomes idle and all data sent has been acknowledged, the variables SND.NXT, RCV.NXT, and SND.UNA will be equal. These variables are maintained in the TCB.

The sending TCP increments the TCB variable SND.NXT every time it sends a segment on down the road to the IP. When the receiving TCP accepts a segment, it increments RCV.NXT and returns an acknowledgment segment to the sending TCP. The amount SND.NXT and RCV.NXT change is the number of data octets present in the segment.

When the original sending TCP receives the return acknowledgment, it increments its SND.UNA variable. The mathematical difference between the SND.NXT and the SND.UNA is a measure of the communication delay between the two TCPs.

An unacceptable segment is a segment received that contains a sequence number that is out of the receiving TCP's window or an acknowledgment number that is unacceptable. If a connection is in the ESTABLISHED, FIN WAIT 1, FIN WAIT 2, CLOSE WAIT, CLOSING, LAST ACK, or TIME WAIT state and an unacceptable segment is received, the receiving TCP returns to the other TCP a segment containing only an acknowledgment. The segment must also contain the current send sequence number and the correct acknowledgment number of the next sequence number expected. The connection does not change state.

Retransmission Time-out

Retransmission time-out is the time a TCP should wait to receive an acknowledgment before resending a segment.

Retransmission time-out can be determined in a variety of ways. Perhaps the simplest way is to measure the time it takes to receive an acknowledgment of a segment during various times of the day. Network load is variable over a 24-hour period. The busiest period, if some portion of the network is connected to the public switched telephone network, is Monday morning from 5 a.m. to 11 a.m. Central Standard Time. If the network is privately switched, the busiest time must be determined. Even in this case, Monday morning is the most likely candidate, unless your company is a financial management company, in which case Friday evenings might be the peak traffic period.

After measuring the time it takes to get an acknowledgment, the time-out variable could be set to the measured time plus some safety factor, say two times the amount measured. To ensure the TCP connection is efficient, the data flow should be monitored to determine if the time-out is too low or too high. A time-out too low results in sending packets again before the other TCP has had a chance to acknowledge the original segment, resulting in a loop condition where one TCP is repeatedly acknowledging the same segment over and over. Setting the time-out too high may result in the TCPs' retransmission buffers growing too large, possibly even overflowing, as each TCP waits, and waits, and waits…. So, there is a trade-off that the network manager must evaluate: buffer space versus loop conditions.

The original TCP specification, RFC 791, includes a calculation to determine the appropriate time-out value. It is included here, with several corrected typos, for the curious:

> "Measure the elapsed time between sending a data octet with a particular sequence number and receiving an acknowledgment that covers that sequence number (segments sent do not have to match segments received). This measured elapsed time is the Round Trip Time (RTT). Next compute a Smoothed Round Trip Time (SRTT) as:
>
> $SRTT = (ALPHA * RTT) + ((1-ALPHA) * RTT)$
>
> and based on this, compute the retransmission timeout (RTO) as:
>
> $RTO = min[UBOUND, max[LBOUND,(BETA*SRTT)]]$

where UBOUND is an upper bound on the timeout (e.g., 1 minute), LBOUND is a lower bound on the timeout (e.g., 1 second), ALPHA is a smoothing factor (e.g., .8 to .9), and BETA is a delay variance factor (e.g., 1.3 to 2.0)."

After all of the above is accomplished, there is still no guarantee that the RTO is a valid RTO. So much depends upon the network characteristics that the above calculation is not really useful except for very stable, constant bit rate networks. While some such networks exist, most network traffic is very variable from moment to moment, hour to hour, and even day to day.

Seems a lot easier to just multiply the measured two-way transmit time, determined during a network traffic peak, by a good fudge factor and "let it be." Of course, the good fudge factor must be acquired through some trial and error and good networking management by observing what is happening on the network.

Precedence and Security

TCP includes a mechanism for providing a degree of transmission security. This mechanism is of use to the Department of Defense where the level of security classification is indicated by the value. Security and precedence are intended to allow only connections between ports operating with identical security values or with the higher of the two precedence levels of the two ports if the two ports have differing security levels.

TCP also includes a mechanism for providing transmission precedence. Ever wonder why your home connection to the Internet is suddenly disconnected? Perhaps a business customer with a higher precedence just dialed into your ISP and the ISP needs your connection to service the higher precedence connection. Have you checked with your ISP to determine if it uses precedence? Would you be surprised to learn that businesses get precedence over personal user accounts? You shouldn't be, since businesses usually pay a higher fee for their connection. Connection attempts that have mismatched security or precedence values will be rejected. If precedence and security level are not set by the user, the TCP supplies default values.

Is the use of precedence and security important? Decidedly so, regardless of any one person's perspective of the equation. Right now, as this book is written, the U.S. Army is undergoing field trials of a battlefield management system at the Army corps level that makes extensive use of TCP/IP and internetworking. This battlefield management system is supposed to work so well that corps-level efficiency will result in a reduced force of several thousands of troops per division. Can you imagine sitting in your office and instead of plugging into your favorite Internet service provider you get plugged into the Army's battlefield management system and now YOU can direct the troops? Much better than your favorite simulated computer game. This is the real stuff! Let us assume you are not an avid war game hound. Security and precedence are still issues of grave national concern. We don't want the captain to get precedence over the general unless the captain has something really important to communicate.

Of great concern, not only to the military but also to business, is the unauthorized access to privileged information. For the military, privileged information might be the state of the battlefield and status of individual units. Any commander worth his rank would love to have that information about his opponent. Business is concerned about access to corporate data including financial information, trade secrets, strategic plans, etc.

To prevent unauthorized access to privileged information, internetwork users erect "firewalls." The typical firewall approach to safeguarding sensitive data is the use of passwords. Passwords may use any number of character-based text and/or numerical values to try to befuddle the hacker intent on crashing into the system. This approach to network security generally requires the user to frequently change passwords in the mistaken belief that frequent password changes will keep the system free from unwanted intrusions. Any hacker with the time and patience can overcome any password-based system.

Another solution for network and data security is encryption. Unsophisticated hackers sitting for long hours at a PC in their attic (or basement or bedroom) and typing in typical passwords (names of children, birthdays, etc.) can eventually overcome the password-based system and get into the target network but they cannot decipher encrypted data if the encryption process is a sophisticated encryption algorithm. However, sophisticated hackers sitting in expensive foreign government offices can, and routinely do, hack into networks and acquire sensitive information and/or destroy data. Deciphering encrypted data is relatively easy for these types of operations. And they are numerous. The best solution to network security is to keep all sensitive information on computing devices that are not connected via any networking to the outside world. Then access control involves controlling the physical access to the computing devices, a much easier situation to manage.

Of course, for the security attributes of TCP to be implemented, the higher-level processes must be able to manage the security attributes. Higher-level processes should specify who gets to connect to the socket and when. Otherwise, anyone can connect. When security is implemented, TCP only performs the initial check to verify authorized access. This is just a basic go/no-go test. Additional pass-codes, such as those used by the U.S. military, may be necessary to protect especially sensitive information.

Basic Data Transfer

TCP is responsible for packaging the data stream received from the upper layer process into segments that have as the fundamental components a series of 8-bit data octets. Usually the upper layer data stream is also based upon some multiple of 8-bit data octets. But the upper layer data stream format is immaterial to the function of TCP. TCP considers the data received from the upper layer process as a bit stream. There is no concept of text, character, or record formatting of data. You could say all data are almost equal in the eyes of TCP, just binary ones and zeroes.

TCP acts as the speed cop during the transmission between users. TCP accomplishes the speed cop duties by blocking or forwarding data segments to and from the IP as necessary to maintain the flow of data without overrunning the receive buffers at either user end of the connection.

When TCP sends a segment to the IP for transport across the medium, TCP attaches a sequence number and an acknowledgment number to the segment header. The combination of segment sequence and acknowledgment numbers serves to establish a reliable host-to-host connection between two user processes. UDP does not concern itself with such reliability features.

A sequence number uniquely identifies each TCP segment. All segments can be distinguishable from all other segments by its unique sequence number. The acknowledgment number is the value of the next expected sequence number. In other words, when a receiving TCP looks at the segment it will see a sequence number and an acknowledgment number that is equal to the sequence number +1. Upon receiving a segment, the receiving TCP returns an "acknowledgment" segment back to the sending TCP with the sequence number equal to the acknowledgment number of the received segment, as shown in Figure 7.4.

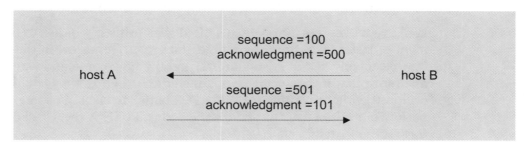

Figure 7.4 Reliable communications

When TCP sends a segment, it places a copy in a holding buffer and starts a time-out clock. If the TCP has not received an acknowledgment for a segment from the remote host before the time-out value, the TCP will resend the segment, again placing it back in the holding buffer and resetting the time-out clock. If an acknowledgment is received, TCP deletes the segment from the holding buffer.

PUSH

The PUSH function makes sure all the data received by the sending TCP from the upper layer process is transported to the remote host. The transmitting host sets the Push flag in the SEND call. A sending TCP can collect data from the upper layer process, sending the data to IP for transport when it is convenient. And the receiving TCP usually waits until the receive buffer is full before sending that data on to its upper layer process.

PUSH clears the data in the sending TCP buffer by pushing it all out to the IP, which must immediately package the data and place it on the data link layer for transport. The PUSH function appends a marker to the end of the data, so the receiving end has visibility that a PUSH occurred. The receiving TCP, upon receiving the segment with the Push flag set, immediately "pushes" that segment of data and any additional segments waiting in the receive buffer on to the upper layer process. What good is this?

In the beginning of time (circa late '60s), many different types of computers were (and still are) networked. These different computers operated at different speeds and had different size buffers for receiving and transmitting data. Since TCP causes the users to exchange buffer size information when the connection is first established, each user knows how much data can be sent before the receive buffer overflows. This is called overflow control, which is one of the features of TCP that is lacking in UDP. The sending TCP buffer may be full because the receiving user's buffer is smaller or the receiving user's clock speed could be much slower than the transmitting end. So, there must be a traffic cop ready to make sure no one goes too fast.

Well, in the good ol' days when TCP/IP was primarily of use to the Department of Defense, buffers were large, data rates were slow in the hinterlands but reasonably fast at headquarters, and the high command wanted some assurance that if they needed to launch the BIG ONE, they could get the order off without waiting for some TCP buffer to clear. Or some such scenario. To put it in easy-to-understand terms, PUSH is the TCP laxative that flushes the system.

A locally issued call to close (user CLOSE call) the connection requires a PUSH call. All data in the sending buffer should be pushed out to the receiving TCP before the connection is closed.

Also, the reception of a segment with the FIN control flag set, indicating the remote TCP wants to close the connection, requires a PUSH call. All data in the local buffer should be pushed out to the receiving TCP before the connection is closed.

URGENT

The sending TCP has the ability to identify segments as "urgent," meaning the segments contain data that is of some special significance. When the sending TCP marks a segment as urgent, the sending TCP is telling the remote host that the data following the segment containing the Urgent flag is urgent. The idea is to give the receiving host time to prepare for the reception of the urgent data. The receiving host could then process all the current segments in the receive buffer, then wait for the urgent data. TCP itself does not take any particular action upon reception of the Urgent flag other than notifying the upper layer process of the flag reception. Rather, the receiving upper layer process must be able to specify what specific action must occur as a result of the urgent notification.

The sending TCP has the ability to identify to the receiving TCP the transmission of urgent data. TCP uses a "pointer" to identify the end of urgent data. The urgent mechanism uses an Urgent field in every segment. When the Urgent control flag is set, the receiving TCP understands the Urgent field is not empty, or meaningless. The Urgent pointer is determined by adding the Urgent field value to the segment sequence number.

When the Urgent pointer is ahead of the receive sequence number (RCV.NXT), the receiving TCP recognizes the data between the "pointer" and the receive sequence number as urgent and so notifies the higher-level user process. When the Urgent "pointer" and the receive sequence number are equal, TCP notifies the higher-level user process of the end of urgent data. TCP makes no use of the urgent data and assumes the higher-level user process makes productive use of the urgent data.

At least one data octet must be included in the segment for the Urgent field to be valid.

By combining the URGENT functionality with the PUSH function, data delivery to the end user process can be speeded up.

Segment Arrives

Now, we are in a position to diagram what happens when a segment arrives at a TCP/IP. The following flowcharts describe the operations performed when a segment arrives and the TCP/IP are in the CLOSED state and when they are in the LISTEN state. The flowcharts are self-explanatory (I think—but maybe not).

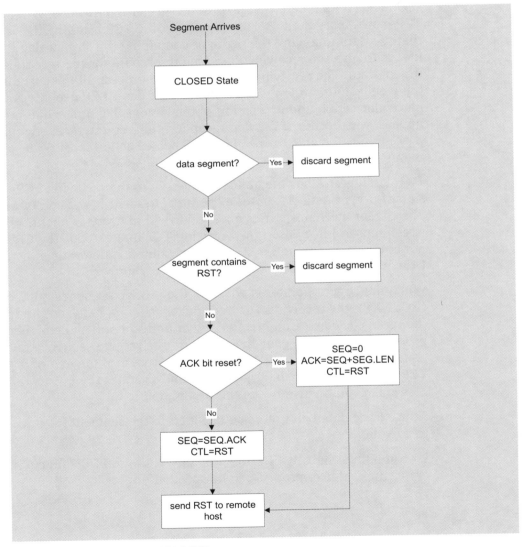

Figure 7.5 Segment arrives/CLOSED state

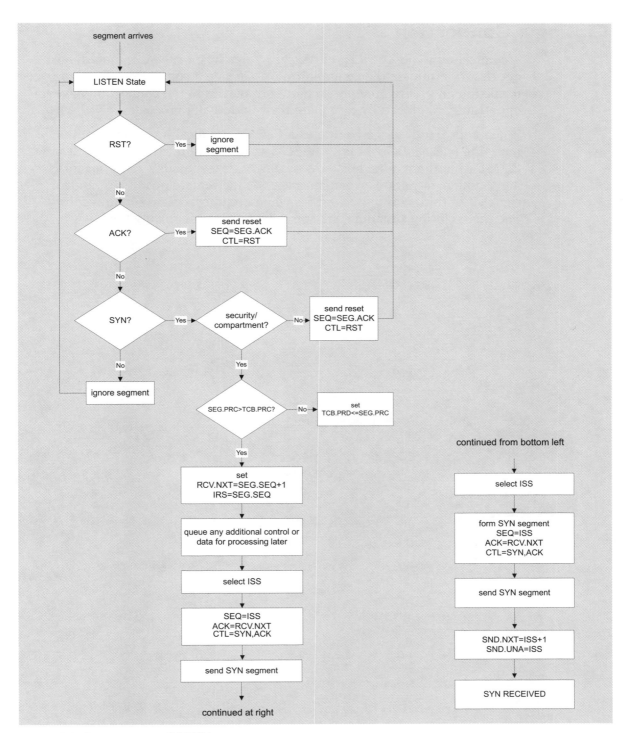

Figure 7.6 Segment arrives/LISTEN state

Closing a Connection

A connection is closed when either the source host or the destination host decides to terminate the communication. Closing a connection should be performed in an orderly manner so that both parties to the connection have the opportunity to gracefully terminate their underlying processes.

When a local user process initiates a CLOSE, the local host may continue receiving packets (stay in the RECEIVE status) until it receives a confirming CLOSE from the remote host. This is one of three possible scenarios for closing. Another scenario is when a host sends the remote host a FIN control signal. The third closing scenario is when both hosts close simultaneously. The three closing situations are summed up in the following figures.

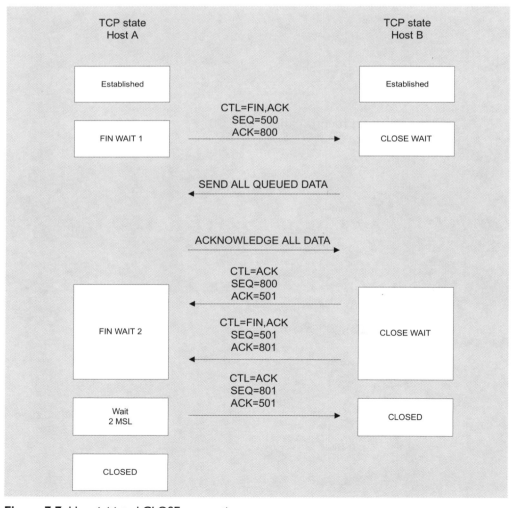

Figure 7.7 User-initiated CLOSE connection

Figure 7.7 illustrates the mechanism for managing a user process-initiated CLOSE connection request. In the user-initiated CLOSE connection request, Host A user process sends a CLOSE request to its TCP. When the Host A TCP receives the CLOSE request, it places a FIN segment in the outgoing segment buffer and enters the FIN WAIT 1 state. At this point, the Host A TCP will not recognize any more SENDs initiated by the Host A user process. In the FIN WAIT 1 state, the Host A TCP may receive. If any previous segments are not acknowledged by Host B, including the FIN segment, the Host A TCP will retransmit the segments until acknowledged. The Host B TCP will RECEIVE the Host A FIN segment and will queue an ACK. In the meantime, all queued segments including ACKs are sent to Host A. Then, Host B will close its connection and send a FIN to Host A. Host A receives Host B's FIN and returns an ACK to Host B. When Host B receives the FIN ACK from Host A, it completes the CLOSE process by actually closing, or deleting, the connection.

As you may discern from the user-initiated CLOSE connection scenario, CLOSE does not really mean close in that the connection is disabled immediately. CLOSE state is the state of not accepting SEND segments from the user process anymore. The connection is closed when both TCPs have deleted the connection information. Remember the connection information is stored in a connection record called the TCB.

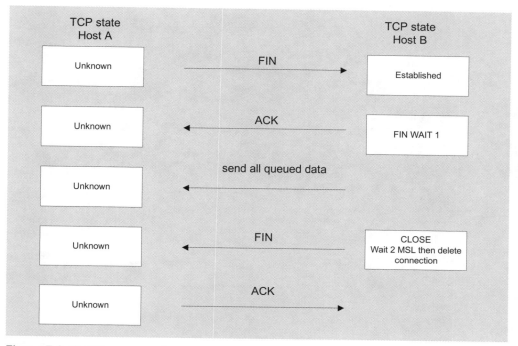

Figure 7.8 CLOSE source unknown

When a FIN of unknown origin arrives at Host B, Host B TCP will ACK the FIN and inform its user process the connection is closing. This process is illustrated in Figure 7.8. Host B user process will send a CLOSE request to its TCP and enter the CLOSE state. Host B TCP now sends all queued data followed

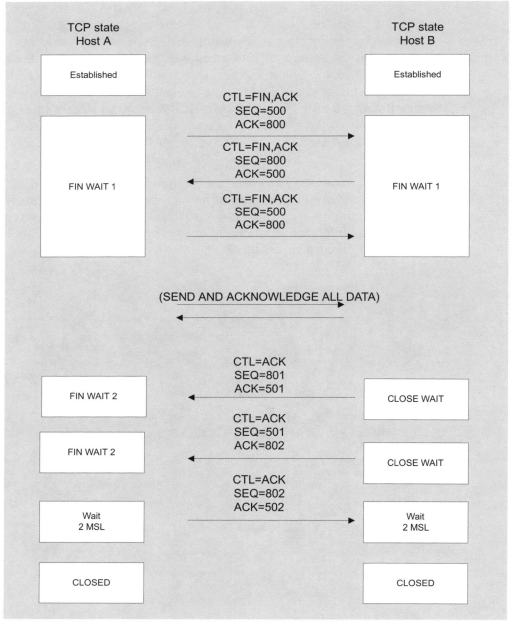

Figure 7.9 CLOSE Simultaneously

by a FIN to Host A TCP. Host B TCP now waits two MSL (maximum segment lifetimes) to receive the FIN ACK. If the ACK is received, or if the two MSL has passed, whichever occurs first, Host B TCP will delete the connection.

When both hosts send a FIN simultaneously, all data queued by both hosts will be SENT and ACK. Then, each host will send a FIN and receive a FIN ACK. When each host receives the FIN ACK, it will delete the connection.

Figure 7.9 shows the sequence of events that occurs when both TCPs send a CLOSE simultaneously.

Summary

TCP progresses through a series of defined steps, or states, to establish a connection, verify the authority of a user to use the connection, or user process, receive data, send data, and gracefully close the connection upon the command of either TCP using the connection. When establishing the TCP connection, it is critical for each TCP to accurately inform the other TCP of the sequence numbers it will use. The use of sequence numbers to identify packets is crucial to the success of TCP's flow control and reliability features.

Chapter 8

Introduction to FTP

Questions answered in this chapter:

What is FTP?

How does FTP work?

What is the relationship between FTP and TCP/IP?

What are the FTP user commands?

Introduction

File Transfer Protocol (FTP) is a popular application providing a means to copy files from any host implementing TCP/IP to any other host implementing TCP/IP. Files are not transferred in the sense they are removed from a system; rather, a file is copied from the source host to the destination host. The original file is neither moved nor changed, only read.

FTP is considered a user application and is fairly easy to use. It is like Telnet in that it has a client and server which constitute the FTP application. The FTP client is used to initiate a file transfer and the FTP server is used to serve FTP client requests, thus making the logical connection between the client and server. Consider Figure 8.1.

Most hosts that have a TCP/IP protocol suite have at least an FTP client. Some also include an FTP server or daemon.

The FTP protocol remains one of the most useful protocols on the Internet. Its strength is that it makes it possible to exchange files between computers from different manufacturers running different operating systems. The full definition of the FTP protocol is specified in RFC 959, available at **ftp://ds.internic.net/rfc/** as rfc0959.txt.

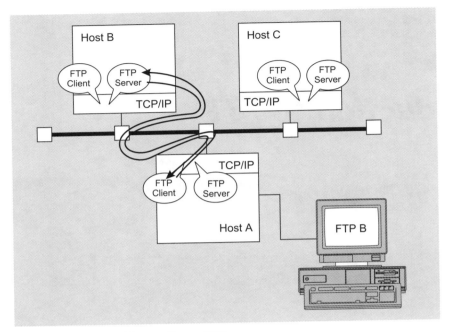

Figure 8.1 The world according to FTP

What Types of Files Can FTP Transfer?

FTP was created to allow computers from different manufacturers, running different operating systems and using different systems of character representation (i.e., ASCII and EBCDIC), to exchange information in a vendor-neutral manner. The FTP specification defines four data transfer types: ASCII, EBCDIC, image, and local. The details of the file types are presented in a later section.

There are two software parts to the FTP system, the client and the server. The server runs either as a stand-alone program, or as part of an operating service system such as *inetd*.

How are FTP Clients Implemented?

FTP clients come in a variety of forms. FTP is frequently implemented as a stand-alone program using either a character or graphical user interface. Although the character-mode interface remains valuable for remote controlling an FTP session across a slow communications link, most users prefer to use an FTP client with a graphical user interface. Although Microsoft's Windows products don't come with graphical FTP client software, a number of independent developers have stepped up to fill the void with both commercial and shareware products. Typical of the available offerings is the WSFTP program, a limited edition of which is available free to certain academic, government, and home users.

Files are moved between the client machine and server machine by highlighting the files and clicking the directional arrows in the center of the screen. More information on availability and licensing of both the limited edition and professional versions of WSFTP is available from **http://www.ipswitch.com**.

The ability to "get" a file from a remote system through FTP is a part of Web browsers. FTP has been integrated into the desktop metaphor of client operating systems as an FTP folder that allows files to be dragged and dropped between the client desktop and the server. FTP additionally has an API (application programming interface) that allows FTP functionality to be embedded within another application. For example, some word processors, such as Lotus Wordpro, have Load from Internet and Save to Internet options on the File menu that implement FTP in the background to load and save files from an Internet FTP server.

What Basic Functions Can FTP Perform?

The following are basic functions available with FTP:

▲ The ability to copy a single file from one host to another. Consider Figure 8.2.

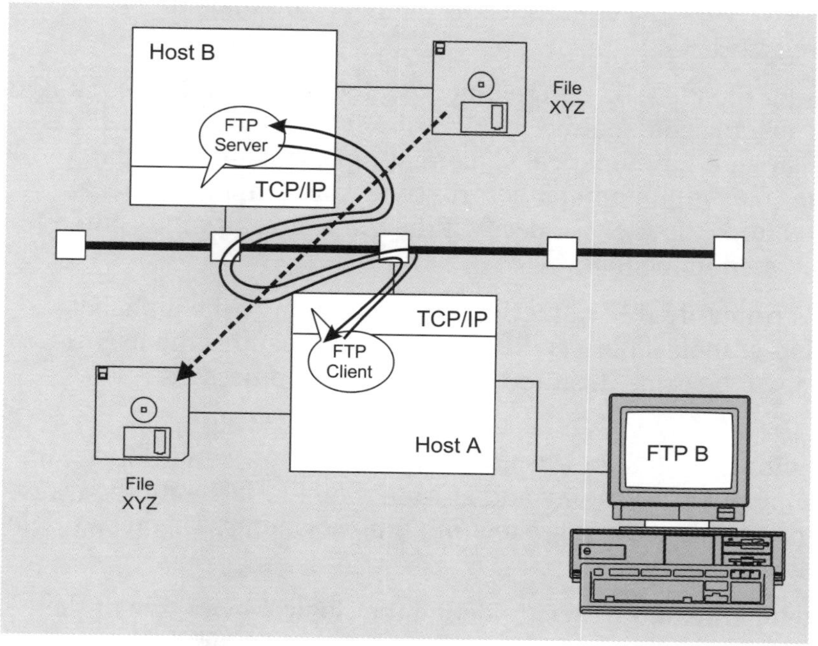

Figure 8.2 shows the XYZ file copied from host B to host A. The display on host A shows the FTP client being invoked to establish the session.

Figure 8.2 FTP and the file copy process

- The ability to copy multiple files from one host to another host
- The ability to list all accessible files in a target host
- The capability to create and/or remove directories in a target host
- The ability to identify the current directory in a target host
- The ability to append a local file to a file located in a remote (target) host
- The ability to append a file from a local host to a file located in a target host

In addition to providing these functions, commands can be executed against an FTP client. When this prompt is present, an FTP client is active:

    ftp>>

A number of commands are executable from the FTP client prompt. Some of those commonly used are listed later in this chapter.

FTP File Types

RFC 959 defines certain types of files. The need to define file types stems from the various ways formatted data can be stored. Depending upon the file type, data that may look like a great outdoor scene if interpreted correctly on one machine may look like a lot of gibberish characters and symbols, if misinterpreted, on another machine. So, to help the process of human evolution along and ensure we view the data as it was intended (by some other human), files are typed.

ASCII is the default file type. By designating ASCII as the default type, all FTP servers must be able to send and receive files of ASCII type. An ASCII file is nothing more than an 8-bit numerical value that represents the familiar alphabet and the (maybe) unfamiliar control codes and graphical objects. ASCII file type requires the user to specify if the file will be printed, stored for later use, or processed immediately.

EBCDIC type is a primarily IBM numerical representation of the alphabet, control codes, and graphical objects. EBCDIC file type requires the user to specify if the file will be printed, stored for later use, or processed immediately.

Image type specifies that all data is transmitted as one contiguous bit stream. However, in the interest of economy and efficiency and to facilitate the transfer of the data, the data stream is broken into 8-bit segments. This type of file is commonly called a binary file.

Local type is intended to allow users to define the "logical byte" size of the transfer. The users may define a logical byte as any value desired. Typical choices are 22-bit and 36-bit sizes. A user would store a 22-bit logical byte in a 32-bit word using zeroes to pad the unused bit positions. When using Local type, the user must specify what the logical byte size will be.

FTP Data Structures

In the interest of accurate data duplication at the destination, FTP permits the designation of file structures. There are three file structures defined. For those familiar with programming, there are no surprises. File, record, and page structures are defined.

File structure defines the data as a sequence of data bytes, record structure defines the data as a set of sequential records, and page structure defines the data as a set of indexed, unrelated pages of data. File structure is useful for transmitting ASCII and EBCDIC text files and sequential binary files. Record structure is useful for transmitting data organized as native type records. Page structure is useful for transmitting random access files. The default data structure is file structure.

Files of page structure type can be various sizes. To accommodate files of page structure, FTP defines a page structure header. Each page is transmitted with a preceding header. The byte size is a logical byte which is defined by the TYPE command. See Figure 8.3.

1st byte	2nd byte	3rd byte	4th byte	5th byte
header length	page index	data length	page type	page options

Figure 8.3 Page structure header

Header length specifies the number of logical bytes in the header. The header length includes the header length byte. The minimum header length is four.

The page index identifies where the page fits into the file. Do not confuse this with the transmission sequence number of the data segment. They are not the same.

The data length specifies the number of logical bytes in the page data. The minimum value is zero.

The page type identifies the type of page this page is. FTP defines four page types: last page, simple page, descriptor page, and access controlled page. See Figure 8.4.

last page value	simple page value	descriptor page value	access controlled page value
0 0 0 0 0 0 0 0	0 0 0 0 0 0 0 1	0 0 0 0 0 0 1 0	0 0 0 0 0 0 1 1

Figure 8.4 Page type values

Last page marks the end of a paged structure transmission. The header length is four bytes, and the data length is zero bytes.

Simple page is the normal type for simple paged files. Simple paged files contain no control information associated with the page. The header length is four bytes.

Descriptor page is used to transmit the file descriptive information.

Access controlled page uses the optional field to designate paged files with page level access control information. The header length is five bytes.

The options field is used to specify page control information, including access control.

FTP Transmission Modes

FTP includes provision for selecting one of three transmission modes. The three modes are stream mode, block mode, and compressed mode. Users must choose the appropriate mode of transmission. Each mode is useful for a particular purpose, depending upon the needs of the users and the data type of the data transferred. All data transfers must include an end-of-file (EOF) marker. TCP/IP will automatically place an EOF marker at the end of any data transferred if the connection is closed and an EOF was not received prior to the connection closing. When a file of record type is transferred, it must include an end-of-record (EOR) at the end of each record. When a file of page type is transferred, it must include an end-of-page (EOP) marker at the end of each page. If an ASCII file of any type other than record type is transferred, an end-of-line character represented as a carriage return/line feed character pair (CRLF) must be at the end of each line. If an EBCDIC file of any type other than record type is transferred, an end-of-line character represented as a null character (NL) must be at the end of each line.

In stream mode the data is transferred as a stream of data bytes. Stream mode does not impose any restrictions concerning the type of file transferred.

In block mode the data is a series of data blocks of any arbitrary length. A data block header specifies the length of the data block and a data block descriptor. The data block header size is 24 bits. The length field occupies 16 bits and specifies the number of bytes the data block contains. The descriptor field is 8 bits and specifies the meaning of the data block. See Figure 8.5.

descriptor	length
8 bits	16 bits

Figure 8.5 Data block header format

The data block descriptor can have one of four meanings. Each meaning is assigned a unique binary value. See Table 8.1. Data block restart (DBR) specifies the intent of the user to cancel the current file transfer and begin sending the file again. Data block errors (DBE) signifies the sending user thinks there may be errors in the block. DBE is not a TCP/IP error control mechanism; rather it is a user process error control device. Data block end-of-file signifies if the block is the last block (EOF) of the file. Data block end-of-record (EOR) signifies if the block is the end of a record (EOR).

Binary Value	Meaning
00010000	data block restart (DBR)
00100000	data block errors (DBE)
01000000	data block end-of-file (EOF)
10000000	data block end-of-record (EOR)

Table 8.1 Data block header descriptor values

Compressed mode accommodates three types of data: regular data, compressed data, and control data. Regular data is transmitted as a byte string. Compressed data is, of course, compressed. Control data is either one or two bytes, depending upon the circumstances.

If the data type in compressed mode is regular data, then the control byte specifies how many bytes of data follow the control byte. The maximum is 127 bytes. See Figure 8.6.

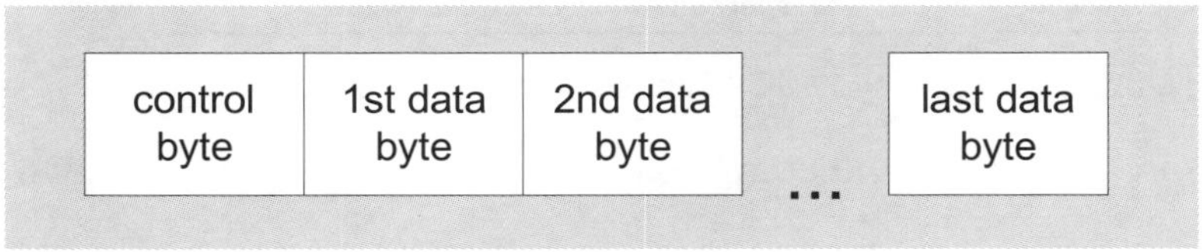

Figure 8.6 Compressed mode, regular data

The format of the control byte is shown in Figure 8.7. The figure shows the most significant bit (MSB) is a zero, while the remaining bits designate the number of data bytes following the control byte. The "x" designates either a binary zero or one, as appropriate.

8th bit	7th bit	6th bit	5th bit	4th bit	3rd bit	2nd bit	1st bit
0	x	x	x	x	x	x	x

Figure 8.7 Compressed mode, regular data control byte

When compressing a string of data bytes, it is common to encounter a string of identical bytes. That is why compressing data usually, but not always, yields such good compression ratios. The format for compressing a string of identical data bytes is shown in Figure 8.8. The figure represents two bytes with the first, or higher-order, byte containing control information and the number of identical bytes that are compressed. The second, or lower-order, byte contains a single byte of the actual data that is compressed.

control byte	data byte

Figure 8.8 Compressed mode, compressed data

In Figure 8.9, the two higher-order bits (eighth and seventh bits) specify that the data is compressed. The remaining bits in the higher-order byte, shown as "x," specify the number of bytes of identical data that are compressed, as represented by the single data byte. The number of bytes that can be compressed into one byte is limited by the number of bits available in the control byte to represent the quantity compressed. In this case, the maximum number of bytes that can be compressed into a single byte is 63 bytes (binary 111111=63).

8th bit	7th bit	6th bit	5th bit	4th bit	3rd bit	2nd bit	1st bit
1	0	x	x	x	x	x	x

Figure 8.9 Compressed mode, control byte

Compressed mode will compress ASCII "filler" bytes as shown in Figure 8.10.

Control Byte	ASCII Filler String Byte
1 1 x x x x x x	all spaces (ASCII character code 32)

Figure 8.10 Compressed ASCII filler string

Compressed mode will compress EBCDIC "filler" bytes as shown in Figure 8.11.

Control Byte	EBCDIC Filler String Byte
1 1 x x x x x x	all spaces (EBCDIC character code 64)

Figure 8.11 Compressed EBCDIC filler string

Compressed mode will compress Local and Image "filler" bytes as shown in Figure 8.12.

Control Byte	Filler String Byte
1 1 x x x x x x	0 0 0 0 0 0 0 0

Figure 8.12 Compressed filler string for Local or Image file types

Compressed mode includes an escape sequence, shown in Figure 8.13.

1st Byte	2nd Byte
escape byte	block mode descriptor code
0 0 0 0 0 0 0 0	see Table 8.1

Figure 8.13 Compressed mode escape sequence

Compressing data is useful for speeding up the transfer of files from machine to machine. If compression is used, expensive system resources are more quickly assigned other tasks. The time saved usually translates directly into dollars. The industry buzzword for "time" is "bandwidth." When you save time, you save bandwidth. And bandwidth costs money.

FTP Commands

Within the FTP system there are a number of commands. Not all FTP implementations support all of the commands. The use of FTP commands is apparent in character-mode FTP programs where the commands are typed at an ftp>> prompt. The use of FTP commands is less apparent when using a graphical FTP client where your interface with FTP commands is through drop-down menus and dialog boxes. The FTP commands are largely invisible when using a Web browser, graphical FTP desktop folder, or application (such as a word processor) to move files between systems. However, regardless of the client interface, these commands define how the client software and the server software communicate. Some clients simply do an excellent job of hiding the details from the user.

RFC 959 contains the definitive FTP commands and their meaning and purpose. FTP includes many response codes that are also defined in RFC 959. Each command must generate at least one reply code.

 CAUTION: FTP has no confirmation mechanism to prevent overwriting existing files with the same name. It is important to exercise extra care with the Prompt property disabled, as it is easy to accidentally overwrite valuable files.

FTP Commands

ftp [*options*] *host*

> File transfer program to move files to and from a remote *host*. When executed, FTP will prompt the user for additional optional commands.

> *options*

> **-d**
> Debugging is enabled.

-g
Filename globbing is disabled.

-i
Interactive prompting is disabled.

-n
Auto-login upon initial connection is disabled.

-v
All responses (verbose) from remote host are displayed.

-t
Packet tracing is enabled.

FTP Commands (user prompted)

! [*command*[*arguments*]]
Interactive shell on local host is executed.

$ *macro* [*arguments*]
Macro, as defined with the **macdef** command, is executed.

? [*command*]
Same as **help**. **?** displays help information. Typing **?** by itself displays a list of available commands, which may vary slightly from implementation to implementation. Typing **?** followed by the name of a specific FTP subcommand displays the help available for that subcommand. It is important that the subcommands be typed in lowercase characters only.

account [*password*]
The user supplies a password to the remote host to access files and services on the remote host.

append [*filename1*] [*filename2*]
Append a local file of *filename1* to a file of *filename2* on the remote host. If *filename2* is not present, the remote host will use *filename1*.

ascii
The file transfer type is set to ASCII. This is the default file transfer type.

bell
Beep the user after completion of each file transfer.

binary
The file transfer type is binary. This file type is formally called "Image" in the RFC documents.

bye
Close FTP session and exit FTP.

case
Toggle (turn on if off/turn off if on) remote host filename case mapping. This command is used with **mget**.

cd [*remote directory*]
Change directory on remote host to the directory specified.

cdup
Change directory of the remote host to the next higher directory (parent directory). This is equivalent to typing **cd**, pressing the spacebar, and typing two periods.

chmod [*mode*] [*filename*]
Change the permissions of the remote file of *filename*.

close
End the FTP session and return to the command line interpreter. The FTP shell is still active.

cr
Toggle (turn on if off/turn off if on) stripping of the carriage return character from files during ASCII type file transfer.

debug [*value*]
Toggle (turn on if off/turn off if on) debugging mode. Use *value* to set the debug level.

delete [*filename*]
Delete the file of *filename* from the remote host.

dir [*directory*] [*filename*]
Print the contents of the remote host's current directory and write the contents to local host file of *filename*. If *filename* is not specified, the contents are displayed on the local host's monitor. If *directory* is not specified, the remote host's current working directory is used.

disconnect
Same as **close**.

form *format*
The file transfer type is set to *format*. The default type is file type *file*.

get file [*filename1*] [*filename2*]
Retrieve file of *filename1* from the remote host and store it on the local host as *filename2*. If *filename2* is not specified, then store the remote file on the local host as *filename1*.

glob
Toggle (turn on if off/turn off if on) filename expansion. Used with **mdelete**, **mget**, and **mput** commands.

hash
Toggle (turn on if off/turn off if on) hash sign (#) printing when each data block is transferred.

help [*command*]
Print help information for the specified command. When *command* is not present, all FTP commands are printed.

idle
Toggle (turn on if off/turn off if on) idle timer on the remote host.

image
Same as **binary**.

lcd [*directory*]
Change directory on local host. If *directory* is not specified, the local host changes to the user's home directory.

ls [*directory*] [*file*]
Abbreviated listing of contents of remote host directory on remote host is printed to local host filename *file*. If *directory* is not specified, the current working directory is assumed. It gives a more abbreviated listing of the directory contents than does the **dir** command. Use the optional *file* specification, which supports the wildcard characters "*" and "?" to restrict the list of filenames to exactly those of interest.

macdef *macro name*
Define a macro with name *macro name*.

mdelete *filename*
Deletes remote host file *filename*.

mdir *files file*
Same as **dir**, except multiple files may be specified.

mget *files*
Expand *files* on remote host, then execute a **get** for each subsequent file.

mkdir *name*
Make a directory with directory name *name* on the remote host.

mls *files file*
Same as **nlist** except the local host *file* must be specified and multiple remote host *files* may be specified.

mode [*type*]

Set file transfer mode to mode *type*. The default mode name is **stream**. Type **mode** by itself to display the current transfer mode (ASCII or binary). Type **mode** followed by either **ascii** or **binary** to set the mode to ASCII or binary.

modtime [*filename*]

Show the last time file *filename* on the remote host was modified.

mput [*files*]

Expand wildcards in the local host files list of *files* and execute a **put** for each subsequent file. Transfers multiple files from the local client computer to the remote host computer. The *files* parameter may be a single file specification using the wildcard characters "*" and "?," a list of individual filenames separated by spaces, or a combination of the two specification techniques.

newer *filename1* [*filename2*]

Get remote host file *filename1* if file *filename1* is newer than local host file *filename2*.

nlist [*directory*] [*filename*]

Print the list of files in remote host *directory* to local host file *filename*. If the directory is not specified, the current working directory is assumed.

nmap [*inpattern outpattern*]

Toggle (turn on if off/turn off if on) the filename mapping capability. Default mapping is off.

ntrans [*inchars*[*outchars*]]

Toggle (turn on if off/turn off if on) the filename character translation capability. If a character, during file transfer (**mput**, **put**, **mget**, **get**), is in *inchars*, it is replaced by the corresponding character in *outchars*.

open *hostname* [*portnumber*]

This command establishes a connection between the local host and a remote host with *hostname* and optional port *portnumber*. The *hostname* parameter may be specified either as an IP address or as a name.

prompt

Toggle (turn on if off/turn off if on) interactive prompting. When transferring multiple files with **mget** or **mput**, FTP will prompt for confirmation before transferring each file.

proxy *ftp command*

Execute the FTP command *ftp command* on a secondary control connection. Forwards commands to another server, allowing logical connections between servers. As a result, files are transferred between the two server computers.

put *filename1* [*filename2*]
Store the local host file of *filename1* on the remote host as *filename2*.

pwd
Print the name of the current working directory on the remote host. **pwd** is the acronym for "print working directory."

quit
Same as **bye**. **quit** closes the FTP session and exits from the FTP command shell.

quote *argument1, argument2...*
Transmit the arguments as listed to the remote host.

recv [*filename1*] [*filename2*]
Same as **get**. **recv** transfers a file from the FTP server to the client. The *filename* parameter must refer to a single file. Wildcard characters are not allowed. For file transfer, use the **mget** command.

restart [*number*]
Restart the transfer of a file from byte count *number*.

rhelp [*command*]
Request the remote host to provide help for FTP command *command*.

rename [*filename1*] [*filename2*]
On the remote host, rename *filename1* to *filename2*.

reset
Clear the local host reply queue. Clears any pending operations between the client and the server.

rmdir [*directory*]
Remove directory *directory* from the remote host.

rstatus [*filename*]
Display status of remote host file *filename* If *filename* is omitted, then **rstatus** displays status of the remote host.

runique
Toggle (turn on if off/turn off if on) file storage on the local host with unique filenames.

send [*filename1*] [*filename2*]
Equivalent to the **put** command, it transfers a file from the client to the FTP server.

sendport
Toggle (turn on if off/turn off if on) port commands. Enables automatic transmission of the server port command.

site [*command*]
Get or set site-specific information from or on a remote host.

size *filename*
Display the size of remote host file *filename*.

status
Display the current FTP status.

struct [*name*]
Set the file transfer structure to structure *name*. The default structure is **stream**.

sunique
Toggle (turn on if off/turn off if on) remote host file storage under unique filenames.

system
Display the remote host operating system in use.

tenex
Set file transfer type to **tenex**. Informs the FTP server that the byte size is 8 bits.

trace
Toggle (turn on if off/turn off if on) packet tracing.

type [*name*]
Set the file transfer type to *name*. If *name* is not specified, the current type in use is printed. The default type is **ASCII**.

unmask [*mask*]
Set the user file generation mode mask on the remote host. If *mask* is omitted, the current mask value is printed.

user *name* [*password*] [*account*]
Identify the user to the remote host. If the user makes an error in specifying the userid or password when the connection is first opened, the **user** subcommand allows the user to resend the userid and password. The alternative is to close the connection to the remote host and reopen it. The **user** command saves a step in this instance.

verbose
Toggle (turn on if off/turn off if on) verbose mode.

How Do You Use FTP Commands?

To start a logical connection with FTP, issue the FTP command at the operating system prompt. Assuming configuration has been performed properly, a prompt similar to the following appears:

ftp>>

Many users issue FTP and a host name or an appropriate address with it. For example, FTP RISC6000.

Once at the FTP prompt, the FTP subcommands available from that client implementation are available.

When performing file transfers, messages appear on the display at different times. For example, after a user has established an FTP session, the ftp>> prompt is present. If a user enters "get" and a valid filename on the target host, messages will be displayed stating the status of the connection. Messages will also reflect the Internet and port address, name of the file being received, size of the file, and the time it took for file transfer (copying) to take place.

Minimum FTP Functionality

RFC 959 defines the minimum FTP functionality required of all FTP servers. The minimum functionality definition is necessary to ensure all FTP servers can transfer files, in a minimal sort of way. Does that make sense?

Type	ASCII non-print
Mode	stream
Structure	file, record
Commands	USER, QUIT, PORT, TYPE, MODE, STRU, RETR, STOR, NOOP

The default values for transfer parameters are:

Type	ASCII Non-print
Mode	stream
Structure	file
Commands	RETR, STOR, NOOP.

Why Would I Want to Be Anonymous?

Security is an important part of many computer operations. Various FTP server programs provide security subsystems to provide restrictions on who can upload and download files from an FTP server. However, the FTP protocol is widely used to establish archives of files for general distribution. Archives of shareware programs are frequently available via FTP. Many hardware and software vendors use FTP servers to distribute updated device drivers, bug fixes, and enhancements. It is increasingly common for these archives to be associated with a Web-based front end that provides filenames and descriptions, with links to the actual files on an FTP server.

To provide open access to a file archive, a tradition has developed to provide a user name of "anonymous" that, when used in conjunction with any Internet e-mail address as the password, provides read-only access to a file archive. Various FTP servers enforce this convention differently: Some ignore the password field completely, some check to make certain that the name contains an "@" character, and others actually attempt to check the validity of the host by sending an ICMP (i.e., a "ping" request) to the host portion of the address to verify the existence of the computer system.

One of the most common problems that users have in accessing an FTP service through their Web browser is that they have failed to provide their e-mail address within the Web browser's configuration. Sometimes their FTP attempts will work; other times they will fail. The success or failure of a particular attempt corresponds to the configuration used in setting up the FTP server site.

What is the Mystery Behind FTP?

There is none. It is simply a file transfer mechanism that enables users to transfer (copy) files from one machine to another. In many ways its simplicity is its complexity. Commands like put, get, open, and close do what they imply, but other commands are not that intuitive. In some instances commands can be customized, depending upon the vendor's implementation of the TCP/IP stack.

The ease of use behind FTP is the fact that it operates the same on virtually any machine. Once Telnet, FTP, and other native applications and functions are started, their operation is the same, regardless of the operating system or hardware platform.

Summary

FTP is a user application for transferring (copying) files from any machine using TCP/IP to another machine using TCP/IP. FTP provides for the orderly transfer of files of various types including text, record, binary, and random access files.

A variety of commands can be issued at the FTP prompt. Those listed in this chapter will help readers new to this topic. No mystery exists with FTP. It operates in a straightforward fashion. Normally, it is the newness of TCP/IP applications and the accompanying acronyms that tend to create some initial discomfort with new users. However, this is the case with practically any networking protocol that is new to a user.

Chapter 9

Introduction to Telnet

Questions answered in this chapter:

What is Telnet?

How does Telnet work?

What is the relationship between Telnet and TCP/IP?

What are the Telnet user commands?

Introduction

The Telnet protocol was one of the first Internet protocols, first proposed in RFC 0097 in February 1971. The full definition of the Telnet protocol is available at **ftp://ds.internic.net/rfc/** as rfc0097.txt. The Telnet protocol provides a remote character-mode terminal that operates over the network. Although fundamentally a character-mode service, most Telnet clients have been enhanced by hosting the character-mode interface in a graphical shell with drop-down menus for the performance of common Telnet commands.

Most services that are available on a local character-mode terminal are also available across the network using the Telnet protocol. Historically, creative programmers wrote character-mode scripts to provide custom information services through the Telnet interface. However, the development of new applications using such interfaces has declined into obscurity with the availability of the rich, graphical interfaces provided by World Wide Web browsers.

Telnet is an application that provides logon capabilities to remote systems. It consists of two parts, a client and a server, as shown in Figure 9.1.

Why are remote logon capabilities important? A fundamental idea behind a network environment is sharing resources. This implies multiple computers and related devices connected together in such a manner that access from multiple sources is possible. For a user on any given computer to access resources on another computer requires a remote logon capability. This is what Telnet does.

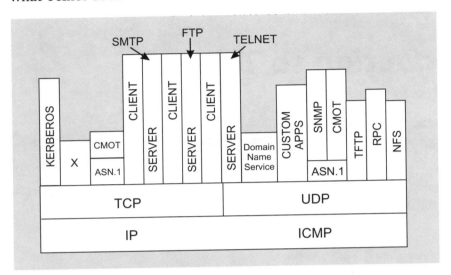

Figure 9.1 TCP/IP protocol suite

For example, consider a small network with three computer servers. Let us assume each computer has a primary purpose. Computer A is a machine dedicated for training. It has training programs on it that anyone on the network can use. Computer B is a machine used to archive customer files; it has a large database running on it. Computer C has users connected to it performing interactive tasks. This means users are directly attached to computer C and they do most of their work on this machine. But because of the network, users on machine C have access to computers A and B. Take a look at Figure 9.2.

Notice the computers in the figure have TCP/IP on each of them, and they are all connected to a common medium. So, for users on computer C to access a training program on computer A, the user on computer C would type Telnet A at the command prompt on computer C.

Once the user on computer C enters the Telnet A command, the Telnet client gets invoked on computer C. After the Telnet client is invoked, it examines a file commonly known as /etc/hosts (particularly UNIX-based computers) searching for a device name A. Assuming it finds it, it then examines its corresponding Internet address as the computer is known to all TCP/IP software. Next, sparing much detail, the Telnet server located on machine A answers the client's request (from computer C) for a logical connection to be

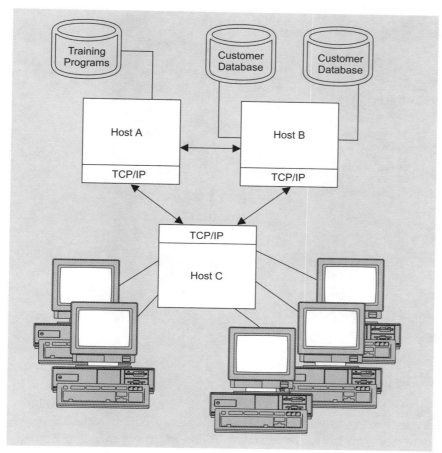

Figure 9.2 Networking via Telnet

established. It is, and then the logon prompt from computer A is displayed on the user's terminal connected to computer C.

Another possibility for what a Telnet client does once it gets invoked is quite common in many networks. It interacts with what is called a Domain Name Server. The Domain Name Server maintains a database that contains device names and Internet addresses on the local network and references to Domain Name Servers with name and address associations for devices in more remote areas of the network. When employed, Telnet clients use this instead of the typical /etc/hosts file to find the address for the target host. The reason behind this is efficiency. In large networks the Domain Name System is used. The consequence if a Domain Name System is not used in a network is that all /etc/hosts files and other pertinent files must be updated anytime new hosts are added to the network.

What are the Characteristics of Telnet?

Telnet is an application and a protocol. From an application perspective, Telnet provides the ability for a user to invoke it and perform a remote logon with another host as shown in Figure 9.3.

The figure shows the Telnet client on host A requesting a logical connection with the Telnet server in host B. The important thing to observe is both Telnet client and server are part of the TCP/IP stack on each network device.

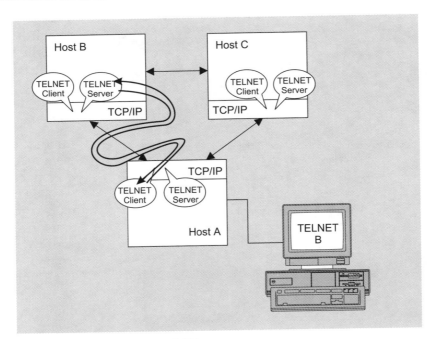

Figure 9.3 Remote logon with Telnet

What is a Raw Telnet?

Figure 9.3 depicts three hosts with a TCP/IP stack, each with a native Telnet client and server. It also shows a user invoking a Telnet client from the TCP/IP protocol stack on host A by entering Telnet at an operating system prompt. In many technical circles this use of Telnet client is referred to as a *raw Telnet*, specifically referring to the Telnet client. The Telnet client is considered native because the Telnet client is inherent to the TCP/IP protocol stack.

Since Telnet is also a protocol, additional explanation is in order. So far, focus has been upon the Telnet application. But the Telnet protocol can be used to create a program called a TN3270 client application. Operational differences exist between a raw Telnet client and a TN3270 client application.

A raw Telnet client is popular for logons to hosts that use ASCII for data representation. For example, if you are working on a Windows computer you can issue a raw Telnet to a Sun computer (using the UNIX operating system). Both systems use ASCII for data representation. This is a typical scenario where TCP/IP is implemented and Telnet is used.

A different requirement exists when a user needs to log on to a computer that uses EBCDIC for data representation and the source computer uses ASCII for data representation. In today's heterogeneous networking environments, a variety of hosts (with different operating systems) may be attached to any given network, particularly TCP/IP. Assume three hosts are attached to a network. Assume two of these hosts are UNIX-based and use ASCII data representation by default. Assume one of the hosts is an IBM system using the VM operating system and it has TCP/IP operating on it. The VM host uses EBCDIC data representation by default. Figure 9.4 depicts such an example.

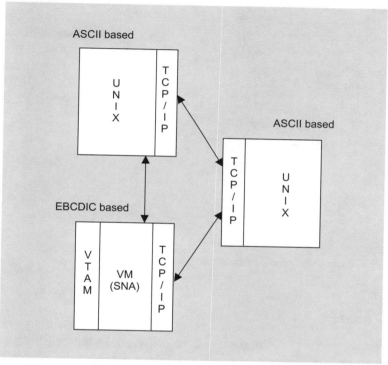

Figure 9.4 Networking and data representation

Figure 9.4 shows hosts that use different methods of representing data; two use ASCII and one uses EBCDIC. The figure also shows that two UNIX hosts and one VM host are present. All hosts are connected to the same network and use TCP/IP as the network protocol.

In Figure 9.5 the Telnet client is invoked on a UNIX (ASCII-based host) and the Telnet server on the VM machine answers the request of the client. Additionally, the TCP/IP stack on the VM machine performs protocol conversion. This means that TCP/IP protocol is converted to SNA on the VM machine. It also performs data translation (ASCII to EBCDIC and vice versa outbound from the VM machine).

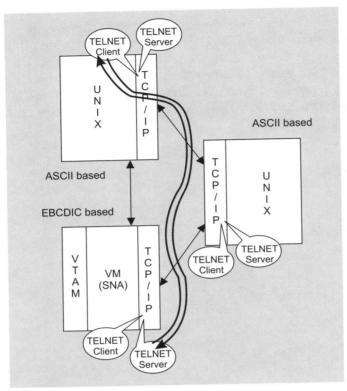

Figure 9.5 Networking and protocol conversion

In summary, Figure 9.5 shows the VM machine performing two functions. It performs protocol conversion and data translation. However, with the appropriate product, data translation can be performed on the UNIX host. Consequently, over time, savings will be realized when measured by CPU cycles.

What is TN3270?

A Telnet protocol is defined, and if an individual with required knowledge wishes to design a program based on Telnet protocol, he or she can. The most common program written using Telnet protocol is an emulator application providing data translation services between ASCII and EBCDIC and vice versa. This program (application) is called a TN3270 client.

Telnet (within a native TCP/IP protocol stack) typically uses ASCII-based data, and it does not fit into SNA natively, which is dominated by EBCDIC. In the SNA world, the EBCDIC goes a step further and defines what are called data streams. A few specific data streams exist, but a dominant one is the 3270 data stream. It is used with terminals and printers.

Because of the differences in ASCII and EBCDIC, converting ASCII into EBCDIC, specifically into a 3270 or a 5250 data stream, is required. The question is where this process takes place. With the data stream dilemma between TCP/IP networks and SNA networks, this fundamental issue must be resolved.

So, how do users on a TCP/IP-based network have ASCII data converted into EBCDIC? Two possible solutions exist.

First, a raw Telnet client can be used to establish a logical connection between a Windows, OS/2, UNIX, or other non-EBCDIC client and an EBCDIC-based host. If this is the case, then ASCII to EBCDIC translation will occur on the EBCDIC host (with the exception of when a gateway is used between the two and translation services are provided or other scenarios).

Second, a TN3270 client application can be used like a raw Telnet to gain entry into the SNA environment, but a TN3270 client application performs data translation. This means it sends an EBCDIC (3270 or 5250 data stream to the destination host). The point is the TN3270 client application translates ASCII data into an EBCDIC, that being a 3270 or 5250 data stream. Figure 9.6 shows two UNIX hosts and a VM host connected to a network. On one UNIX host a TN3270 client application exists.

In the figure, the TN3270 client is shown establishing a logical connection with the Telnet server native to the TCP/IP protocol on the VM machine. But notice that the data stream leaving the ASCII-based host is EBCDIC! Magic? No, it works because data format (be it ASCII or EBCDIC) gets formatted at layer six within a network. By the time the data gets down to the interface card connecting it to the network, the data is represented by voltages or light pulses, whichever the network is based upon.

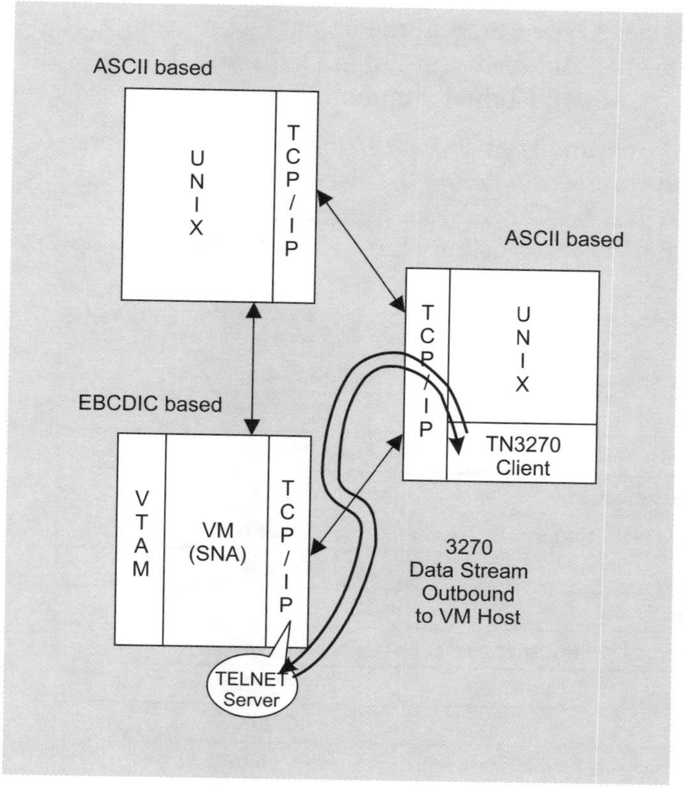

The net effect of having TN3270 clients is that they do pay for themselves over a period of time if used in a scenario such as Figure 9.6. But there are many instances where they (TN3270 applications) are not needed and provide little if any benefit to the end user. Both a raw Telnet and a TN3270 client provide the user with remote logon capability. Both the raw Telnet and TN3270 client are client applications. The difference is merely where data translation is performed.

Figure 9.6 Networking and data translation

How is Telnet Used?

As mentioned previously, Telnet consists of a client and server. A client always initiates a logical connection and a server always answers the client's request. To use Telnet, a command must be entered to invoke the Telnet client. The command to invoke the Telnet client from the TCP/IP suite is Telnet. Assuming TCP/IP has been installed properly and normal setup occurred, entering the Telnet command invokes the Telnet client from the TCP/IP protocol stack.

If the Telnet command is entered without a target host name, alias, or Internet address, the following prompt appears:

    telnet>>

This command is generated from the Telnet client on that host. When the prompt appears, valid Telnet client commands can be entered.

What are the Valid Telnet Client Commands?

Valid Telnet client commands can be entered at the Telnet client prompt. If you forget which commands are valid from the Telnet client prompt, enter the question mark to display a list of valid Telnet commands.

Telnet includes a number of optional connection attributes that may be negotiated when establishing the connection. Table 9.1 lists the currently supported option attributes. The referenced RFCs specify the Telnet options. Individual Telnet implementations may or may not offer any particular option choice.

Option #	Attribute	Reference
Option 0	Binary Transmission	RFC856
Option 1	Echo	RFC857
Option 2	Reconnection	NIC50005
Option 3	Suppress Go Ahead	RFC858
Option 4	Message Size Negotiation	ETHERNET
Option 5	Status	RFC859
Option 6	Timing Mark	RFC860
Option 7	Remote Controlled Transmit and Echo	RFC726
Option 8	Output Line Width	NIC50005
Option 9	Output Page Size	NIC50005
Option 10	Output Carriage-Return Disposition	RFC652
Option 11	Output Horizontal Tab Stops	RFC653
Option 12	Output Horizontal Tab Disposition	RFC654

Option #	Attribute	Reference
Option 13	Output Form-feed Disposition	RFC655
Option 14	Output Vertical Tab Stops	RFC656
Option 15	Output Vertical Tab Disposition	RFC657
Option 16	Output Linefeed Disposition	RFC657
Option 17	Extended ASCII	RFC698
Option 18	Log-out	RFC727
Option 19	Byte Macro	RFC735
Option 20	Data Entry Terminal	RFC1043, RFC732
Option 21	SUPDUP	RFC736, RFC734
Option 22	SUPDUP Output	RFC749
Option 23	Send Location	RFC779
Option 24	Terminal Type	RFC1091
Option 25	End of Record	RFC885
Option 26	TACACS User Identification	RFC927
Option 27	Output Marking	RFC933
Option 28	Terminal Location Number	RFC946
Option 29	Telnet 3270 Regime	RFC1041
Option 30	X.3 PAD	RFC1053
Option 31	Negotiate About Window Size	RFC1073
Option 32	Terminal Speed	RFC1079
Option 33	Remote Flow Control	RFC1372
Option 34	Linemode	RFC1184
Option 35	X Display Location	RFC1096
Option 36	Environment Option	RFC1408
Option 37	Authentication Option	RFC1409
Option 38	Encryption Option	Classified
Option 39	New Environment Option	RFC1572
Option 40	TN3270E	RFC1647
Option 255	Extended-Options-List	RFC861

Table 9.1 Telnet options

Telnet Commands

An abbreviated list of valid Telnet client commands and a brief explanation of each is listed below:

telnet [*options*] [*host* [*port*]]

User command to connect to a remote host using the Telnet protocol. If *host* is not included when **telnet** is invoked, the command line prompt (telnet>>) is displayed. Then the user can execute the *options* commands. Otherwise, an **open** command is performed with whatever *options* are specified.

options

-8
Enables an 8-bit input data path.

-a
Automatically logon to the remote host.

-d
Toggle (turn on if off/turn off if on) socket level debugging.

-e [*escape_character*]
Sets the Telnet escape character to *escape_character*. If *escape_character* is omitted, then there is no defined escape character.

-E
Prevents the recognition of any character as an escape character.

-l *user*
If the remote host recognizes **environ**, *user* is the value of **user** sent to the remote host.

-L
Enables an 8-bit output data path.

-n *tracefilename*
tracefilename is open and records the trace information.

-r
Enable a user interface similar to **rlogin**. This mode sets the escape character to ~ (tilde), unless modified by **-e**.

Commands

Ctrl-Z
Suspend **telnet** execution.

! [*command*]
Execute *command* in a subshell on the local host. If *command* is not specified, an interactive subshell is invoked.

?[*command*]
Print help information for *command*. If *command* is omitted, print a summary of help information.

check
Verify settings for special characters.

close
This command closes a current Telnet connection if one is established and returns to the command prompt mode.

display *argument xxxx*
This command displays the **set** and **toggle** operating values as specified in *xxxx* in use for Telnet. Because these parameters can be changed, they are site dependent.

export
Use local host defaults for special characters.

import
Use remote host defaults for special characters.

mode [*type*]

mode—This command indicates whether an entry can be made in line-by-line or one-character-at-a-time mode.

?
Print help information for the **mode** command.

character
If remote host understands option, disable **telnet linemode** option; otherwise, enter a mode where one character at a time is entered.

edit/-edit
Enable/disable the **telnet linemode edit** mode.

isig/-isig
Enable/disable the **telnet linemode trapsig** mode.

line
If remote host understands option, enable **telnet linemode** option; otherwise, enter a mode where one line at a time is entered.

softtabs/-softtabs
Enable/disable the **linemode soft_tab** mode.

open *host* [*user*] [[-]*port*] [**-a**] [**-l** *user*]
Open a connection to the named remote *host*. If the *port* is not specified, the local host will use the default port number.

quit
Close the Telnet connection and exit **telnet.**

status
Display the current status of the Telnet connection. The display will include the current mode and the remote host name.

send *arguments*
Transmit one or more special character sequences to the remote host.

arguments

?
Print the help information for the **send** command.

abort
Transmit the **telnet abort** sequence.

ao
Transmit the **telnet ao** sequence. The **ao** sequence causes the remote host to flush all output from the remote system and send it to the local host.

ayt
"Are you there" sequence is transmitted to the remote host.

brk
Transmit **telnet brk** (break) sequence.

ec
Transmit **telnet ec** (erase character) sequence. **ec** sequence causes the remote system to erase the last character received.

el
Transmit the **telnet el** (erase line) sequence. **el** sequence causes the remote system to erase the last line received.

eof
Transmit **telnet eof** sequence. **eof** sequence designates the file end-of-file.

eor
Transmit **telnet eor** sequence. **eor** sequence designates the file end-of-record.

escape
Transmit the **telnet escape** character. Initially the **escape** character is "[".

ga
Transmit the **telnet ga** sequence. The **ga** sequence designates the remote host to "go ahead."

getstatus
The local host requests the remote host to transmit its current status.

ip

Transmit **telnet ip** sequence. The **ip** sequence interrupts the currently running remote host process.

nop

Transmit **telnet nop** sequence. The **nop** sequence informs the remote host there is "no operation."

susp

Transmit **telnet susp** sequence. The **susp** sequence informs the remote host to suspend the currently running process.

synch

Transmit **telnet synch** sequence. The **synch** sequence informs the remote host to ignore all previously typed but unread data.

?

Display **set** and **unset** commands.

set *argument value*
unset *argument value*

set or **unset** Telnet variables to specific values. The *value* **off** turns the variables off and the *value* **on** turns them on. **set** enables the variables while **unset** disables them. The **display** command will display the value of the variables.

ayt

In **localchars** mode, this character becomes the alternate **ayt** character.

echo

Echoes entered characters on the local host.

eof

In **linemode**, or line-by-line mode, entering this character sequence as the first characters on a new line will cause the end-of-file character to be transmitted to the remote host.

erase

In **localchars** character-at-a-time mode, a **telnet ec** sequence is transmitted to the remote host.

escape

The local host will transmit the Telnet escape character to the remote host. The escape character is initially "[". The escape character places the remote host in the Telnet command prompt mode.

flushoutput

In **localchars** mode, the **telnet ao** character is transmitted.

forw1
In **localchars** mode, the **forw1** character is transmitted to the remote host which interprets the character as the alternate end-of-line character.

forw2
In **localchars** mode, the **forw2** character is transmitted to the remote host which interprets the character as the alternate end-of-line character.

interrupt
In **telnet ao localchars** mode, the **telnet ip** sequence is transmitted to the remote host.

kill
In **telnet ip localchars** character-at-a-time mode, the **telnet eb** sequence is transmitted to the remote host.

lnext
In **telnet el linemode** mode or line-by-line mode, this character becomes the remote host's **lnext** character.

quit
When the **quit** character is entered in **telnet el localchars** mode, the **telnet brk** sequence is transmitted to the remote host.

reprint
In **telnet brk linemode** or line-by-line mode, this character is the remote host's reprint character.

start
If **telnet toggle-flow-control** is enabled, this character becomes the remote host's **start** character.

stop
If **telnet toggle-flow-control** is enabled, this character becomes the remote host's **stop** character.

susp
When the **suspend** character is entered in **telnet localchars** or **linemode** mode, the **telnet susp** sequence is transmitted to the remote host.

tracefile
File used by **netdata** to write output to.

worderase
In **telnet brk linemode** or line-by-line mode, the **worderase** character becomes the remote host's **worderase** character.

slc [*state*]
In **telnet linemode** mode, set the state of special characters.

environ [*argument*[*xxxx*]]
In **telnet environ** mode, act upon variables *argument* [*xxxx*]. *xxxx* represents the argument variables as defined below:

argument

> **define** *variable value*
> Define the *variable* as an environmental variable with *value*.
>
> **undefine** *variable*
> Remove the *variable* from the environmental variable list.
>
> **export** *variable*
> Tag *variable* for **export** to the remote host.
>
> **inexport** *variable*
> Tag *variable* to be excluded from **export** to the remote host, unless the remote host specifically requests it.
>
> **send** *variable*
> Send *variable* to the remote host.

toggle *argument* [*xxxx*]
Toggle (turn on if off/turn off if on) various Telnet flags. Flags may also be enabled or disabled using the **set** or **unset** commands. These flags determine how Telnet will respond to events. *xxxx* represents the argument variables as defined below:

argument

> **?**
> Display **toggle** commands.
>
> **autoflush**
> When **autoflush** and **localchars** are TRUE and **ao** or **quit** characters are recognized by the remote host, data on the local host will not be displayed until the remote host acknowledges to the local host that it has processed all Telnet character sequences.
>
> **autosync**
> When **autosynch** and **localchars** are TRUE and the **intr** or **quit** character is entered, the Telnet sequence transmitted will be followed by the **telnet synch** sequence. Inital **autosync** value is FALSE.
>
> **binary**
> Enable/disable the **telnet binary** local host variable on the input and output.

inbinary
Enable/disable the **telnet binary** local host variable on the input.

outbinary
Enable/disable the **telnet binary** local host variable on the output.

crlf
If **crlf** is TRUE, carriage returns are transmitted as CR-LF. If **crlf** is FALSE, carriage returns are transmitted as CR-NUL. The initial **crlf** value is FALSE.

crmod
Toggle (turn on if off/turn off if on) **crmod** (carriage return mode) mode. The initial **crmod** value is FALSE.

debug
Toggle (turn on if off/turn off if on) socket level debugging mode. The initial **debug** value is FALSE.

localchars
When TRUE, **interrupt**, **flush**, **quit**, **kill**, and **erase** characters are recognized by the local host.

netdata
Toggle (turn on if off/turn off if on) the display of all network data. The initial **netdata** value is FALSE.

options
Toggle (turn on if off/turn off if on) the display of Telnet protocol processing having to do with Telnet options. The initial **options** value is FALSE.

prettydump
When **netdata** toggle and **prettydump** are enabled, the **netdata** output is formatted into a better user friendly format. For example, a space is placed between each character and any Telnet sequence is preceded by an asterisk.

skiprc
The ~/**telnetc** file is not processed. The initial **skiprc** value is false.

termdata
Toggle (turn on if off/turn off if on) hexadecimal printing format for host data. The initial **termdata** value is false.

Helpful Hints for Using Telnet

Using Telnet is fairly straightforward. Once users break through the newness of the technology it is not difficult. Learning Telnet is easier when one understands basic Telnet operation, Telnet commands, and how to log on to hosts appropriately.

Since Telnet is part of the TCP/IP protocol suite, it does work with other components in the suite. For example, if one attempts to establish a remote logon with a target host, and after a period of time a response is displayed on the terminal something to the effect of "host unreachable" or some other message, this indicates problems are not necessarily related to Telnet. In this example, the "host unreachable" message comes from the Internet Control Message Protocol (ICMP) component. This is an integral part of the IP layer. It provides messages responding to different conditions. Here, a destination host is not reachable by the Telnet client. The obvious question is, why? With this example a couple of reasons are possible. It could be the host is unreachable because of a break in the network connection. Or it could be that the host is located on another segment of the network and, for some reason, inaccessible at the moment. Other possibilities exist.

When messages such as these appear they are most often generated from the ICMP portion of the TCP/IP suite. It would be helpful to familiarize yourself with common messages and understand their meaning. They can prove to be valuable troubleshooting tools.

Is Telnet Just for Computers?

We frequently need to configure and manage a number of computer-related devices across our networks, including network infrastructure devices such as concentrators, bridges, routers, and switches. The designers of such equipment have several options when designing the user interfaces to these devices. They may use jumpers and switches augmented by written documentation for the function of each jumper. They may provide a series of push buttons with an LCD panel for performing the configuration. Many devices have a serial port that can be cabled either directly or through a modem to a computer terminal or computer running terminal emulation software. The screen on the following page shows the Telnet interface to an Ascend Pipeline ISDN router, typical of the interfaces found on such equipment.

Many such network devices additionally provide the ability to establish a terminal session with the device's configuration interface through a Telnet session. The ability to Telnet to network devices such as concentrators, bridges, routers, and switches to perform configuration tasks makes it possible to perform routine configuration and status monitoring tasks from a central site across the network. Such management, commonly referred to as "in-band" management, is never a complete solution to managing such devices, however. An alternative, or "out-of-band," interface is required for configuring the device to initially communicate across the network, and to address reconfiguration issues in times of network disruption.

Figure 9.7
Telnet interface

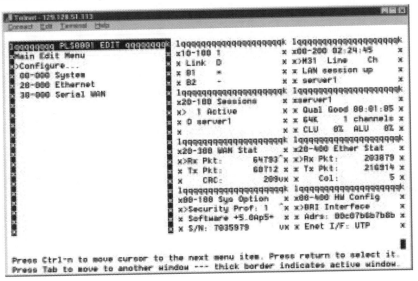

Summary

Telnet is a very popular application in the TCP/IP protocol suite. It provides remote logon capabilities and operates on a client-server method of communication. Each Telnet, native to the majority of TCP/IP protocol stacks, consists of a client and server. A client is used to initiate a request. Servers always respond to the request of a client.

Telnet is both an application and a protocol. It is an application in its native sense. It is also a protocol in its native sense; they are not diametrically opposed. The Telnet protocol can be used to write a TN3270 client application.

A TN3270 client application provides a user with the advantage of performing data translation on the host where the TN3270 client resides. To use a TN3270 client application requires communication with a Telnet server. This may be a Telnet server in a TCP/IP stack on an EBCDIC host, or it may be a customized program called a TN3270 server. The latter does little more than provide the necessary ability to establish a logical connection with a TN3270 client.

Chapter 10

Introduction to SMTP

Questions answered in this chapter:

What is SMTP?

How does SMTP work?

What is the relationship between SMTP and TCP/IP?

What are the SMTP user commands?

Introduction

Simple Mail Transfer Protocol (SMTP) is part of the TCP/IP suite of protocols. It is a mechanism for electronic mail transfer. The concept of sender and receiver is used with SMTP and is parallel to the client-server relationship used in Telnet and FTP. SMTP specifies an end-to-end delivery system. Specifically, the source SMTP client makes a connection directly with the recipient's SMTP system. This is different from the operation of many LAN-based e-mail systems. LAN-based mail systems, such as cc:mail, Lotus Notes, Groupwise, and Microsoft Mail, operate on a store-and-forward principle, where messages are copied across a series of servers to move from the sender to the receiver. In the SMTP system, the sending system holds the content of the mail message until it can directly contact the receiving system—with a provision for eventually discarding messages intended for receiving systems that are repeatedly unreachable.

SMTP Components

Electronic mail is fairly simple in concept and operation. Its basic structure appears like Figure 10.1. Figure 10.1 shows two hosts connected to a network. Each host has the same components for mail. Host A is the sending host and host B is the receiver.

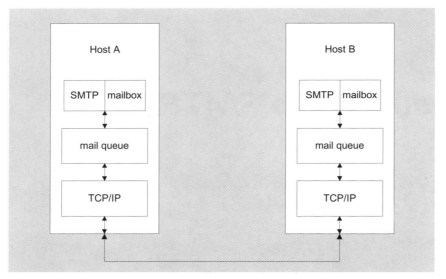

Figure 10.1 SMTP at work with TCP/IP

The following events occur once a mail program has been invoked:

▶ The User Agent is the component that causes the mail program to begin. It is invoked by a command and it provides an editor for the sender to create a message to be sent.

▶ After the message is created, it is passed to a Message Transfer Agent. The Message Transfer Agent is responsible for setting up communications with remote hosts and subsequently transmitting the message.

▶ On the receiving host another Message Transfer Agent accepts the message and stores it on the message queue of the individual receiving the message.

▶ The recipient of the message views it by invoking the User Agent on his/her machine.

Mail systems are straightforward to use. Besides the SMTP mail system, X.400 is popular. The X.400 mail system is now an ISO standard. Although the X.400 standard is popular, the SMTP system has recently surged in popularity as a result of corporations looking to Internet standards to meet corporate needs at minimum costs. X.400 differs from SMTP in characteristics such as the ability to convert messages to a different medium like faxes, the ability to trace messages via a formal envelope, and a priority system, for example.

Why Do I Need a Mail Server?

The SMTP e-mail system works at its best between computers that are constantly powered on and connected to the Internet through a persistent TCP/IP connection. Although the SMTP protocol has provisions for repeatedly trying to connect to hosts that are unreachable, this feature was designed to accommodate the periodic downtime associated with performing routine maintenance on computer systems and to compensate for communications problems on the network. Pressing it to accommodate intermittent TCP/IP connections associated with a dial-up modem connection is going beyond the level of robustness designed into the system. Additionally, mail must be addressed to a receiving machine that has a constant IP address—not typically associated with dial-up modem connections.

Beyond the issue of constant network connectivity, most users enjoy the freedom of being able to access their e-mail from more than one place—not just from the machine where the mail has been sent. The typical desktop Windows computer found on the majority of users' desks is not configured to provide this service. In practice, therefore, the SMTP mail system has the greatest functionality when the mail is stored on mail servers running on multiuser systems that in turn provide mail services to clients via the POP3 or IMAP protocol. Where SMTP defines the mechanism that is used to move Internet mail between host systems, POP3 and IMAP are used by mail client software to interact with the SMTP host. It's not that you can't run your desktop computer as an SMTP mailer, it's just that there is likely more full-featured functionality to be had by using a mail server.

How Does SMTP Mail Interact with LAN-based Mail Systems?

Because the SMTP mail system operates on a connection basis rather than a store-and-forward basis, moving mail between SMTP and LAN-based systems is normally accomplished through a mail gateway. When an SMTP client sends mail to a recipient on a LAN-based mail system, the SMTP client actually makes its connection with the SMTP gateway machine serving the LAN-based system. The SMTP protocol only guarantees delivery to the gateway; it is up to the LAN-based system to complete the delivery to the user's inbox.

An SMTP connection is frequently used as an intermediary between users of LAN-based mail systems in different organizations. The sender's LAN-based system delivers mail to its SMTP gateway, which uses an SMTP connection to send the message to the recipient's SMTP gateway, which in turn passes the message on to the user through the LAN-based system on the far end.

Common SMTP Commands

SMTP has a limited number of commands because sending a message is not that complex. Some commands that can be executed with SMTP include:

helo—This command identifies the sender to the receiver.

mail—This invokes SMTP.

send—This causes a message to be delivered directly to the designated recipient if the intended receiver is currently logged on.

soml—This causes message delivery direct to the recipient's display, assuming the recipient is logged on; if not, the message is treated as mail and stored in the recipient's mailbox.

help—This asks a recipient for a list of commands supported by the mail system on the host to which he/she is attached.

rcpt—This command can be used to identify an individual recipient or multiple recipients.

turn—This command is entered by the mail sender to request the recipient to become the sender rather than the receiver.

saml—This command performs two functions. First, it delivers a message to the intended receiver's mailbox. And, second, if the intended recipient is logged on, it will deliver the message to the user's display.

Other SMTP commands can be obtained by entering **help** at the mail prompt.

Although it is possible to interact with an SMTP mailer by using Telnet to access the host on port 25, the well-known port number for SMTP mail, this is rarely done. In general, the command-level interaction with the SMTP system is performed exclusively by SMTP mail computers. However, directly accessing the SMTP daemon through Telnet can be of assistance when debugging mail transport difficulties.

What Kind of Information Can I Mail?

The base definition of SMTP mail, as described in RFC 821, provides for the transmission of 7-bit ASCII data with line lengths of less than 1,000 characters per line. This is the lowest common denominator for Internet mail. It provides for the basic transmission of information in the English language. It does not, however, make provision for information that is not in English or consists of something other than text. There are two mechanisms for overcoming this limitation.

SMTP Service Extensions

The SMTP Service Extensions specify a means to extend the capabilities of SMTP to overcome the limitations of RFC 821. The first piece of the puzzle is RFC 1651, which provides the SMTP receiver a mechanism to communicate to the SMTP sender program which extensions it supports. An original set of extensions was published in RFC 1123, and is modified by RFC from time to time. The optional RFC 1652 specifies SMTP Service Extensions for 8-bit MIME transport, which allows systems supporting this extension to exchange data using 8-bit encoding schemes rather than encoding everything as 7-bit mail-safe ASCII. A final piece, RFC 1653, provides a mechanism for declaring the size of a message, overcoming the message size limitations associated with the original RFC 821 specification.

MIME

The Multipurpose Internet Mail Extensions (MIME) provide a mechanism to embed binary data inside an SMTP mail message. MIME was initially defined in RFCs 1521 and 1522. The MIME and SMTP Service Extensions are not mutually exclusive—they complement each other. MIME is designed to maintain compatibility with previously issued RFCs to as great an extent as possible. It is also equipped to handle the reality that many of the mail systems in operation on the Internet fail to provide strict compliance with even RFC 821: They convert tabs to spaces, wrap lines longer than 76 characters, pad all the lines of a message to a uniform length, and commit related sins of failure to maintain strict adherence to the standard.

The MIME system specified in RFC 1521 was designed from the outset to be extensible. It begins by defining the parts of a mail message into various content types, such as text, audio, graphics, etc., each of which have subtypes. The RFC defines a system for registering values for various content-type/subtype pairs, with provision for both permanent and experimental pairs.

The MIME specification additionally provides a method for including a pointer to information that is external to the message itself. These references can be specified as FTP links, where the user is expected to provide a user ID and password, or as anonymous FTP links. Additionally, the links can reference files on the local file system or files that are accessible through a mail server.

Note:

Yes, there is a relationship between MIME in the context of SMTP mail and MIME in the context of the World Wide Web. MIME originated as an extension to SMTP for the purpose of transmitting binary and multimedia data as part of an electronic mail message. The concept of a mime type is an integral part of this e-mail equation in that it provides a standardized way of describing the type of data being transmitted. When the World Wide Web was undergoing its metamorphosis from a text-only system to a multimedia-enabled system, the designers chose to lift the mime-type specification from the world of e-mail and apply it to the Web. This precluded the need to reinvent the wheel and create a competitive system for describing the data type of nontext information. The original MIME specification remains, however, as a transport specification describing how SMTP mail systems can be extended to accommodate the exchange of multimedia data through electronic mail.

Where Does the Domain Name System Fit into Mail?

The Domain Name Server (DNS) provides a record type called an MX record that handles many of the details of the SMTP mail system. When the sending computer wants to send a message to a receiving computer, it contacts the DNS server to gain the address of the host system set up to receive incoming SMTP mail. Appropriately constructed MX records can provide two useful services. First, they can provide a list of multiple host computers and an order of preference to be used in delivering mail. If the most preferred host is unavailable, the mail is delivered to the secondary or tertiary host, as available. An MX record can also provide an e-mail alias function, allowing a user to publish only an aliased address, which is resolved at each connection to the machine address where the user actually wants to receive mail. Such an alias allows published electronic mail addresses to remain constant over time, as machine upgrades, e-mail preferences, and job assignments change within an organization.

Summary

SMTP is the electronic mail system specified by RFCs in the TCP/IP protocol suite. The SMTP e-mail system is an end-to-end delivery system, in contrast to most LAN-based e-mail systems. Originally designed for the exchange of English-only text messages of limited length, extensions now allow the inclusion of multimedia (graphics and sound) data elements of significant size.

Chapter 11

ICMP

Questions answered in this chapter:

What is ICMP?

How does ICMP work?

What is the relationship between ICMP and TCP/IP?

What are the ICMP messages?

Introduction

Gateways use Internet Control Message Protocol (ICMP) to help manage the intranetwork-to-internetwork and internetwork-to-internetwork connections. ICMP's primary management function is reporting to the sending host any processing errors. A processing error message might be necessary due to the inability of the router to determine the destination address from the information provided by IP and therefore telling the sending host that the destination is unreachable. Other possible error messages might be necessary to tell the sending IP the router's buffer is full and to pause sending, or that the destination route specified in the IP header is too long.

ICMP is part of IP and must be implemented by every host using IP, which includes all routers and gateways. ICMP is not intended to make IP a reliable communications protocol, but only to provide some pertinent information about the status of the network, when appropriate. Upper layer protocols must still receive the ICMP message and take appropriate action based upon the message content. The action the host takes is entirely up to the programming team that designed the host. Good, robust programs utilize these messages to help resolve whatever caused the message to be generated.

Due to the possibility of a never-ending message loop, ICMP does not report processing errors concerning ICMP messages. Also, ICMP only sends messages about the first fragment (fragment zero = fragment offset of zero) of fragmented datagrams.

227

ICMP version 6 (ICMPv6) was introduced to fulfill some special needs of IPv6. The ICMPv6 differences are identified where applicable.

ICMP Message Format

ICMP uses the IP datagram for sending ICMP messages. A non-ICMP message header is shown in Figure 11.1. For a normal data-carrying datagram, the protocol bit field is set to 00000000. To designate the IP datagram as an ICMP message datagram, the IP header protocol bit field is set to 00000001.

0 1 2 3	4 5 6 7	8 9 10 11 12 13 14 15	16 17 18 19 20 21 22 23 24 25 26 27 28 29 30 31	
version	IHL	type of service	length	
identification			flags	fragment offset
time to live		00000000	header checksum	
source address				
destination address				
options (variable length)			padding (variable length)	
data				

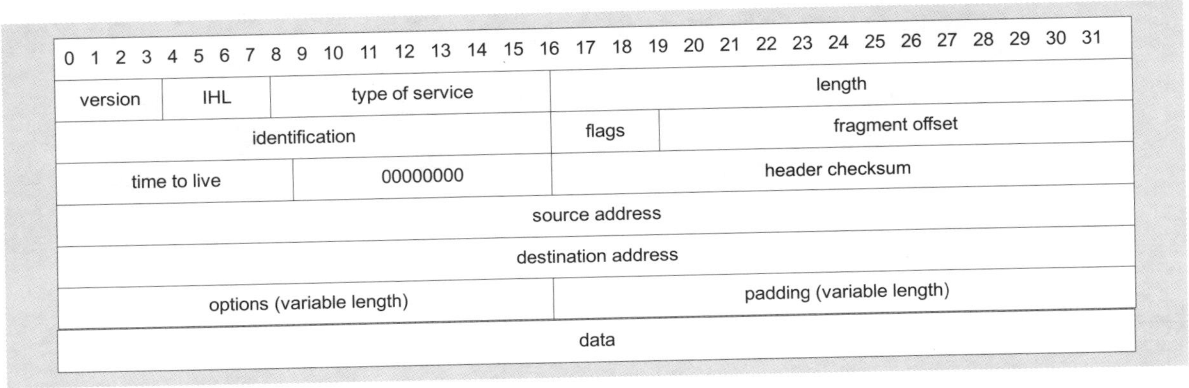

Figure 11.1 IP datagram header

Figure 11.2 illustrates the use of the IP header when utilized for ICMP messaging. The protocols bit field is set to 00000001. The first octet of the IP data bit field is used to define the ICMP type field in all datagrams generated by IP. The value of this field determines whether the information carried in

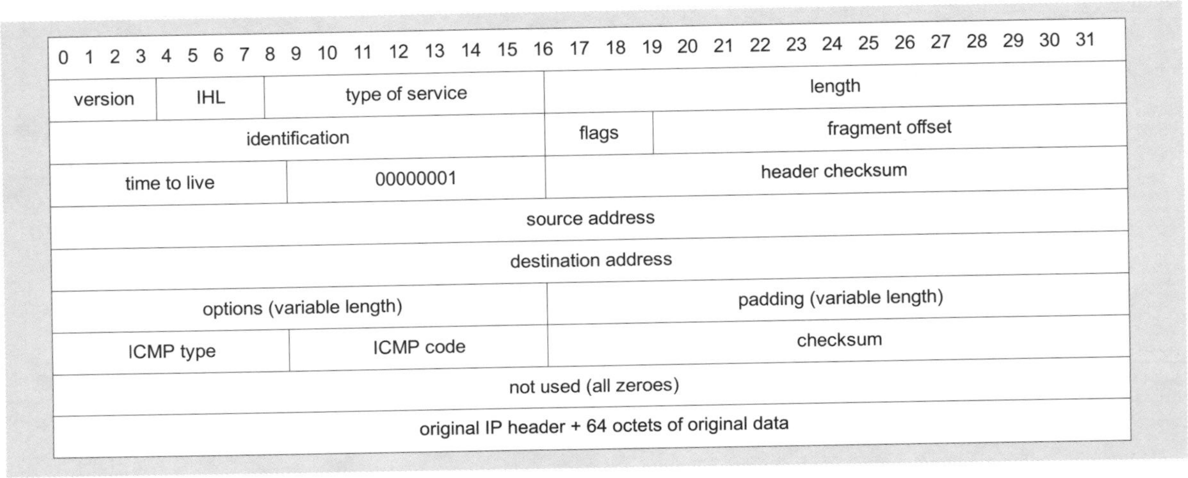

0 1 2 3	4 5 6 7	8 9 10 11 12 13 14 15	16 17 18 19 20 21 22 23 24 25 26 27 28 29 30 31	
version	IHL	type of service	length	
identification			flags	fragment offset
time to live		00000001	header checksum	
source address				
destination address				
options (variable length)			padding (variable length)	
ICMP type		ICMP code	checksum	
not used (all zeroes)				
original IP header + 64 octets of original data				

Figure 11.2 IP datagram header with valid ICMP message

the data bit field should be interpreted by any receiving IP as bona-fide user data or ICMP messages. Figure 11.1 illustrates the general use of the IP datagram header.

ICMP version 6 allows the last field (original IP header and 64 octets of original data) to be as large as 576 octets (bytes).

Notice the first data octet is the ICMP message type bit field followed by the ICMP code bit field. Both bit fields are 8 bits. Following the code bit field is the 16-bit checksum field. Between the checksum field and the original IP header plus the first 64 octets of original data is a 32-bit field of all zeroes. This field is reserved for later extensions and is only used when the receiving host calculates the checksum.

Table 11.1 lists the various ICMP types and codes. In the "Message" column, the device that may generate the message is included in parentheses.

Message	ICMP Type	ICMP Code
echo reply message (both)	0	0
unassigned	1	
unassigned	2	
packet too big (ICMPv6) (both)	2	0
net unreachable (gateway)	3	0
hop limit exceeded in transit (ICMPv6) (both)	3	0
host unreachable (gateway)	3	1
fragment reassembly time exceeded (ICMPv6) (both)	3	1
protocol unreachable (host)	3	2
port unreachable (host)	3	3
fragmentation needed & DF set (gateway)	3	4
source route failed (gateway)	3	5
destination Network Unknown	3	6
destination Host Unknown	3	7
source Host Isolated	3	8
communication with destination network is administratively prohibited	3	9
communication with destination host is administratively prohibited	3	10
destination network unreachable for type of service	3	11
destination host unreachable for type of service	3	12
source quench (both)	4	0
bad header field (ICMPv6) (both)	4	0
bad next header type (ICMPv6) (both)	4	1
bad IPv6 option (ICMPv6) (both)	4	2

Message	ICMP Type	ICMP Code
redirect datagrams (gateway)	5	0
redirect datagrams (host)	5	1
redirect datagrams (service & gateway)	5	2
redirect datagrams (service & host)	5	3
alternate host address (both)	6	0
unassigned	7	
echo message (both)	8	0
router advertisement (both)	9	0
router solicitation (both)	10	0
time-to-live exceeded in transit (gateway)	11	0
fragment reassembly time exceeded (gateway)	11	1
pointer indicates the error (both)	12	0
missing a required option (both)	12	1
bad length (both)	12	2
time-stamp message (both)	13	0
time-stamp reply message (both)	14	0
information request message (both)	15	0 obsolete
information reply message (both)	16	0 obsolete
information request message (both)	17	0
information reply message (both)	18	0
reserved (for security)	19	
reserved (for experiments)	20-29	
traceroute (both)	30	
datagram conversion error (both)	31	
mobile host redirect (both)	32	
IP version 6 where-are-you (both)	33	
IP version 6 I-am-here (both)	34	
mobile registration request (both)	35	
mobile registration reply (both)	36	
reserved	37-127	
echo request message (ICMPv6) (both)	128	0
echo reply message (ICMPv6) (both)	129	0
reserved	130-255	

Table 11.1 ICMP message types and codes

The IP header bit fields are used in the same manner as described in the chapter on IP. That is, the version number, IHL, TOS, length, identification, flags, fragment offset, time-to-live, header checksum, and source and destination addresses are used for the same purposes as outlined in Chapter 5. For ICMP messages the TOS is always zero. Perhaps it should be stated that the source address is always the router originating the ICMP message and the destination is always the host from which the original datagram was received by the router.

Any gateway along the transmission path may generate ICMP messages. If a gateway other than the initial gateway connected to the host generates an ICMP message, then the ICMP message is returned to the gateway forwarding the packet to the gateway generating the ICMP message. In other words, gateways may generate ICMP messages to other gateways, each following the return path to the original sender of the datagram causing the ICMP message to be generated. In this manner, a host can be notified of routing problems far from the immediate gateway connected to the host.

It is convenient to classify ICMP messages into four categories:

▲   ICMP error messages

    ICMPv6 message type 2 Packet Too Big
    ICMP message type 3 Destination Unreachable
    ICMP message type 4 Source Quench
    ICMP message type 5 Redirect
    ICMP message type 6 Alternate Host Address
    ICMP message type 11 Time Exceeded
    ICMP message type 12 Parameter Problem
    ICMP message type 31 Datagram Conversion Error
    ICMP message type 32 Mobile Host Redirect

ICMP error messages are always transmitted with the default TOS (0000).

▲   ICMP request messages

    ICMP message type 8 Echo
    ICMP message type 10 Router Solicitation
    ICMP message type 13 Time-stamp
    ICMP message type 15 Information Request
    ICMP message type 17 Information Request
    ICMP message type 30 Traceroute
    ICMP message type 33 IP version 6 Where-Are-You
    ICMP message type 35 Mobile Registration Request
    ICMPv6 message type 128 Echo Request

ICMP request messages are transmitted with any value in the TOS field.

▲   ICMP reply messages

    ICMP message type 0 Echo Reply
    ICMP message type 9 Router Advertisement

ICMP message type 14 Time-stamp Reply
ICMP message type 16 Information Reply
ICMP message type 18 Information Reply
ICMP message type 34 IP version 6 I-Am-Here
ICMP message type 36 Mobile Registration Reply
ICMPv6 message type 129 Echo Reply

ICMP reply messages are transmitted with the same value in the TOS field as the TOS value used in the corresponding ICMP request message.

▲ ICMP unassigned and reserved messages

ICMP message type 1 Unassigned
ICMP message type 2 Unassigned
ICMP message type 7 Unassigned
ICMP message type 19 Reserved (for security)
ICMP message type 20-29 Reserved (for experiments)
ICMP message type 37-255 Reserved except 128 and 129

ICMP Messages

Type 0 (Echo or Echo Reply)

When a receiving device receives a type 0 ICMP message, it must immediately return the information included in the data bit field of the datagram to the transmitting device. The device generating the type 0 ICMP message may use the header identifier to keep track of echo requests and responses. The echoing device returns the same identifier and data values in the echo reply.

Table 11.1 shows gateways or hosts generate type 0, code 0 messages.

Type 1

Type 1 messages are currently unassigned.

Type 2

Type 2 messages are currently unassigned for versions of ICMP versions less than version 6. ICMPv6 defines a type 2 "packet too big" error message that is returned to the source if the packet received is too large for the interface to process.

Type 3 (Destination Unreachable)

When a gateway is unable to reconcile the route from the gateway to the destination specified in the IP header, the gateway returns this message type to the originating host.

Gateways use internal routing tables that do not necessarily have up-to-date routing information about the internetwork. So, a cutting-edge kind of operation might want to go somewhere on the Internet but may be blocked from reaching the destination because routers do not have the path to the destination in their routing tables. A more likely scenario is the temporary loss of a communications link between a destination and a gateway or the loss of a link from gateway to gateway. A good example of the latter is the accidental cutting of fiber cables by construction crews. ICMP type 3 messages are generated when a gateway must fragment a datagram to accommodate the size requirements, yet the "don't fragment" flag is set.

At times, a datagram can be delivered to the intended destination, yet the receiving host may still generate a type 3 ICMP message. An example is the receipt of a datagram by a host that cannot deliver the datagram because the IP protocol is incorrect or the connection is not established.

Table 11.1 shows that gateways may generate type 3, code 0, 1, 4, and 5 messages, and hosts may generate type 3, code 2 and 3 messages.

The two ICMPv6 type 3 error messages are basically the same as those defined for other flavors of ICMP. The code 0 message is returned to the source if a router receives a datagram with the hop limit equal to zero or if it decrements the hop limit to zero. The code 1 message is returned to the source if the fragment reassembly time limit is exceeded by the interface assembling the fragment.

Type 4 (Source Quench)

Devices receiving datagrams have a finite amount of buffer space to receive datagrams and store them until their turn for processing. Buffer size is dependent upon system resources and the function performed by the device. The more traffic expected, the larger the buffer. Client hosts typically have the smallest buffers, server hosts have larger buffers, and gateways have the largest buffers. TCP/IP has a mechanism for sharing information about the size of the receive buffer with the expectation that the transmission rate of the transmitting device will not exceed the ability of the receiving device to buffer, then process the datagrams. However, even the best of plans go awry. So, TCP/IP includes type 4 ICMP messages to tell transmitting devices to slow down. If the transmitting device does exceed the rate at which the receiving device can buffer the datagrams, the datagrams are discarded and the receiving device generates an ICMP type 4 "source quench" message.

A device can send a source quench message for every message discarded. When the transmitting device receives a source quench message, the device should throttle back its transmission rate until it no longer receives source quench messages from the device.

A better solution is for a receiving device to send the source quench message when it approaches its buffer size limit rather than waiting until the limit is exceeded. Rather than discarding datagrams and triggering additional traffic on the network, this approach to traffic management results in delivered datagrams and less network traffic overall.

Table 11.1 shows that both gateways and hosts may generate type 3, code 0 messages.

ICMPv6 changes the definition of code 0 messages and adds code 1 and 2 messages to the type 4 category. Also, ICMPv6 adds a 32-bit pointer field immediately after the ICMP checksum field. An IPv6 type 4 message is sent when an interface encounters a problem with an IPv6 header field if the IPv6 cannot continue processing the datagram. The code user in conjunction with the ICMPv6 pointer field identifies the particular IPv6 header field that is causing the error.

Type 5 (Redirect)

When a gateway receives a datagram, it checks its routing tables for the address of the next gateway on the way to the datagram's destination. If the gateway discovers that another gateway is closer to the intended destination and is directly connected to the network where the sending device is located, the gateway will generate a "redirect" message to the sending device advising the sending device of the shorter, or more direct, path. The gateway generating the type 5 message does not discard the datagram. When the IP source route option is included in the datagram and the gateway address is listed in the destination address field, a redirect message is not returned to the sending device.

Table 11.1 shows that gateways generate type 5, code 0 and 2 messages, and hosts generate type 5, code 1 and 3 messages.

Type 6 (Alternate Host Address)

A type 6 message informs any listening interfaces that the source address is an alternate address for the source address.

Type 7 (Unassigned)

Type 7 messages are unassigned.

Type 8 (Echo or Echo Reply)

When a receiving device receives a type 0 ICMP message, it must immediately return the information included in the data bit field of the datagram to the transmitting device. The device generating the type 0 ICMP message uses the header sequence number to keep track of echo requests and responses. The echoing device returns the same sequence number and data values in the echo reply.

Table 11.1 shows gateways and hosts generate type 8, code 0 messages.

Type 9 (Router Advertisement)

Router advertisement is a response to a received router solicitation message. Typically, router advertisement is unicast to the interface issuing the router solicitation. It is used to announce the interface's (node, router, etc.) presence on the network. One use for this type of message occurs when a network powers up after a power loss.

Type 10 (Router Solicitation)

Router solicitation is a request for all routers receiving the solicitation request to respond with a router advertisement. Typically, router solicitation is multicast and is used to discover the interfaces (nodes, routers, etc.) connected to the network. One use for this of type message occurs when a network powers up after a power loss.

Type 11 (Time Exceeded)

When a gateway receives a packet, one of its first chores is to check the IP datagram time-to-live value. If the time-to-live is zero, the gateway must discard the packet. If the gateway discards the packet, it will notify the device that sent the datagram to it using the "time exceeded" message.

When a host receives datagram fragments, it must reassemble them within a certain time frame. If it does not receive all the fragmented parts within the specified time period and cannot complete the reassembly of the fragmented parts, it will discard the fragmented parts and send a "time exceeded" message. An exception occurs when fragment zero is not received. In this case, an ICMP message is not sent.

Table 11.1 shows that gateways generate type 11, code 0 messages, and hosts may generate type 11, code 1 messages.

Type 12 (Parameter Problem)

When a gateway or host processes a datagram and discovers problems with the information in the datagram, such as when the checksum comparison fails or when the options field has incorrect or incompatible entries, the gateway or host will discard the datagram and notify the device sending the datagram by using the "parameter problem" message. If the code equals zero, the pointer value points to, or identifies, the offending octet in the original datagram header.

As an example, if the ICMP message is type 12, code 0, and the pointer equals 11 (or 12), the datagram generating the ICMP message has an incorrect checksum value. Another example: If the ICMP message is type 12, code 0, and the pointer equals 2, the datagram generating the ICMP message has an incorrect Type of Service. The pointer can also identify the problems with TOS options.

If the ICMP message is type 12, code 1, the datagram generating the ICMP message has an option missing from the header. If the ICMP message is type 12, code 2, the datagram generating the ICMP message has an incorrect length parameter.

Table 11.1 shows that both gateways and hosts may generate type 12, code 0, 1, and 2 messages.

Type 13 and 14 (Time-stamp Request and Time-stamp Reply)

A device sends a type 13 ICMP message to a destination and includes in the data bit field a time-stamp value. The time-stamp value is in milliseconds past midnight Universal Time (UT) and is 32 bits long. The destination returns the ICMP type 13 message as an ICMP type 14 message to the original source device with the original data and with two additional 32-bit time-stamps in the data field that represents the time the ICMP message was received and the time it was returned to the source device.

One possible use for type 13 and 14 ICMP messages is to determine the forward and return path transit time for a datagram from source to destination. These messages can also be used to determine the amount of time the destination device required to process a datagram, information useful for traffic management purposes. However, the traffic load of many networks is so bursty and the traffic load varies so greatly daily and hourly that setting datagram time-to-live values in concrete based upon type 13 and 14 ICMP data might result in less effective network throughput.

Code 0 specifies a sequence number may be used to aid in matching time-stamp queries and replies.

Table 11.1 shows both gateways and hosts generate type 13 and 14, code 0 messages.

Type 15 and 16 (Information Request and Information Reply)

A source device sends a type 15 ICMP message with the source and destination address bits fields consisting of all zeroes. Remember all zeroes in source and destination address fields means "all devices this network." All IP modules that reply to the sender of this broadcast message include their correct source and destination address in a type 16 ICMP "information reply" message. The use of this message type provides a way for a device to discover its own network address.

Code 0 specifies a sequence number may be used to aid in matching information request queries and replies.

Table 11.1 shows both gateways and hosts generate type 15 and 16 ICMP messages.

Type 15 and 16 messages are now obsolete but will be found still in use in older equipment. They are replaced by types 17 and 18.

Type 17 and 18 (Information Request and Information Reply)

These ICMP messages are similar to types 15 and 16.

Table 11.1 shows both gateways and hosts generate type 17 and 18 ICMP messages.

Type 19-29 (Reserved)

ICMP message types 19-29 are reserved for special purposes.

Type 30 (Traceroute)

Type 30 ICMP messages are an older version of type 33 and 34 messages.

Table 11.1 shows both gateways and hosts generate type 30 ICMP messages.

Type 31 (Datagram Conversion Error)

Type 31 ICMP messages are sent in response to errors the receiving device may encounter when processing the datagram. Such errors include wrong protocol numbers, checksum errors, length errors, etc.

Table 11.1 shows both gateways and hosts generate type 31 ICMP messages.

Type 32 (Mobile Host Redirect)

Type 32 messages are similar to type 5 messages except the host generating the ICMP message is a mobile computing device. Any guesses where one will find mobile computing devices? How about the U.S. Army and very mobile battlefields?

Table 11.1 shows both gateways and hosts generate type 32 ICMP messages.

Type 33 and 34 (Where are you and I am here)

A source device sends a type 33 ICMP message with the source and destination address bits fields appropriately filled out. The object is to find the path to the destination address. All IP modules that reply to the sender of this ICMP message include the route the datagram followed to get to the destination. The use of this message type provides a way for a device to discover the path to any other internetwork device.

Code 0 specifies that a sequence number may be used to aid in matching queries and replies.

Table 11.1 shows gateways and hosts generate type 33 and 34 ICMP messages.

Type 35 and 36 (Mobile Registration Request and Mobile Registration Reply)

ICMP type 35 and 36 messages allow mobile computing devices to be moved from network to network or subnet to subnet while keeping their original internet addresses. Just like type 32 messages, these types of messages are of particular interest to networking armies on the move.

Table 11.1 shows gateways and hosts generate type 35 and 36 ICMP messages.

Type 128 (Echo Request)

An interface may use the echo request to verify the reliability of the connection with another interface. The validity of a connection is determined upon analyzing the echo reply message received from the echoing interface. An identifier field is used to match echo replies to this echo request.

After the checksum field, type 128 messages add a 16-bit identifier field followed by a 16-bit sequence number field and a data field.

Table 11.1 shows gateways and hosts generate type 128, code 0 messages.

Type 129 (Echo Reply)

When a receiving device receives a type 0 ICMPv6 echo request message, it must immediately return the information included in the data bit field of the datagram to the transmitting device as an echo reply message. The echoing device returns the same sequence number and data values in the echo reply. An identifier field is used to match echo replies to a specific echo request.

After the checksum field, type 129 messages add a 16-bit identifier field followed by a 16-bit sequence number field and a data field.

Table 11.1 shows gateways and hosts generate type 129, code 0 messages.

Summary

ICMP provides a means for user processes to be informed of the status of IP connections. Connection status reporting is crucial to the maintenance of a reliable data communications link between the IPs. ICMP performs its task by sending error and control codes to the IP. ICMP must be implemented on every platform/computing device that also contains IP.

Chapter 12

SNMP

Questions answered in this chapter:

What is managed information?

What is a Managment Information Base?

What is SNMP?

What information is managed by SNMP?

What are the common SNMP commands?

Introduction

A network requires some form of network management capability so network resources can be effectively and economically used. Network management includes, but is not necessarily limited to, the ability to monitor the network for compliance to desired characteristics, such as throughput, error rates, and congestion. Based upon the network status, network managers can make intelligent choices concerning where resources can be most effectively utilized. The Internet Architecture Board of the IETF recommends that all TCP/IP implementations include provision for network management.

To accomplish TCP/IP network management, the host must implement several IETF network management protocols. RFC 1213 defines the protocol for "Management Information Base for Network Management of TCP/IP-based Internets—MIB II" and describes the managed objects contained in the management information base (MIB). RFC 1155 is the protocol for "Structure and Identification of Management Information for TCP/IP-based Internets (SMI)" and describes how managed objects contained in the MIB are defined. RFC 1157 is the protocol for Simple Network Management Protocol and defines the protocol used to manage the MIB objects.

Here is the short story on how MIB-II became the current MIB protocol. In August 1988, the network management information base was defined by RFC

1066. RFC 1066 is now called MIB-I since it was the first defined MIB. Prior to RFC 1066, network management, if it existed at all, was a vendor proprietary tool. In May 1990 RFC 1156 clarified and modified some things to the MIB but it was still called MIB-I. Then along came RFC 1158, which made major changes to the MIB. The changes were sufficient to justify renaming the original MIB to MIB-II. Further refinements and additions to the MIB-II were made in March 1991 by RFC 1213. The next generation MIB is expected to be called MIB-III.

The SNMP, SMI, and MIB protocols are Standard protocols with Recommended status. Networks do not have to implement these protocols, but it is recommended that they do. And if they do implement the protocols, the implementation must conform to the protocol requirements.

SNMP (manages objects) RFC 1157
SMI (defines managed objects) RFC 1155
MIB (contains managed objects) RFC 1213

Figure 12.1 Network management architecture

Figure 12.1 shows the relationship between the MIB, SMI, and SNMPv1 protocols. This particular grouping of protocols is known as SNMPv1, or SNMP version one. Each of these three protocols is concerned with management of internetworking information. SMI is probably the information management cornerstone, as it defines the objects that will be managed. The MIB contains the managed objects and SNMPv1 is responsible for actually performing the management tasks. SNMPv1 is really the user portal for extracting management information from the MIB. To understand what it is we are trying to manage (the MIB objects), we will look at the SMI managed object definitions later.

In January 1996, several RFCs were published that defined an SNMPv2, or SNMP version two. The applicable RFCs are listed in Table 12.1:

Structure of Management Information for Version 2 of the Simple Network Management Protocol (SNMPv2)	RFC 1902
Textual Conventions for Version 2 of the Simple Network Management Protocol (SNMPv2)	RFC 1903
Conformance Statements for Version 2 of the Simple Network Management Protocol (SNMPv2)	RFC 1904

Protocol Operations for Version 2 of the Simple Network Management Protocol (SNMPv2)	RFC 1905
Transport Mappings for Version 2 of the Simple Network Management Protocol (SNMPv2)	RFC 1906
Management Information Base for Version 2 of the Simple Network Management Protocol (SNMPv2)	RFC 1907

Table 12.1 SNMPv2 RFCs

What is Managed Information?

Managed information is nothing more, or less, than the storage and retrieval of data (aka information) for human analysis and action when the (or some) human deems such storage, retrieval, analysis, and action appropriate. To manage information in the network environment, network management stations utilizing network management application software are placed at points in the network deemed best by some discerning individual.

A network is composed of network elements such as clients and servers operating on hosts. Also unseen by the network user are a multitude of other network elements such as bridges, routers, gateways, and switches. Each of these network elements will have a software program running that will store, retrieve, and send data to and from network management applications. The network element software responsible for the data storage/retrieval, etc., is called a management agent.

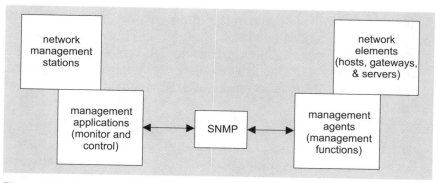

Figure 12.2 Network management interfaces

Management agents and management applications are called network interfaces, or just interfaces, in the RFCs. The common bond linking the interfaces is SNMP. Figure 12.2 illustrates the relationship among the various SNMP entities. SNMPv1 is the (ideal) messenger boy continually running back and forth delivering network messages without ever requesting a break or a pay raise. But where does the messenger boy fetch and store his messages? A database called a Management Information Base (MIB).

The MIB is used to accomplish the data storage and retrieval and provides a limited ability, by triggering events and toggling logic switches, to act upon the results of the data analysis. So, the MIB has two basic functions. One is to provide a network troubleshooting capability by measuring the health of the network and the other is to provide a limited network management capability.

To accomplish the basic MIB goals, managed objects are kept in the MIB. Each of the data objects stored in the MIB must comply with the data notation defined by Abstract Syntax Notation One. ASN.1 is specified in the Open Systems Interconnection document "Specification of Abstract Syntax Notation One (ASN.1)," International Organization for Standardization, International Standard 8824, December 1987. ASN.1 requires that each object type have a name and an encoding. The object name is called the object identifier since it, logically, identifies the object by name. The object type defines the data structure of the object type. Example object types include integer and string.

Object names are used to identify managed objects. An object name is a textual representation of the object. Object identifiers may be used in lieu of names for objects.

Object identifers are used as a convenient shorthand notation to identify any object associated with networking. Object identifiers identify abstract data structures and not-so-abstract internetworking documents. An object identifier is an ordered sequence of integers that represents a hierarchial view of the object identifer's place in the internetworking world. Each object identifier includes a paired label that contains an abbreviated object description. Figure 12.3 shows the internetworking hierarchy and the object identifier associated with each level. The object identifier is the integer enclosed in parentheses and the adjacent associated label. Notice the root node is unlabeled.

The management of internetworking is organized as a hierarchical, or tree, structure with the international governing bodies at the apex of the hierarchy. Each governing body and the ultimate users of the internetworks are nodes on the tree. In the overall scheme of things, it was decided that each node on the internetworking management tree should assign the object identifiers to all the nodes immediately under the assigning node's purview. So, ISO assigns object identifiers to national and international organizations, while the U.S. Department of Defense assigns object identifiers to the Internet. In Figure 12.3, the Internet Management node assigns object identifiers to all the IETF RFCs.

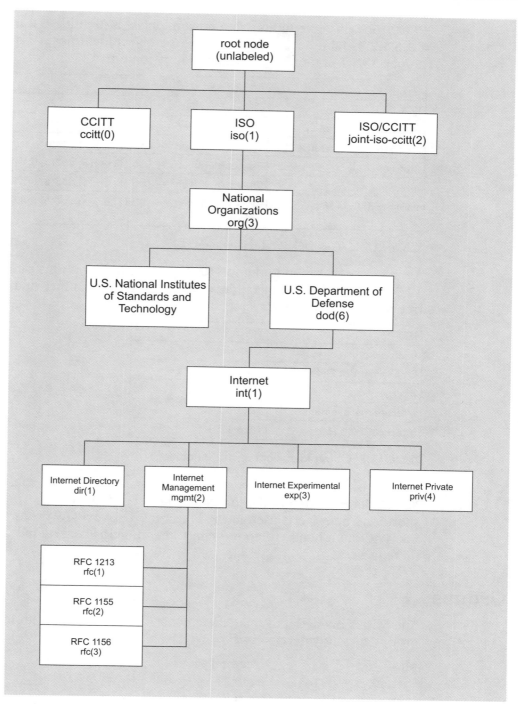

Figure 12.3 Internetworking management tree

RFC 1156 will serve to illustrate how an object is identified. It is identified as 1.3.6.1.2.3. Table 12.2 illustrates how the object identifier is derived and the proper ASN.1 notation for each subsidiary identifier.

Group	Identifier
ISO	Object Identifier ::= {iso (1)}
National Organization	Object Identifier ::= {iso (1) org(3)}
Department of Defense	Object Identifier ::= {iso (1) org(3) dod(6)}
Internet	Object Identifier ::= {iso (1) org(3) dod(6) int(1)}
Internet management	Object Identifier ::= {iso (1) org(3) dod(6) int(1) mgmt(2)}
Internet RFC 1156	Object Identifier ::= {iso (1) org(3) dod(6) int(1) mgmt(2) rfc(3)}

Table 12.2 Object identification notation

A numerical shorthand notation for object identifiers is illustrated in Table 12.3. Notice how the object hierarchy gives the appearance of an inverted tree as the objects are traversed from top to bottom.

ISO	1.
National organization	1.3
Department of Defense	1.3.6
Internet	1.3.6.1
Internet management	1.3.6.1.2
Internet RFC 1156	1.3.6.1.2.3

Table 12.3 Object identifier numerical notation

The use of the numerical shorthand notation shown above extends down the object identifier tree to the lowest level of object identifiers. The numerical shorthand notation is used in the literature to save a few drops of printer's ink. Without a handy reference chart, the numerical shorthand notation is quite useless.

Groups

The MIB is divided into related elements, or objects, called groups. The groups currently defined are:

MIB	{mgmt 1}
System	{mib 1}
Interfaces	{mib 2}
Address Translation	{mib 3}
IP	{mib 4}

ICMP	{mib 5}
TCP	{mib 6}
UDP	{mib 7}
EGP	{mib 8}
CMOPT	{mib 9}
Transmission	{mib 10}
SNMP	{mib 11}

If any particular node implements a group, then it must implement all the objects within the group. No picking and choosing. In other words, a user might decide that UDP is consuming resources better utilized elsewhere and remove UDP from the system. That is okay. However, if UDP is implemented, then all objects in the UDP group must be implemented.

SMI Objects

We are primarily concerned with the SMI object identifiers found in the Internet. The Internet includes four categories of object identifiers:

directory	Object Identifier ::= {int 1}
management	Object Identifier ::= {mgmt 2}
experimental	Object Identifier ::= {exp 3}
private	Object Identifier ::= {priv 4}

The directory (int (1)) node is reserved for future use. It is envisioned that the Internet will somehow incorporate OSI protocols one day and this node will be used for ISO identifiers.

The management (mgmt (2)) node identifies objects that are defined in IAB-approved documents. The Internet Assigned Numbers Authority (IANA) is delegated the responsibility for administering the assignment of object identifiers within the internet management node. When objects are defined in RFCs, the IANA assigns them an object identifier.

The experimental (exp (3)) node is used to identify objects used in Internet experiments. The IANA is delegated the responsibility for administering the assignment of object identifiers within the internet experimental node.

The private (priv (4)) node is used to identify objects defined by private organizations. The IANA is delegated the responsibility for administering the assignment of object identifiers within the internet private node. This node has at least one node which is the private enterprises node:

enterprises   Object Identifier ::= {private 1}

The enterprises (private (1)) node is used to register networking subsystem products. Under the enterprises node, individual enterprises may be assigned nodes allowing networking designers and builders the opportunity for defining new MIB objects (that only their networking products may understand).

SMI Object Types

The syntax used in defining SMI object structure and types is specified in ASN.1 type Object definition. The format to be used for managed objects is defined so consistency across multiple vendor environments is maintained. A full object type definition consists of five fields:

Object
Syntax
Definition
Access
Status

Every object has a type assignment. Type assignments are necessary to ensure the object resolves into something the machine can recognize when it is operating on the object. Type assignments are Constructor, Counter, Gauge, DisplayString, Implicit, Integer, IpAddress, NetworkAddress, PhysAddress, Opaque, Primitive, and TimeTicks. Constructor type contains a subtype called Sequence which contains several subtypes itself. The following is a short description of each type:

Constructor types

Sequence subtype:

Sequence is allowed only if it is used to generate either lists or tables.

The sequence for lists is:
Sequence {type(1), ..., type(n)}
Each <type> must be one of the allowed ASN.1 primitive types such as integer.

The sequence for tables is:
Sequence OF <entry>
where <entry> must be an allowed ASN.1 constructor type.

Bits subtype:

Bits subtype represents a directory of named bits. The directory is assigned non-negative, contiguous values, starting at zero. Only the named bits are valid for use in a value. A label for a Bits contruct value consists of one or more letters or digits up to a maximum of 64 characters. Hyphens are not allowed and the initial character must be a lowercase letter.

Counter32 types

Counter32 types represent non-negative integers which increase by one until they reach a maximum value, then they revert to zero and start increasing again. The maximum value of counter types is $(2^32)-1$. Counter values must be initialized by the management agent to some initial value, otherwise the initial value is unknown. Counter is the SNMPv1 counter type name and Counter32 is the SNMPv2 counter type name.

Counter64 types

Counter64 types represent non-negative integers which increase by one until they reach a maximum value, then they revert to zero and start increasing again. The maximum value of counter types is $(2^64)-1$. Counter values must be initialized by the management agent to some initial value, otherwise the initial value is unknown. Counter64 is the SNMPv2 counter type name.

Unsigned32

Unsigned32 types represent integer values between 0 and 2^32-1 inclusive.

Gauge types

Gauge types represent non-negative integers which may increase or decrease, but will latch at a maximum value. The maximum value is $(2^32)-1$. Gauge32 is the SNMPv32 gauge type name.

DisplayString type

DisplayString types represent ASCII text information in character strings with 8-bit bytes. The data representation of character strings with 8-bit bytes is commonly referred to as an octet string in the RFCs. The size of the octet string is zero to 255 characters.

Implicit types

Implicit types are application-defined types that must resolve into an implicitly defined ASN.1 primitive type, list, table, or other application-defined types.

Integer types

Integer types are the positive counting numbers 0 to 255.

IpAddress types

IpAddress types represent 32-bit Internet addresses. IpAddress is represented by the primitive octet string, length 4 bytes, and is in network byte-order.

NetworkAddress type

NetworkAddress types represent addresses from one of several protocol families. Currently, only the Internet family is used.

PhysAddress

PhysAddress types represent media addresses as (usually) binary octet strings.

Opaque types

Opaque types allow any ASN.1 to be passed through the network. The value of interest is encoded into a string of octets using the ASN.1 basic rules. Then the result is encoded as an octet string. Any conforming implementation will accept and recognize Opaque type data. Conforming implementations do not need to decode and interpret the Opaque type data.

Primitive types

These are Integer, Octet, String, Object Identifier, and Null. No other primitive types are allowed.

TimeTick types

TimeTick types represent non-negative integers which count the time in hundredths of a second since some epoch. The syntax of the object type must identify the reference epoch used. Typical epochs used are midnight January 1, 1900, and midnight January 1, 1970.

Each of the object type fields is further defined by including the following information as part of the object definition:

xxxxx

This is a text name, xxxxx, called the Object DESCRIPTOR and the object's corresponding Object Identifier. Names are unique and descriptive of the object. A subidentifier of 0 (zero) is not allowed as it is reserved for future use.

Bits construct

The Bits construct represents a directory of named bits. The directory is assigned non-negative, contiguous values, starting at zero. Only the named bits are valid for use in a value. A label for a Bits contruct value consists of one or more letters or digits up to a maximum of 64 characters. Hyphens are not allowed and the initial character must be a lowercase letter.

Definition

This is an ASCII text of the object's purpose or function.

Access

Access identifies what operations the user process may perform on the object. Access categories are:

  read only
  read/write
  write only
  not accessible

Status

Status identifies the current situation regarding the necessity of implementing the object. The statuses are:

mandatory	these objects must be implemented if the group is implemented
deprecated	all deprecated objects are slated for obsolescence
optional	user decides whether or not to implement optional objects
obsolete	do not use

Objects have an associated object type defined by the object, a text definition, an associated access, and an associated status. Each of these object elements are included in the object identifier. No other object elements are necessary, or allowed, for the object to be included in the MIB.

UTC Format

Time is important in network management. The standard method used to measure time is to measure the number of ticks past some arbitrary starting point (see TimeTick types). Time is recorded in Universal Time Coordinate (UTC) format: YYMMDDHHMMZ.

Abbreviation	Meaning	Range of Values
YY	last two digits of year	00..99
MM	month	01..12
DD	day of month	01..31
HH	hours	00..23
MM	minutes	00..59
Z	Greenwich Mean Time (GMT)	n/a

Table 12.4 UTC format

When the "Z" is appended to the UTC, the time is given in 24-hour time, also known as military time. In this method of recording time, the beginning of each day is midnight and is 0000. The hour is incremented as time progresses from midnight through the day and evening until the next midnight hour when the clock resets to 0000. That is, 0800 is 8:00 a.m. and 2000 is 8:00 p.m. As an example, "9903010830Z" represents 8:30 a.m. GMT on March 1, 1999.

MIB

The MIB stores all the information that is known about the condition or status of the network. Here is $10,000 worth of consulting advice. When the honchos want to know something important about the network and demand a report of this or that, go ask engineering (or open your copy of this book to this chapter and check yourself) if the desired information is in the MIB. If the answer is no, then the honchos are not going to get what they want without some amount of effort, time, and financial expenditures.

The information maintained in the MIB is, for the most part, generated/created at the lowest level of the network, the physical devices performing the tasks. In order for a human, sometimes called a network manager (other times called something less glorifying), to use the MIB information, it must be displayed in a human readable format. Software programmers write code called "middleware" to extract the information from the MIB and make it available for human consumption in, usually, nice graphical user interfaces (GUIs). Also, these middleware programs can write to the MIB objects that have a write status.

Proprietary vendor implementations are free to add to or subtract from the network management requirements specified in RFC 1155, RFC 1157, and RFC 1213. Vendors are free to do as they please. No one has yet been executed, or even imprisoned (as far as I know), for deviating from the requirements as specified in the RFCs. However, market forces tend to cause vendors to move toward equipment that does comply with the RFC requirements, as wise customers tend to move away from expensive single-vendor solutions.

MIB Groups

Each MIB group and the objects it contains is described in the following sections and tables. Remember that the purpose of the MIB is twofold. The MIB contains objects used to collect information for the purpose of understanding the health of the network and the associated connections. A less prevalent MIB role is to allow some control, by switching a variable "on" or "off," of a few network variables. Understanding the structure and the purpose of the MIB objects that follow will be a lot easier if the two reasons for the MIB's existence is kept in focus.

SNMPv1 System Group

The System Group provides administrative, contact, location, and service information concerning the managed node. The managed node is also called a "node" in the RFCs and literature. Table 12.5 contains all System Group objects and a short definition of their purpose. Implementation of the System Group is mandatory for all systems.

Object	Syntax	Definition	Access
sysDescr {system 1}	Display STR	node id	ro
sysObjectID {system 2}	OID	vendor's id	ro
sysUpTime {system 3}	TimeTicks	time since last reinitialization	ro
sysContact {system 4}	DisplayStr	system admin contact #	ro
sysName {system 5}	DisplayStr	node's domain name	ro
sysLocation {system 6}	DisplayStr	physical node location	ro
sysServices {system 7}	Integer	specific primary services of node	ro

The following abbreviations are used: OID = Object Identifier, ro = read only

Table 12.5 System Group objects

The sysDescr is a string of printable ASCII characters that contain a text description of the system. The character string length is 0 to 255 characters. sysDescr identifies the system's hardware type, software operating system, and the networking software used.

sysObjectID is the manufacturer's ASCII text identification of the network management subsystem the device utilizes. The sysObjectID is assigned in the SMI enterprise's subtree (1.3.6.1.4.1).

sysUpTime is the time since the network management portion of the system was last reinitialized. sysUpTime is measured in hundredths of a second.

sysContact is the contact person assigned responsibility for this managed node. Included in the printable ASCII text is information on how to contact that individual.

sysName is the assigned name for this managed node. It is the node's fully qualified domain name.

sysLocation is the physical location of this node and can be as detailed as desired. sysLocation might be a street address in a city and may also include additional locating details. An example might be, "basement, 2621 E. Park Blvd., Nowhere, Texas."

sysServices is a numerical value that describes the set of services this node offers. The numerical value is a sum calculated as follows:

initial value of sum = 0
if OSI protocol layer 1 services are performed then
exp1 := 1 else exp1 := 0
if OSI protocol layer 2 services are performed then
exp2: = 2 else exp2 := 0
if OSI protocol layer 3 services are performed then
exp3: = 3 else exp3 := 0
if OSI protocol layer 4 services are performed then
exp4: = 4 else exp4 := 0
if OSI protocol layer 5 services are performed then
exp5: = 5 else exp5 := 0
if OSI protocol layer 6 services are performed then
exp6: = 6 else exp6 := 0
if OSI protocol layer 7 services are performed then
exp7: = 7 else exp7 := 0

calculate sum now:

$$\text{sum} := 2^{(exp1-1)} + 2^{(exp2-1)} \ldots 2^{(exp7-1)}$$

Note: Do not include any OSI layer exponents (exp1, exp2, etc.) if the exponent equals zero.

An example could be a node offering end-to-end application services such as a file service. The sum is calculated as:

$$\text{sum} := 2^{(4-1)} + 2^{(7-1)}$$
$$\text{sum} := 8 + 64$$
$$\text{sum} := 72$$

In terms of OSI protocol models the following functions are defined:

Exponent/layer	Functionality	Example
1	physical	repeaters
2	data link	bridges
3	internet	IP gateways
4	end-to-end	IP hosts
7	applications	file/mail services

Table 12.6 OSI layer functions

OSI protocol layers 5 and 6 may be counted, but it is not customary to do so. Layers 5 and 6 may or may not be used, depending upon the system configuration and whether or not Layer 7 is used.

The SNMPv1 Interfaces Group

The Interfaces table, Table 12.8, contains information on the node's network interfaces. The RFC says each interface is considered to be attached to a subnetwork that is not the same as the subnetwork address partitioning scheme used in the Internet protocol. The Interfaces Group table, Table 12.7, contains all the Interfaces Group objects and a short definition of their purpose. Implementation of the Interfaces Group is mandatory for all systems.

Object	Syntax	Definition	Access
ifNumber {interfaces 1}	I	# of send/receive nodes on this network	ro
ifTable {interfaces 2}	Seq	list of IP nodes	na
ifEntry {ifTable 1}	ifEntry	subnetwork node entry objects	na
ifIndex {ifEntry 1}	I	unique node value	ro
ifDescr {ifEntry 2}	OS	detailed node information	ro
ifType {ifEntry 3}	sb	physical link protocol type	ro
ifMtu {ifEntry 4}	I	maximum IP datagram size	ro
ifSpeed {ifEntry 5}	G	node's current bandwidth	ro
ifPhysAddress {ifEntry 6}	OS	node's physical link address	ro
ifAdminStatus {ifEntry 7}	sb	node state	rw
ifOperStatus {ifEntry 8}	I	current operational state	ro
ifLastChange {ifEntry 9}	TT	time of current operational state	ro
ifInOctets {ifEntry 10}	C	# of data octets received	ro
ifInUcastPkts {ifEntry 11}	C	# of subnet unicast pkts delivered	ro
ifInNUcastPkts {ifEntry 12}	C	# of subnet non-unicast pkts delivered	ro
ifInDiscards {ifEntry 13}	C	# of rcvd error-free pkts disc	ro
ifInErrors {ifEntry 14}	C	# of rcvd pkts disc due to errors	ro
ifInUnknownProtos {ifEntry 15}	C	# of rcvd pkts disc due to unknown protocol	ro
ifOutOctets {ifEntry 16}	C	# of octets transmitted	ro
ifOutUcastPkts {ifEntry 17}	C	# of pkts trans subnet unicast address	ro
ifOutNUcastPkts {ifEntry 18}	C	# of pkts trans subnet non-unicast address	ro
ifOutDiscards {ifEntry 19}	C	# of trans error-free pkts disc	ro
ifOutErrors {ifEntry 20}	C	# of trans pkts disc due to errors	ro
ifOutQLen {ifEntry 21}	G	output packet queue length	ro
ifSpecific {ifEntry 21}	OI	identifies implementation specific MIB	ro

C = Counter, disc = discarded, G = Gauge, I = Integer, man = mandatory, na = not accessible, OI = Object Identifier, OS = octet string, pkts = packets, rcvd = received, ro = read only, rw = read/write, sb = see below, Seq = Sequence, trans = transmitted, TT = TimeTicks

Table 12.7 Interfaces Group objects

ifNumber is the number of entries in the ifTable. All connected interfaces are counted, including connected network devices that do not use IP, such as media access control (MAC) layer bridges. An interface is defined as a network.

ifTable is a list of connected network interfaces. The ifTable syntax is Sequence of IfEntry.

ifEntry is the bucket, or subtable, for collecting a particular connected interface's properties.

ifIndex identifies a specific interface and its associated properties listed in the table. The value of ifIndex must be equal to or less than ifNumber.

ifDescr is an ASCII character string describing the interface particulars including the name of the interface manufacturer, product name, and product version.

ifType is a numerical value that specifies the type of interface's physical layer. Table 12.8 lists the interface types and their associated ifType value.

Type of Interface	Value	Notes
other	1	if other = 1 then the type is none of the following types
regular1822	2	
hdh1822	3	
ddn-x25	4	
rfc877-x25	5	
ethernet-csmacd	6	
iso88023-csmacd	7	
iso88024-tokenBus	8	
iso88025-tokenRing	9	
iso88026-man	10	
starLan	11	
proteon-10Mbit	12	
proteon-80Mbit	13	
hyperchannel	14	
fddi	15	
lapb	16	
sdlc	17	
ds1	18	T-1
e1	19	E1 is the European equivalent of T-1
basicISDN	20	
primaryISDN	21	

Type of Interface	Value	Notes
propPointToPointSerial	22	
ppp	23	
softwareLoopback	24	
eon	25	eon is CLNP over IP
ethernet-3Mbit	26	
nsip	27	nsip is XNS over IP
slip	28	slip is generic SLIP
ultra	29	ultra is ULTRA technologies
ds3	30	ds3 is T-3
sip	31	sip is SMDS
frame-relay	32	

Table 12.8 Interface types and ifType values

ifMtu specifies the largest datagram, in octets, that can be sent or received by the interface. If the ifMtu value is 455, then up to 455 octets may be sent or received on the interface.

ifSpeed is a measure of the interface's current speed in bits per second. This value is an estimation except for those interfaces that do not vary (constant bit rate) in speed.

ifPhysAddress specifies the interface's address at the protocol layer immediately beneath the network layer in the protocol stack. If the interface does not have such an address, the ifPhysAddress should contain an octet string of zero length.

ifAdminStatus places the interface into a desired operating state. The states and their associated numerical values are given in Table 12.9. ifAdminStatus is read/write which allows the network manager to place the interface into the operating state desired by writing to the object the numerical value representing the state desired.

Operating State	ifAdminStatus/ifOperStatus Value	Meaning
up	1	ready to pass packets
down	2	not ready to pass packets
testing	3	in some test mode

Table 12.9 ifAdmin Status and ifOperStatus values

ifOperStatus specifies the current operational state of the interface. ifOperStatus numerical values and their meaning are the same as ifAdminStatus and are given in Table 12.9. Notice the only difference between this object and ifAdminStatus is this object is read only while ifAdminStatus is read/write. This object reads the actual operational state of the interface while ifAdminStatus is used to place the object into a desired state.

ifLastChange is the numerical value of sysUpTime at the time the interface entered the current operational state.

ifInOctets is the total number of octets received by the interface. The number of octets received includes framing characters.

ifInUcastPkts specifies the number of subnetwork unicast packets that were delivered to a higher-level protocol.

ifInNUcastPkts specifies the number of non-unicast packets that were delivered to a higher-level protocol.

ifInDiscards specifies the number of discarded inbound packets that were discarded even though no packet errors were detected.

ifInErrors specifies the number of inbound packets containing errors.

ifInUnknownProtos specifies the number of packets received that were discarded due to an unknown or unsupported protocol.

ifOutOctets specifies the total number of transmitted octets. The number of transmitted octets includes framing characters.

ifOutUcastPkts specifies the total number of packets transmitted at the request of a higher-level protocol to a subnetwork unicast address. The number of transmitted packets includes the packets that were discarded or not sent.

ifOutNUcastPkts specifies the total number of packets transmitted at the request of a higher-level protocol to a subnetwork non-unicast (i.e., multicast or broadcast) address. The number of transmitted packets includes the packets that were discarded or not sent.

ifOutDiscards specifies the number of outgoing packets that were selected to be discarded even though no errors were detected to prevent the transmission of the packet.

ifOutErrors specifies the number of outgoing packets that could not be transmitted because of an error.

ifOutQLen specifies the output packet queue length in packet units.

ifSpecific is a reference to MIB definitions specific to the particular media used to realize the network interface. If the interface is realized by frame relay, then the value of ifSpecific will refer to an RFC document which defines frame relay objects.

ifInDiscards {ifEntry 13} and ifOutDiscards {ifEntry 19} discard packets for no apparent reason. Yet it is not in the best interest of an interface to drop packets needlessly. We might dispose of that interface and get a more well-behaved replacement. Why would a network interface discard error-free packets when transmitting or receiving? Remember from earlier chapters that there are receive and transmit buffers. A TCP/IP with a full buffer is well-advised to discard packets, thereby triggering the retransmit function of TCP/IP rather than overwriting the buffer contents with the new data. And the same logic applies to the receive buffer—it gets full and we start dropping packets. Remember the transmit and receive windows?

SNMPvI Address Translation Group

The Address Translation Group provides the ability for TCP/IP to translate IP addresses to physical addresses. Physical addresses are sometimes called subnetwork addresses and IP addresses are called network addresses.

The Address Translation Group was used to map only from IP addresses to physical addresses. The one-way mapping was found to be a problem with MIB-II objects. CLNP requires two-way address mapping. To accommodate the CLNP mapping requirements, the Address Translation Group functionality was replaced in MIB-II with two-way address mapping in the IP Group. So, the Address Translation group status is "deprecated." Deprecated status means that the group is included only to ensure compatibility with MIB-I implementations and will not be used for the next generation (MIB-III) protocol.

Table 12.10 contains all the Address Translation Group objects and a short definition of their purpose. Implementation of the Address Translation Group is mandatory on all systems.

Object	Syntax	Definition	Access
atTable {at 1}	Seq	mult network address to physical address eq	na
atEntry {atTable 1}	atEntry	single network address to physical address eq	na
atIfIndex {atEntry 1}	I	owning node of address equivalence	rw
atPhysAddress {atEntry 2}	OS	media-dependent physical address	rw
atNetAddress {atEntry 3}	NA	IP address of media-dependent physical address	rw

eq = equivalence, I = Integer, mult = multiple, na = not accessible, NA = NetworkAddress, O = octet string, Seq = Sequence, rw = read/write

Table 12.10 Address Translation Group objects

atTable contains the network address to physical layer address equivalences of each possible interface. Some interfaces do not use address translation tables to determine address equivalences. If all interfaces are this type, then the Address Translation table is empty with all zero values.

atEntry contains one network address to physical address equivalence for each atEntry object.

atIfIndex specifies the particular interface for which this entry's equivalence applies to. This is the same interface identifed by ifIndex.

atPhysAddress specifies the media-dependent physical address. If atPhysAddress is set to a null string, the corresponding physical address in atTable is invalidated.

atNetAddress specifies the network IP address that matches the media-dependent physical address.

SNMPv1 IP Group

The IP Group provides much information about the health of the connection. Such things as the number of successful and unsuccessful datagram sends and receives are logged and reported. Table 12.11 contains all the IP Group objects and a short definition of their purpose. Implementation of the IP Group is mandatory for all systems.

 Note: ipNetToMediaTable provides the address translation functionality in MIB-II that was formerly performed by the Address Translation Group in MIB-I.

Object	Syntax	Definition	Access
ipForwarding {ip 1}	I	node is/is not a gateway	rw
ipDefaultTTL {ip 2}	I	default time-to-live value	rw
ipInReceives {ip 3}	C	total # of datagrams received	ro
ipInHdrErrors {ip 4}	C	# of disc datagrams due to IP header errors	ro
ipInAddrErrors {ip 5}	C	# of disc datagrams due to invalid node address	ro
ipForwDatagrams {ip 6}	C	# of datagrams forwarded to next hop	ro
ipInUnknownProtos {ip 7}	C	# of disc rcvd datagrams due to invalid protocol	ro
ipInDiscards {ip 8}	C	# of disc rcvd datagrams with no errors	ro
ipInDelivers {ip 9}	C	# of datagrams delivered to user processes	ro
ipOutRequests {ip 10}	C	# of datagrams IP requested to transmit	ro

Object	Syntax	Definition	Access
ipOutDiscards {ip 11}	C	# of trans datagrams disc with no errors	ro
ipOutNoRoutes {ip 12}	C	# of trans datagrams disc due to invalid destination address	ro
ipReasmTimeout {ip 13}	I	max seconds for fragment keep alive before disc	ro
ipReasmReqds {ip 14}	C	# of fragments rcvd to be reassembled	ro
ipReasmOKs {ip 15}	C	# of datagrams successfully reassembled	ro
ipReasmFails {ip 16}	C	# of datagrams unsuccessfully reassembled	ro
ipFragOKs {ip 17}	C	# of datagrams successfully fragmented	ro
ipFragFails {ip 18}	C	# of datagrams unsuccessfully fragmented	ro
ipFragCreates {ip 19}	C	# of datagram fragments created	ro
ipAddrTable {ip 20}	Seq	table of IP address info	na
ipRoutingTable {ip 21}	Seq	IP routing table for this node	na
ipNetToMediaTable {ip 22}	Seq	IP address mapping table	na
ipRoutingDiscards {ip 23}	C	# routing entries disc	ro

C = Counter, disc = discarded, I = Integer, na = not accessible, rcvd = received, ro = read only, rw = read/write, trans = transmitted

Table 12.11 IP Group objects

ipForwarding specifies whether or not the interface will forward datagrams. Since the designation of an interface as a host or gateway determines whether or not it will forward datagrams, unless the datagram is source routed via the host, this object determines the use, either as a host or gateway, of an interface. See Table 12.12.

Interface Type	ipForwarding Value	Meaning
gateway	1	interface forwards all datagrams
host	2	interface does not forward any datagrams

Table 12.12 ipForwarding values

ipDefaultTTL specifies the default value to be inserted into the time-to-live field of the IP header whenever a value is not supplied by the transport layer protocol.

ipInReceives specifies the total number of incoming datagrams received from interfaces.

ipInHdrErrors specifies the number of incoming datagrams discarded due to errors in the IP header.

ipInAddrErrors specifies the number of input datagrams discarded because the IP address in the IP header's destination field was not a valid address for this interface.

ipForwDatagrams specifies the number of incoming datagrams to be forwarded on to the next hop. If the interface does not act as a gateway, the count includes the number of packets that were successfully source routed by this interface.

ipInUnknownProtos specifies the number of locally addressed datagrams that were received successfully yet discarded due to an unknown or unsupported protocol.

ipInDiscards specifies the number of incoming IP datagrams discarded even though the datagram had no errors.

ipInDelivers specifies the total number of incoming datagrams delivered to IP user protocols (including ICMP).

ipOutRequests specifies the total number of IP datagrams local IP user protocols (including ICMP) sent to IP for transmission.

ipOutDiscards specifies the number of outgoing IP datagrams discarded even though the datagram had no errors.

ipOutNoRoutes specifies the number of outgoing IP datagrams discarded due to an unknown route to the requested destination.

ipReasmTimeout specifies the maximum number of seconds received fragments will be kept while they are awaiting reassembly.

ipReasmReqds specifies the number of IP fragments received which needed to be reassembled at this node.

ipReasmOKs specifies the number of IP datagrams successfully reassembled.

ipReasmFails specifies the number of datagram reassembly failures detected by the IP reassembly algorithm.

ipFragOKs specifies the number of IP datagrams that were successfully fragmented by this interface.

ipFragFails specifies the number of IP discarded datagrams this interface needed to fragment but could not due to some particular reason, such as a "do not fragment" flag in the IP header.

ipFragCreates specifies the number of IP datagram fragments generated.

ipAddrTable is the table of addressing information relevant to this interface's IP addresses.

ipRoutingTable is this interface's IP Routing table.

ipNetToMediaTable is the IP Address Translation table used for mapping IP addresses to physical addresses.

ipNetToMediaTable provides the address translation functionality in MIB-II that was formerly performed by the Address Translation group in MIB-I.

ipRoutingDiscards specifies the number of routing entries that were discarded even though the entry was valid.

SNMPvI IP Address Table

The IP Address Table is a subelement of the IP Group. See the ipAddrTable {ip 20} entry in Table 12.11. The IP Address Table is shown separately for clarity.

Table 12.13 contains all the IP Address Table objects and a short definition of their purpose. Implementation of the IP Address Table is mandatory for all systems.

Object	Syntax	Definition	Access
ipAddrTable {ip 20}	Seq	table of IP address info	na
ipAddrEntry {ipAddrTable 1}	ipAddrEntry	address info for one IP address	na
ipAdEntAddr {ipAddrEntry 1}	ipAddress	IP address of this table entry	ro
ipAdEntIfIndex {ipAddrEntry 2}	I	interface index value	ro
ipAdEntNetMask {ipAddrEntry 3}	ipAddress	IP address subnet mask	ro
ipAdEntBcastAddr {ipAddrEntry 4}	I	IP broadcast address LSB	ro
ipAdEntReasmMaxSize {ipAddrEntry 5}	I	max reassembled datagram possible	ro

I = Integer, LSB = least significant bit, na = not accessible, ro = read only, Seq = sequence

Table 12.13 IP Address Table objects

ipAddrTable specifies the table of addressing information relevant to this interface's IP addresses.

ipAddrEntry specifies the addressing information applicable to one of this interface's IP addresses.

ipAdEntAddr specifies the particular IP address for which this interface's address information is applicable to.

ipAdEntIfIndex specifies the index value which uniquely identifies the interface for which this table entry is applicable.

ipAdEntNetMask specifies the subnet mask associated with the IP address of this table entry. The mask value is an IP address with all the network bits set to 1 and all the host bits set to 0.

ipAdEntBcastAddr specifies the value of the least significant bit of the IP broadcast address.

ipAdEntReasmMaxSize specifies the largest IP datagram this node is able to reassemble from incoming IP datagram fragments received on this interface. The range of values the object may assume is from 0 to 65,535.

SNMPv1 IP Routing Table

The IP Routing Table is a subelement of the IP Group. See the ipRouting Table {ip 21} entry in Table 12.11. The IP Routing Table is shown separately for clarity.

The IP Routing Table holds the information necessary to identify each route known to this node. Table 12.14 contains all the IP Routing Table objects and a short definition of their purpose. Implementation of the IP Routing Table is mandatory for all systems.

Object	Syntax	Definition	Access
ipRoutingTable {ip 21}	Sequence of ipRouteEntry	IP routing table for this node	na
ipRouteEntry {ipRoutingTable 1}	ipRouteEntry	route to a destination	na
ipRouteDest {ipRouteEntry 1}	ipAddress	destination IP address of this route	rw
ipRouteIfIndex {ipRouteEntry 2}	I	next hop local interface identifier	rw
ipRouteMetric1 {ipRouteEntry 3}	I	primary routing metric for this route	rw
ipRouteMetric2 {ipRouteEntry 4}	I	alternate routing metric for this route	rw
ipRouteMetric3 {ipRouteEntry 5}	I	alternate routing metric for this route	rw
ipRouteMetric4 {ipRouteEntry 6}	I	alternate routing metric for this route	rw
ipRouteNextHop {ipRouteEntry 7}	ipAddress	next hop IP address	rw
ipRouteType {ipRouteEntry 8}	I	route type	rw
ipRouteProto {ipRouteEntry 9}	I	route learning mechanism	ro

Object	Syntax	Definition	Access
ipRouteAge {ipRouteEntry 10}	I	# of seconds since route last updated	ro
ipRouteMask {ipRouteEntry 11}	ipAddress	destination address AND mask	rw
ipRouteMetric5 {ipRouteEntry 12}	I	alternate routing metric	ro
ipRouteInfo {ipRouteEntry 13}	OID	specific routing MIB	ro

I = Integer, na = not accessible, OID = Object Identifier, ro = read only, rw = read/write

Table 12.14 IP Routing Table objects

ipRoutingTable specifies this node's IP routing table.

ipRouteEntry specifies a route to a specific destination.

ipRouteDest specifies the destination IP address of the route in this table entry. A value of 0.0.0.0 is interpreted as a default route. Multiple routes to a single destination may be listed in the table. The network management protocol used determines the ability to access multiple routes in the table.

ipRouteIfIndex specifies the index value which identifies the next node of the route identified in this table entry.

ipRouteMetric1 specifies the primary routing metric for the route identified in this table entry. The routing protocol specified in the route's ipRouteProto value determines the value of this entry. This value should be set to –1 if the metric is not used.

ipRouteMetric2 specifies an alternate routing metric for the route identifed in this table entry. The routing protocol specified in the route's ipRouteProto value determines the value of this entry. This value should be set to –1 if the metric is not used.

ipRouteMetric3 specifies an alternate routing metric for the route identified in this table entry. The routing protocol specified in the route's ipRouteProto value determines the value of this entry. This value should be set to –1 if the metric is not used.

ipRouteMetric4 specifies an alternate routing metric for the route identified in this table entry. The routing protocol specified in the route's ipRouteProto value determines the value of this entry. This value should be set to –1 if the metric is not used.

ipRouteNextHop specifies the IP address of the next hop of the route identified in this table entry.

ipRouteType specifies the type of route identified in this table entry. Table 12.15 lists the values of this table entry and their meaning:

Value	Meaning
1	other or none of the following
2	invalid route
3	route to directly connected (sub)network (direct routing)
4	route to a non-local indirect host/network/subnetwork (indirect routing)

Table 12.15 ipRouteType values

ipRouteProto specifies how the routing information for this table entry and the associated route was acquired or learned. ipRouteProto values 5 through 14 are gateway routing protocols. Table 12.16 lists the values of this table entry and their meaning:

Value	Meaning
1	none of the following; manually configured
2	local, set by a network protocol, acquired by ICMP
3	set by a network management protocol
4	icmp or redirect
5	egp
6	ggp
7	hello
8	rip
9	is-is
10	es-is
11	ciscolgrp
12	bbnSpfIgp
13	spf
14	bgp

Table 12.16 ipRouteProto values

ipRouteAge specifies the number of seconds since this route was last updated or determined to be valid.

ipRouteMask specifies the mask to be logically AND'ed with the destination address before being compared to the value in the ipRouteDest field. If an implementation does not support arbitrary subnet masks, then Table 12.17 shows the values to be used for the ipRouteMask table entry. The ipRouteDest entry is used to determine which class the next hop belongs to.

Network Type	Mask
Class A	255.0.0.0
Class B	255.255.0.0
Class C	255.255.255.0
default route	0.0.0.0

Table 12.17 ipRouteMask values

ipRouteMetric5 specifies an alternate routing metric for the route identified in this table entry. The routing protocol specified in the route's ipRouteProto value determines the value of this entry. This value should be set to –1 if the metric is not used.

ipRouteInfo specifies alternate or additional MIB definitions specific to the particular routing protocol identified in this table for this route. The MIB definitions are specified in RFCs applicable to the routing protocol responsible for this route. The routing protocol specified in the route's ipRouteProto value determines the value of this entry. This value should be set to the Object Identifier if the metric is not used.

SNMPv1 IP Net to Media Table

The IP Net to Media Table is a subelement of the IP Group. See the ipNetToMedia Table {ip 22} entry in Table 12.11. The IP Net to Media Table is shown separately for clarity.

Table 12.18 contains all the IP Net to Media Table objects and a short definition of their purpose. Implementation of the IP Net to Media Table is mandatory for all systems.

Object	Syntax	Definition	Access
ipNetToMediaTable {ip 22}	Sequence of ipNetToMediaEntry	IP Address Translation table	na
ipNetToMediaEntry {ipNetToMediaTable 1}	ipNetToMediaEntry	IP address to physical address equivalence	na
ipNetToMediaIfIndex {ipNetToMediaEntry 1}	I	interface applicable to the address equivalence	rw
ipNetToMediaPhysAddress {ipNetToMediaEntry 2}	phyAddress	transmission media-dependent physical address	rw
ipNetToMediaNetAddress {ipNetToMediaEntry 3}	ipAddress	IP address of {ipNetToMediaEntry 2}	rw
ipNetToMediaType {ipNetToMediaEntry 4}	I	interface status	rw

I = Integer, na = not accessible, rw = read/write

Table 12.18 IP Net to Media Table objects

ipNetToMediaTable is the IP Address Translation table used to map from IP addresses to physical addresses.

ipNetToMediaEntry specifies an IpAddress to physical address equivalence.

ipNetToMediaIfIndex specifies the node for which this table entry's equivalence is valid for.

ipNetToMediaPhysAddress specifies the media-dependent physical address of the node for which this table entry is valid for.

ipNetToMediaNetAddress specifies the IpAddress corresponding to the media-dependent physical address of the node for which this table entry is valid.

ipNetToMediaType specifies the type of mapping for which this table entry is valid. Table 12.19 lists the ipNetToMediaType values and their meaning.

Value	Meaning
I	other; none of the following
2	invalid mapping
3	dynamic mapping
4	static mapping

Table 12.19 ipNetToMediaType values

SNMPv1 ICMP Group

The ICMP Group contains the ICMP send and receive statistics. Table 12.20 contains all the ICMP Group objects and a short definition of their purpose. Implementation of the ICMP Group is mandatory for all systems.

Object	Syntax	Definition	Access
icmpInMsgs {icmp 1}	C	# of ICMP messages rcvd	ro
icmpInErrors {icmp 2}	C	# of ICMP messages rcvd with errors	ro
icmpInDestUnreachs {icmp 3}	C	# of ICMP destination unreachable msg rcvd	ro
icmpInTimeExcds {icmp 4}	C	# of ICMP time exceeded msg rcvd	ro
icmpInParmProbs {icmp 5}	C	# of ICMP parameter problem msg rcvd	ro
icmpInSrcQuenchs {icmp 6}	C	# of ICMP source quench msg rcvd	ro
icmpInRedirects {icmp 7}	C	# of ICMP redirect msg rcvd	ro
icmpInEchos {icmp 8}	C	# of ICMP echo msg rcvd	ro
icmpInEchoReps {icmp 9}	C	# of ICMP echo reply msg rcvd	ro
icmpInTimestamps {icmp 10}	C	# of ICMP timestamp msg rcvd	ro

Object	Syntax	Definition	Access
icmpInTimestampReps {icmp 11}	C	# of ICMP timestamp reply msg rcvd	ro
icmpInAddrMasks {icmp 12}	C	# of ICMP address mask request msg rcvd	ro
icmpInAddrMaskReps {icmp 13}	C	# of ICMP address mask reply msg rcvd	ro
icmpOutMsgs {icmp 14}	C	# of ICMP msg node attempted to transmit	ro
icmpOutErrors {icmp 15}	C	# of ICMP msg node did not send due to errors	ro
icmpOutDestUnreachs {icmp 16}	C	# of ICMP destination unreachable msg sent	ro
icmpOutTimeExcds {icmp 17}	C	# of ICMP time exceeded msg sent	ro
icmpOutParmProbs {icmp 18}	C	# of ICMP parameter problem msg sent	ro
icmpOutSrcQuenchs {icmp 19}	C	# of ICMP source quench msg sent	ro
icmpOutRedirects {icmp 20}	C	# of ICMP redirect msg sent	ro
icmpOutEchos {icmp 21}	C	# of ICMP echo msg sent	ro
icmpOutEchoReps {icmp 22}	C	# of ICMP echo reply msg sent	ro
icmpOutTimestamps {icmp 23}	C	# of ICMP timestamp msg sent	ro
icmpOutTimestampReps {icmp 24}	C	# of ICMP timestamp reply msg sent	ro
icmpOutAddrMasks {icmp 25}	C	# of ICMP address mask request msg sent	ro
icmpOutAddrMaskReps {icmp 26}	C	# of ICMP address mask reply msg sent	ro

C = Counter, msg = message or messages, rcvd = received, ro = read only

Table 12.20 ICMP Group objects

icmpInMsgs specifies the total number of ICMP messages received by this node.

icmpInErrors specifies the number of ICMP messages received by the node that had ICMP errors such as invalid address, bad checksum, bad length, etc.

icmpInDestUnreachs specifies the number of ICMP "destination unreachable" messages received by this node. That is, the packet was unable to reach its intended destination for some reason.

icmpInTimeExcds specifies the number of ICMP "time exceeded" messages received by this node.

icmpInParmProbs specifies the number of ICMP "parameter problem" messages received by this node.

icmpInSrcQuenchs specifies the number of ICMP "source quench" messages received by this node.

icmpInRedirects specifies the number of ICMP "redirect" messages received by this node.

icmpInEchos specifies the number of ICMP "echo request" messages received by this node.

icmpInEchoReps specifies the number of ICMP "echo reply" messages received by this node.

icmpInTimestamps specifies the number of ICMP "timestamp request" messages received by this node.

icmpInTimestampReps specifies the number of ICMP "timestamp reply" messages received by this node.

icmpInAddrMasks specifies the number of ICMP "address mask request" messages received by this node.

icmpInAddrMaskReps specifies the number of ICMP "address mask reply" messages received by this node.

icmpOutMsgs specifies the total number of ICMP messages this node attempted to send.

icmpOutErrors specifies the number of ICMP messages not sent by this node because of problems within ICMP. One reason for not sending an ICMP message is a lack of buffer space.

icmpOutDestUnreachs specifies the number of ICMP "destination unreachable" messages transmitted by this node.

icmpOutTimeExcds specifies the number of ICMP "time exceeded" messages transmitted by this node.

icmpOutParmProbs specifies the number of ICMP "parameter problem" messages transmitted by this node.

icmpOutSrcQuenchs specifies the number of ICMP "source quench" messages transmitted by this node.

icmpOutRedirects specifies the number of ICMP "redirect" messages transmitted by this node. Hosts do not transmit redirects, so the value of this object will always be zero if the node is a host.

icmpOutEchos specifies the number of ICMP "echo (request)" messages transmitted by this node.

icmpOutEchoReps specifies the number of ICMP "echo reply" messages transmitted by this node.

icmpOutTimestamps specifies the number of ICMP "timestamp request" messages transmitted by this node.

icmpOutTimestampReps specifies the number of ICMP "timestamp reply" messages transmitted by this node.

icmpOutAddrMasks specifies the number of ICMP "address mask request" messages transmitted by this node.

icmpOutAddrMaskReps specifies the number of ICMP "address mask reply" messages transmitted by this node.

SNMPv1 TCP Group

The TCP Group contains information about this node's existing TCP connections. Table 12.21 contains all the TCP Group objects and a short definition of their purpose. Implementation of the TCP Group is mandatory for all systems.

Object	Syntax	Definition	Access
tcpRtoAlgorithm {tcp 1}	I	retransmit unacknowledged packet timeout value	ro
tcpRtoMin {tcp 2}	I	minimum retransmission timeout value in millisecs	ro
tcpRtoMax {tcp 3}	I	maximum retransmission timeout value in millisecs	ro
tcpMaxConn {tcp 4}	I	maximum # of TCP connections	ro
tcpActiveOpens {tcp 5}	C	# times node transition CLOSED to SYN SENT	ro
tcpPassiveOpens {tcp 6}	C	# times node transition LISTEN to SYN RCVD	ro
tcpAttemptFails {tcp 7}	C	# times node transition SYN RCVD to CLOSED & # times node transition SYN RCVD to LISTEN & # times node transition SYN SENT to CLOSED	ro
tcpEstabResets {tcp 8}	C	# times node transition CLOSE WAIT to CLOSED & # times node transition ESTABLISHED to CLOSED	ro
tcpCurrEstab {tcp 9}	G	# TCP cc ESTABLISHED or CLOSED WAIT	ro
tcpInSegs {tcp 10}	C	# segments rcvd including errors	ro
tcpOutSegs {tcp 11}	C	# segments sent excluding retransmits	ro
tcpRetransSegs {tcp 12}	C	# retransmitted segments	ro
tcpConnTable {tcp 13}	Sequence of tcpConnEntry	TCP connection-specific table	na
tcpConnEntry {tcpConnTable 1}	tcpConnEntry	current TCP connection info	na
tcpConnState {tcpConnEntry 1}	I	TCP connection state	rw
tcpConnLocalAddress {tcpConnEntry 2}	ipAddress	TCP connection local IP address	ro

Object	Syntax	Definition	Access
tcpConnLocalPort {tcpConnEntry 3}	I	TCP connection local port #	ro
tcpConnRemAddress {tcpConnEntry 4}	ipAddress	TCP connection remote IP address	ro
tcpConnRemPort {tcpConnEntry 5}	I	TCP connection remote port number	ro
tcpInErrs {tcp 14}	C	# segments rcvd with errors	ro
tcpOutRsts {tcp 15}	C	# segments sent with RST flag set	ro

C = Counter, cc = current connections, G = Gauge, I = Integer, na = not accessible, rcvd = received, ro = read only, rw = read/write

Table 12.21 TCP Group objects

The tcpRtoAlgorithm specifies the algorithm for calculating the retransmit unacknowledged timeout value for this node. Table 12.22 lists the values of this object and their meaning.

Value	Meaning
I	other; none of the following
2	constant (user-specified value)
3	MIL-STD-1778
4	Van Jacobson's algorithm

Table 12.22 tcpRtoAlgorithm values

tcpRtoMin specifies the minimum retransmission timeout value, in milliseconds, permitted by a TCP implementation.

tcpRtoMax specifies the maximum retransmission timeout value, in milliseconds, permitted by a TCP implementation.

tcpMaxConn specifies the maximum TCP connections the node can support. For nodes that have a dynamic maximum number of connections, the value of this object should be –1.

tcpActiveOpens specifies the number of times all TCP connections on this node have transitioned from the CLOSED state to the SYN SENT state.

tcpPassiveOpens specifies the number of times all TCP connections on this node have transitioned from the LISTEN state to the SYN RCVD state.

tcpAttemptFails specifies the number of times all TCP connections on this node have transitioned from either the SYN SENT or the SYN RCVD state to the CLOSED state and specifies the number of times all TCP connections on this node have transitioned from the SYN RCVD state to the LISTEN state.

tcpEstabResets specifies the number of times all TCP connections on this node have transitioned from either the ESTABLISHED state or the CLOSE WAIT state to the CLOSED state.

tcpCurrEstab specifies the number of all TCP connections on this node that are currently in the ESTABLISHED or CLOSE WAIT.

tcpInSegs specifies the total number of segments received.

tcpOutSegs specifies the total number of segments sent. The count does not include retransmitted segments.

tcpRetransSegs specifies the total number of segments retransmitted.

tcpConnTable is a connection-specific table containing TCP connection information.

tcpConnEntry contains information about a specific TCP connection. The instance of each tcpConnEntry sequence is transient, existing only as long as the connection remains in a state other than CLOSED.

tcpConnState specifies the state of the TCP connection identified by this tcpConnEntry.

Table 12.23 lists the values tcpConnState may assume and their meaning. RFC 1213 states that the only value a management station may set the tcpConnState to is 12, which places the connection in the CLOSED state. If the management station attempts to set it to any other value, the agent running the underlying program is supposed to return a bad value flag.

Value	Meaning
1	closed
2	listen
3	synSent
4	synReceived
5	established
6	finWait1
7	finWait2
8	closeWait
9	lastAck
10	closing
11	timeWait
12	deleteTCB

Table 12.23 tcpConnState values

tcpConnLocalAddress specifies the local IP address of this TCP connection. If the connection is in a LISTEN state and will accept a connection request from any other IP node, the tcpConnLocalAddress value is 0.0.0.0.

tcpConnLocalPort specifies the local port number for this TCP connection. The valid range of values tcpConnLocalPort may assume is 0 to 65,535.

tcpConnRemAddress specifies the remote IP address for this TCP connection.

tcpConnRemPort specifies the remote port number for this TCP connection. The valid range of values tcpConnRemPort may assume is 0 to 65,535.

tcpInErrs specifies the total number of segments received in error by all current TCP connections.

tcpOutRsts specifies the number of TCP segments sent with the RST flag set.

SNMPv1 UDP Group

Table 12.24 contains all the UDP Group objects and a short definition of their purpose. Implementation of the UDP Group is mandatory for all systems.

Object	Syntax	Definition	Access
udpInDatagrams {udp 1}	C	# UDP datagrams delivered to user process	ro
udpNoPorts {udp 2}	C	# UDP datagrams rcvd - no user process	ro
udpInErrors {udp 3}	C	# UDP datagrams rcvd - cannot deliver	ro
udpOutDatagrams {udp 4}	C	# UDP datagrams sent	ro
udpTable {udp 5}	Sequence of udpEntry	all listener UDP data	na
udpEntry {udpTable 1}	udpEntry	individual listener UDP data	na
udpLocalAddress {udpEntry 1}	ipAddress	IP address for this listener	ro
udpLocalPort {udpEntry 2}	I	local UDP port # for this listener	ro

C = Counter, I = Integer, na = not accessible, rcvd = received, ro = read only

Table 12.24 UDP Group objects

udpInDatagrams specifies the total number of UDP datagrams delivered to UDP users.

udpNoPorts specifies the total number of received UDP datagrams that were addressed to nonexistent applications.

udpInErrors specifies the number of received UDP datagrams with errors that were not delivered. udpInErrors does not include the udpNoPorts count.

udpOutDatagrams specifies the total number of UDP datagrams sent from this node.

udpTable contains information about this node's UDP endpoints on which a local application is currently accepting datagrams.

udpEntry specifies appropriate information about a particular current UDP listener.

udpLocalAddress specifies the local IP address for this UDP listener. If the listener will accept a connection request from any other IP node, the udpLocalAddress value is 0.0.0.0.

udpLocalPort specifies the local port number for this UDP listener. The range of values udpLocalPort may assume is 0 to 65,535.

SNMPv1 EGP Group

The EGP Group contains information about this node's EGP neighbors. Table 12.25 contains all the EGP Group objects and a short definition of their purpose. Implementation of the EGP Group is mandatory for all systems.

Object	Syntax	Definition	Access
egpInMsgs {egp 1}	C	# EGP msgs rcvd with no errors	ro
egpInErrors {egp 2}	C	# EGP msgs rcvd with errors	ro
egpOutMsgs {egp 3}	C	# of EGP msgs created	ro
egpOutErrors {egp 4}	C	# of EGP msgs not sent	ro
egpNeighTable {egp 5 }	Sequence of egpNeighEntry	EGP neighbor table	na
egpNeighEntry {egpNeighTable 1}	egpNeighEntry	specific EGP neighbor info	na
egpNeighState {egpNeighEntry 1}	I	EGP state wrt the EGP neighbor	ro
egpNeighAddr {egpNeighEntry 2}	ipAddress	IP address of EGP neighbor	ro
egpNeighAs {egpNeighEntry 3}	I	EGP neighbor's system number	ro
egpNeighInMsgs {egpNeighEntry 4}	C	#EGP msgs rcvd fm neighbor without errors	ro
egpNeighInErrs {egpNeighEntry 5}	C	#EGP msgs rcvd fm neighbor with errors	ro
egpNeighOutMsgs {egpNeighEntry 6}	C	# local EGP msgs add to the nghbr	ro
egpNeighOutErrs {egpNeighEntry 7}	C	# local EGP msgs add to the nghbr not sent	ro

Object	Syntax	Definition	Access
egpNeighInErrMsgs {egpNeighEntry 8}	C	# EGP error msgs rcvd fm nghbr	ro
egpNeighOutErrMsgs {egpNeighEntry 9}	C	# EGP error msgs sent to nghbr	ro
egpNeighStateUps {egpNeighEntry 10}	C	# EGP sttran to UP with nghbr	ro
egpNeighStateDowns {egpNeighEntry 11}	C	# EGP sttran fm UP to any state with nghbr	ro
egpNeighIntervalHello {egpNeighEntry 12}	I	interval of Hello retrans (t1 timer)	ro
egpNeighIntervalPoll {egpNeighEntry 13}	I	interval of Poll retrans (t3 timer)	ro
egpNeighMode {egpNeighEntry 14}	sb	polling mode (active or passive)	ro
egpNeighEventTrigger {egpNeighEntry 15}	sb	Start/Stop trigger	ro
egpAs {egp 6}	I	EGP autonomous system #	ro

add = addressed, C = Counter, fm = from, I = Integer, na = not accessible, msgs = messages, nghbr = neighbor, retrans = retransmissions, sb = see below, sttran = state transitions, wrt = with respect to

Table 12.25 EGP Group objects

egpInMsgs specifies the number of EGP messages received by this node without error.

egpInErrors specifies the number of EGP messages received by this node that were in error.

egpOutMsgs specifies the total number of EGP messages generated by this node.

egpOutErrors specifies the number of EGP messages generated by this node and not transmitted.

egpNeighTable specifies the EGP neighbor table. The EGP neighbor table contains information about this node's EGP neighbors.

egpNeighEntry contains information about this node's relationship with a specific EGP neighbor.

egpNeighState specifies the local system's EGP state with respect to this entry's EGP neighbor. Each EGP state is represented by a value as shown in Table 12.26.

Value	Meaning
1	idle
2	acquisition
3	down
4	up
5	cease

Table 12.26 EGPNeighState values

egpNeighAddr specifies the IP address of this entry's EGP neighbor.

egpNeighAs specifies the autonomous system of this EGP peer. The value of egpNeighAs is zero if the autonomous system number of the neighbor is unknown.

egpNeighInMsgs specifies the number of error-free EGP messages received from this EGP peer.

egpNeighInErrs specifies the number of EGP messages received from this EGP peer that contained errors.

egpNeighOutMsgs specifies the number of EGP messages generated by this node and transmitted to this EGP peer.

egpNeighOutErrs specifies the number of EGP messages generated by this node and not transmitted to this EGP peer because of resource limitations within an EGP node.

egpNeighInErrMsgs specifies the number of EGP error messages received from this EGP peer.

egpNeighOutErrMsgs specifies the number of EGP error messages transmitted to this EGP peer.

egpNeighStateUps specifies the number of EGP UP state transitions with this EGP peer.

egpNeighStateDowns specifies the number of EGP DOWN state transitions to any other state with this EGP peer.

egpNeighIntervalHello specifies the timing interval between EGP Hello command retransmissions in hundredths of a second.

egpNeighIntervalPoll specifies the timing interval between EGP Poll command retransmissions in hundredths of a second.

egpNeighMode specifies the polling mode of this EGP node. A value of 1 specifies an active polling mode and a value of 2 specifies a passive polling mode.

egpNeighEventTrigger is used to trigger operator-initiated Start and Stop events. A value of 1 specifies a start event on the specified neighbor and a value of 2 specifies a stop event on the specified neighbor.

egpAs specifies the autonomous system number of this EGP node.

SNMPv1 Transmission Group

MIB-II is designed to accommodate the different types of transmission media. The specific Transmission Group utilized is based on the transmission media associated with the transport system utilized by each node on a system. That is, the Transmission Group is implementation specific. The appropriate Transmission Group is mandatory for each implementation.

The transmission object identifier is given as (in the formal ASN.1 notation):
transmission Object Identifier ::= {mib-2 10}

The naming convention for Transmission Group object members is:
type Object Identifier ::= {transmission number}

Type is the symbolic value used for the media in the ifType column if the ifTable object number is the actual integer value corresponding to the symbol.

SNMPv1 SNMP Group

Table 12.27 contains all the SNMP Group objects and a short definition of their purpose. Implementation of the SNMP Group is mandatory for all systems.

The SNMP group is identifed as: snmpObject Identifier ::= {mib-2 11}

Object	Syntax	Definition	Access
snmpInPkts {snmp 1}	C	# SNMPv1 msgs rcvd by node	ro
snmpOutPkts {snmp 2}	C	# SNMPv1 msgs delivered to transport svc	ro
snmpInBadVersions {snmp 3}	C	# incorrect version SNMPv1 msgs rcvd	ro
snmpInBadCommunityNames {snmp 4}	C	# unknown name SNMPv1 msgs rcvd	ro
snmpInBadCommunityUses {snmp 5}	C	# unallowed operations	ro
snmpInASNParseErrs {snmp 6}	C	# of ASN.1 or BER errors rcvd	ro
not used {snmp 7}	nu	nu	nu
snmpInTooBigs {snmp 8}	C	# PDUs rcvd error status fd out of bounds	ro
snmpInNoSuchNames {snmp 9}	C	# PDUs rcvd error status fd incorrect name	ro

Object	Syntax	Definition	Access
snmpInBadValues {snmp 10}	C	# PDUs rcvd error status fd bad value	ro
snmpInReadOnlys {snmp 11}	C	# PDUs rcvd error status fd read only	ro
snmpInGenErrs {snmp 12}	C	# PDUs rcvd error status fd "genErr"	ro
snmpInTotalReqVars {snmp 13}	C	# MIB objects fetched due to valid Get Request/Next PDUs	ro
snmpInTotalSetVars {snmp 14}	C	# MIB objects changed due to valid Set Request PDUs	ro
snmpInGetRequests {snmp 15}	C	# Get Request PDUs processed	ro
snmpInGetNexts {snmp 16}	C	# Get Next PDUs processed	ro
snmpInSetRequests {snmp 17}	C	# Set Request PDUs processed	ro
snmpInGetResponses {snmp 18}	C	# Get Response PDUs processed	ro
snmpInTraps {snmp 19}	C	# Trap PDUs processed	ro
snmpOutTooBigs {snmp 20}	C	# PDUs created error status fd out of bounds	ro
snmpOutNoSuchNames {snmp 21}	C	# PDUs created error status fd: no such name"	ro
snmpOutBadValues {snmp 22}	C	# PDUs created error status fd "bad value"	ro
{snmp 23}	nu	nu	nu
snmpOutGenErrs {snmp 24}	C	# PDUs created error status fd "genErr"	ro
snmpOutGetRequests {snmp 25}	C	# Get Request PDUs created	ro
snmpOutGetNexts {snmp 26}	C	# Get Next PDUs created	ro
snmpOutSetRequests {snmp 27}	C	# Set Request PDUs created	ro
snmpOutGetResponses {snmp 28}	C	# Get Response PDUs created	ro
snmpOutTraps {snmp 29}	C	# Trap PDUs created	ro
snmpEnableAuthenTraps {snmp 30}	I	create authentication failure traps permission	rw

C = Counter, I = Integer, fd = field, msgs = messages, nu = not used, rcvd = received, ro = read only, rw = read/write, svc = service

Table 12.27 SNMP Group objects

snmpInPkts specifies the total number of SNMPv1 messages delivered to the SNMPv1 protocol by the transport service.

snmpOutPkts specifies the total number of SNMPv1 messages which were transmitted from the SNMPv1 protocol to the transport service.

snmpInBadVersions specifies the total number of SNMPv1 messages which were delivered to the SNMPv1 protocol node and were for an unsupported SNMPv1 version.

snmpInBadCommunityNames specifies the total number of SNMPv1 messages with an unknown community name delivered to the SNMPv1 protocol.

snmpInBadCommunityUses specifies the total number of SNMPv1 messages with an unallowed SNMPv1 operation delivered to the SNMPv1 protocol.

snmpInASNParseErrs specifies the total number of SNMPv1 messages with ASN.1 or bit error rate (BER) errors received by the SNMPv1 protocol.

snmp 7 is not used.

snmpInTooBigs specifies the total number of SNMPv1 PDUs received with an error status of tooBig.

snmpInNoSuchNames specifies the total number of SNMPv1 PDUs received with an error status of noSuchName.

snmpInBadValues specifies the total number of SNMPv1 PDUs received with an error status of badValue.

snmpInReadOnlys specifies the total number of SNMPv1 PDUs received with an error status of readOnly.

snmpInGenErrs specifies the total number of SNMPv1 PDUs received with an error status of genErr.

snmpInTotalReqVars specifies the total number of MIB objects that were retrieved by the SNMPv1 protocol due to the reception of an SNMPv1 Get Request or Get Next PDU.

snmpInTotalSetVars specifies the total number of MIB objects that were altered by the SNMPv1 protocol due to the reception of SNMPv1 Set Request PDUs.

snmpInGetRequests specifies the total number of SNMPv1 Get Request PDUs that were accepted and processed by the SNMPv1 protocol.

snmpInGetNexts specifies the total number of SNMPv1 Get Next PDUs that were accepted and processed by the SNMPv1 protocol.

snmpInSetRequests specifies the total number of SNMPv1 Set Request PDUs that were accepted and processed by the SNMPv1 protocol.

snmpInGetResponses specifies the total number of SNMPv1 Get Response PDUs that were accepted and processed by the SNMPv1 protocol.

snmpInTraps specifies the total number of SNMPv1 Trap PDUs that were accepted and processed by the SNMPv1 protocol.

snmpOutTooBigs specifies the total number of SNMPv1 PDUs with an error status field of tooBig which were generated by the SNMPv1 protocol.

snmpOutNoSuchNames specifies the total number of SNMPv1 PDUs with an error status field of noSuchName which were generated by the SNMPv1 protocol.

snmpOutBadValues specifies the total number of SNMPv1 PDUs with an error status field of badValue which were generated by the SNMPv1 protocol.

snmp 23 is not used.

snmpOutGenErrs specifies the total number of SNMPv1 PDUs with an error status field of genErr which were generated by the SNMPv1 protocol.

snmpOutGetRequests specifies the total number of SNMPv1 GetRequest PDUs that were generated by the SNMPv1 protocol.

snmpOutGetNexts specifies the total number of SNMPv1 Get Next PDUs that have been generated by the SNMPv1 protocol.

snmpOutSetRequests specifies the total number of SNMPv1 Set Request PDUs that were generated by the SNMPv1 protocol.

snmpOutGetResponses specifies the total number of SNMPv1 Get Response PDUs that were generated by the SNMPv1 protocol.

snmpOutTraps specifies the total number of SNMPv1 Trap PDUs that were generated by the SNMPv1 protocol.

snmpEnableAuthenTraps specifies if the SNMPv1 agent process is permitted to generate authentication-failure traps. If the snmpEnableAuthenTraps value is 1, traps are enabled. If the snmpEnableAuthenTraps value is 2, traps are disabled.

Other MIBs

So far, we have discussed the basic MIB objects that are common to all implementations. The implementation of these MIB objects is mandatory for all implementations incorporating network management. However, there are additional MIBs containing a multitude of MIB objects whose implementation is not mandatory.

The original purpose (circa RFC 1155/1156/1157) of keeping the MIB simple seems to have gone by the wayside. As networks expanded and network transport technologies developed, more and more traffic-related statistics were desired. There are a variety of MIB specifications now defined in the RFCs. A list of the MIBs is included to give the reader a sense of proportion and a roadmap to find those of particular interest.

Recommended MIB Protocols

The Recommended MIB Protocols are the foundation upon which the SMI and SNMPv1 network management structure is built. The Recommended MIB Protocols form the basis of the MIB information in this chapter and are listed below. Recommended MIB Protocols are general in nature and are applicable to all implementations:

Concise MIB Definitions	1212
Management Information Base II (MIB-II)	1213

Elective MIB Protocols

Elective MIB Protocols are those MIB protocols that are very implementation specific. Due to size constraints, the Elective MIB Protocols are not covered in this chapter. They are, however, listed below for reference:

STD-MIBs	Reassignment of Exp MIBs to Std MIBs	1239
BGP-MIB	Border Gateway Protocol MIB (Version 3)	1269
FDDI-MIB	FDDI-MIB	1285
FRAME-MIB	Management Information Base for Frame	1315
SNMP-PARTY-MIB	Administration of SNMP	1353
DS1/E1-MIB	DS1/E1 Interface Type	1406
DS3/E3-MIB	DS3/E3 Interface Type	1407
IDENT-MIB	Identification MIB	1414
SNMPv2	Party MIB for SNMPv2	1447
SNMPv2	Manager-to-Manager MIB	1451
X25-MIB	Multiprotocol Interconnect on X.25 MIB	1461
PPP/LCP MIB	Link Control Protocol of PPP MIB	1471
PPP/SEC MIB	Security Protocols of PPP MIB	1472
PPP/IP MIB	IP Network Control Protocol of PPP MIB	1473
PPP/Bridge MIB	Bridge PPP MIB	1474
BRIDGE-MIB	BRIDGE-MIB	1493
FDDI-MIB	FDDI Management Information Base	1512
	Token Ring Extensions to RMON MIB	1513
HOST-MIB	Host Resources MIB	1514
	802.3 MAU MIB	1515
SRB-MIB	Source Routing Bridge MIB	1525
DECNET-MIB	DECNET MIB	1559
NSM-MIB	Network Services Monitoring MIB	1565
MAIL-MIB	Mail Monitoring MIB	1566
X500-MIB	X.500 Directory Monitoring MIB	1567
SONET-MIB	MIB SONET/SDH Interface Type	1595
FR-MIB	Frame Relay Service MIB	1604
DNS-S-MIB	DNS Server MIB Extensions	1611
DNS-R-MIB	DNS Resolver MIB Extensions	1612
UPS-MIB	UPS Management Information Base	1628
ETHER-MIB	Ethernet MIB	1643

BGP-4-MIB	BGP-4 MIB	1657
SNANAU-MIB	SNA NAUs MIB using SMIv2	1666
SIP-MIB	SIP Interface Type MIB	1694
ATM-MIB	ATM Management Version 8.0 using SMIv2	1695
MODEM-MIB	Modem MIB - using SMIv2	1696
RDBMS-MIB	RDMS MIB - using SMIv2	1697
RIP2-MIBRIP	Version 2 MIB Extension	1724
AT-MIB	Appletalk MIB	1742
SDLCSMIv2	SNADLC SDLC MIB using SMIv2	1747
802.5-MIB	IEEE 802.5 Token Ring MIB	1748
802.5-SSR	802.5 SSR MIB using SMIv2	1749
RMON-MIB	Remote Network Monitoring MIB	1757
Print-MIB	Printer MIB	1759
OSPF-MIB	OSPF Version 2 MIB	1850
CONV-MIB	Textual Conventions for SNMPv2	1903
CONF-MIB	Conformance Statements for SNMPv2	1904
OPS-MIB	Protocol Operations for SNMPv2	1905
TRANS-MIB	Transport Mappings for SNMPv2	1906
SNMPv2-MIB	MIB for SNMPv2	1907
COEX-MIB	Coexistence between SNMPV1 & SNMPV2	1908
MOBILEIPMIB	Mobile IP MIB Definition using SMIv2	2006
MIB-IP SNMPv2	MIB for IP	2011
MIB-TCP SNMPv2	MIB for TCP	2012
MIB-UDP SNMPv2	MIB for UDP	2013
802.12-MIB	IEEE 802.12 Interface MIB	2020
RMON-MIB	RMON MIB using SMIv2	2021
DLSW-MIB	DLSw MIB using SMIv2	2024
ENTITY-MIB	Entity MIB using SMIv2	2037
SNANAU-APP	SNANAU APPC MIB using SMIv2	2051
RMON-MIB	Remote Network Monitoring MIB	2074
TABLE-MIB	IP Forwarding Table MIB	2096
802.3-MIB	802.3 Repeater MIB using SMIv2	2108
ISDN-MIB	ISDN MIB using SMIv2	2127
DC-MIB	Dial Control MIB using SMIv2	2128

Experimental MIB Protocols

The Experimental MIB Protocols are in-process (read "problematic") specifications and are implemented only if you are a bold soul and/or directly involved in testing, modifying, and otherwise assisting the development process of the specification. They are included here for reference.

OIM-MIB-II	OSI Internet Management: MIB-II	1214
SNMP-MUXSNMPv1	MUX Protocol and MIB	1227
802.4-MIP	IEEE 802.4 Token Bus MIB	1230
CLNS-MIB	CLNS-MIB	1238
TCP/IPXMIB	TCP/IPX Connection MIB Specification	1792
METER-MIB	Traffic Flow Measurement Meter MIB	2064

Management Information Base for SNMPv2

The following sections detail the SNMPv2 Management Information Base. SNMPv2 has obsoleted some portions of SNMPv1 MIB.

{snmpMIBObjects 1} status is obsolete.
{snmpMIBObjects 2} status is obsolete.
{snmpMIBObjects 3} status is obsolete.
snmpMIBObjects{snmpMIB 1} status is current.

SNMPv2 System Group

The System Group is a group of objects common to all managed systems. The status of all the objects in Table 12.28 is "current."

Object	Syntax	Access	Description
sysDescr{system 1}	DisplayString(SIZE (0..255))	ro	textual description of the system
sysObject{system 2}	OID	ro	id of network mgmt subsys
sysUpTime{system 3}	TimeTicks	ro	time of last initialization
sysContact{system 4}	DisplayString (SIZE (0..255))	rw	contact person responsible for node
sysName{system 5}	DisplayString (SIZE (0..255))	rw	node's fully qualified domain name
sysServices{system 6}	I(0..127)	ro	node's set of services

OID = Object Identifier, ro = read only, rw = read/write

Table 12.28 SNMPv2 System Group objects

SNMPv2 Object Resource Information Group

The Object Resource Information Group describes the support of various MIB objects by the SNMPv2 entity. The status of all the objects in Table 12.29 is "current."

Object	Syntax	Access	Description
sysORLastChange{system 8}	TimeStamp	ro	sysUpTime value when sysORID last changed
sysORTable{system 9}	SEQ OF SysOREntry	na	table of node's capabilities
sysOREntry{sysORTable 1}	SysOREntry	na	sysORTable row entry
sysORIndex{sysOREntry 1}	I (1..2147483647)	na	variable for identifying sysORTable entries
sysORID{sysOREntry 2}	OID	ro	node's capabilities
sysORDescr{sysOREntry 3}	DisplayString	ro	text description of node's capabilities
sysORUpTime{sysOREntry 4}	TimeStamp	ro	sysUptime when row last updated

na = not accessible, OID = Object Identifier, ro = read only, rw = read/write

Table 12.29 SNMPv2 Object Resource Information Group objects

SNMPv2 SNMPv1 Group

The SNMPv2 SNMPv1 Group defines the objects used to provide basic control of an SNMPv1 entity by an SNMPv2 entity. These are listed in Table 12.30.

Object	Syntax	Access	Description
snmpInPkts{snmp 1}	Counter32	ro	# msgs delivered to node
snmpOutPkts{snmp 2}	Counter32	ro	# msgs passed to transport service
snmpInBadVersions{snmp 3}	Counter32	ro	# msgs rcvd for unsupported SNMPv1 version
snmpInBadCommunityNames {snmp 4}	Counter32	ro	# msgs rcvd with unknown community name
snmpInBadCommunityUses {snmp 5}	Counter32	ro	# msgs rcvd illegal SNMPv1 operation
snmpInASNParseErrs{snmp 6}	Counter32	ro	# ASN.1 or BER errors
{snmp 7 }	not used		
snmpInTooBigs{snmp 8}	Counter32	ro/obs	# msgs error status "tooBig"
snmpInNoSuchNames{snmp 9}	Counter32	ro/obs	# msgs error status "noSuchName"
snmpInBadValues{snmp 10}	Counter32	ro/obs	# msgs error status "badValue"
snmpInReadOnly{snmp 11}	Counter32	ro/obs	# msgs error status "readOnly"
snmpInGenErrs{snmp 12}	Counter32	ro/obs	# msgs error status "genError"
snmpInTotalReqVars{snmp 13}	Counter32	ro/obs	# MIB objects retrieved
snmpInTotalSetVars{snmp 14}	Counter32	ro/obs	# MIB objects altered
snmpInGetRequests{snmp 15}	Counter32	ro/obs	# Get Request PDUs processed
snmpInGetNexts{snmp 16}	Counter32	ro/obs	# Get Next PDUs processed
snmpInSetRequests{snmp 17}	Counter32	ro/obs	# Set Request PDUs processed
snmpInGetResponses{snmp 18}	Counter32	ro/obs	# Get Response PDUs processed
snmpInTraps{snmp 19}	Counter32	ro/obs	# Trap PDUs processed
snmpOutTooBigs{snmp 20}	Counter32	ro/obs	# PDUs created with error status "tooBig"
snmpOutNoSuchNames{snmp 21}	Counter32	ro/obs	# PDUs created with error status "NoSuchName"
snmpOutBadValues{snmp 22}	Counter32	ro/obs	# PDUs created with error status "badValue"
{snmp 23}	not used		
snmpOutGenErrs{snmp 24}	Counter32	ro/obs	# PDUs created with error status "genError"
snmpOutGetRequests{snmp 25}	Counter32	ro/obs	# Get Request PDUs created
snmpOutGetNexts{snmp 26}	Counter32	ro/obs	# Get Next PDUs created
snmpOutSetRequests{snmp 27}	Counter32	ro/obs	# Set Request PDUs created
snmpOutGetResponses{snmp 28}	Counter32	ro/obs	# Get Response PDUs created
snmpOutTraps{snmp 29}	Counter32	ro/obs	# Trap PDUs created
snmpEnableAuthenTraps{snmp 30}	I	rw	# enable authentication Failure traps

Object	Syntax	Access	Description
snmpSilentDrops{snmp 31}	Counter32	ro	# PDUs dropped due to size constraints
snmpProxyDrops{snmp 32}	Counter32	ro	# PDUs sent nodes and no response rcvd

I = integer, msgs = messages, rcvd = received, ro = read only, ro/obs = read only/obsolete object, rw = read/write **Note:** snmpEnableAuthenTraps I = enabled, 2 = disabled

Table 12.30 SNMPv2 SNMPv1 Group objects

SNMPv2 Notifications Group

The SNMPv2 Notifications Group snmpTrap{snmpMIBObjects 4} defines the objects used to configure an SNMPv2 entity performing the role of a network agent to create SNMPv2 Trap PDUs. The status of all objects is "current."

Object	Syntax	Access	Description
snmpTrapOID{snmpTrap 1}	OID	afn	id of notification currently sent
{snmpTrap 2}		obs	
snmpTrapEnterprise{snmpTrap 3}	OID	afn	enterprise id of trap currently sent
{snmpTrap 4}		obs	

afn = accessible-for-notify, obs = obsolete, OID = Object Identifier

Table 12.31 SNMPv2 Notifications Group objects

SNMPv2 Well-known Traps

SNMPv2 Well-known Traps snmpTraps{snmpMIBObjects 5} defines the objects used to report management SNMPv2 errors and faults. The status of all Well-known Traps objects is "current."

Object	Syntax	Description
coldStart{snmpTraps 1}	nt	node is reinitializing with change config
warmStart{snmpTraps 2}	nt	node is reinitializing with no change config
linkDown{snmpTraps 3}	nt	defined in RFC 1573
linkUp{snmpTraps 4}	nt	defined in RFC 1573
authenticationFailure{snmpTraps 5}	nt	msg rcvd not authenticated
egpNeighborLoss{snmpTraps 5}	nt	defined in RFC 1213

nt = Notification Type

Table 12.32 SNMPv2 Well-known Traps objects

SNMPv2 Set Group

SNMPv2 Set Group snmpSet{snmpMIBObjects 6} defines the objects used to coordinate the SNMPv2 activities of several cooperating SNMPv2 entities, each acting as a network manager. The status of all objects is "current."

Object	Syntax	Access	Description
snmpSetSerialNo{snmpSet 1}	TI	rw	allows multiple access to SNMPv2 on node

rw = read/write, TI = Test and Increment

Table 12.33 SNMPv2 Set Group objects

SNMPv2 Conformance Information Group

The SNMPv2 Conformance Information Group objects are:
snmpMIBConformance{snmpMIB 2}
snmpMIBCompliances{snmpMIBConformance 1}
snmpMIBGroups{snmpMIBConformance 2}

SNMPv2 Compliance Group

The SNMPv2 Compliance Group objects are:
{snmpMIBCompliances 1} – status is obsolete
{snmpMIBCompliances 2} – status is current

Object	Syntax	Description
snmpBasicCompliance	MC	SNMPv2 compliance statement
snmpGroup	GP	
snmpSetGroup	GP	
systemGroup	GP	
snmpBasicNotificationsGroup	GP	
snmpCommunityGroup {snmpMIBCompliances 2}	GP	required for community-based authentication

GP = Group, MC = Module Compliance

Table 12.34 SNMPv2 Compliance Group objects

SNMPv2 Conformance Group

The SNMPv2 Conformance Group objects are:
{snmpMIBGroups 1} status is obsolete
{snmpMIBGroups 2} status is obsolete
{snmpMIBGroups 3} status is obsolete
{snmpMIBGroups 4} status is obsolete

Objects	Syntax	Description
snmpGroup{snmpMIBGroups 8}	OG	SNMPv2 control/instrumentation objects
snmpCommunityGroup {snmpMIBGroups 9}	OG	SNMPv2 community-based instrumentation objects
snmpSetGroup{snmpMIBGroups 5}	OG	allows multiple use of SNMPv2 set operation
systemGroup{snmpMIBGroups 6}	OG	object definition for common objects
snmpBasicNotificationsGroup {snmpMIBGroups 7}	NG	2 SNMPv2 notifications {coldStart & authenticationFailure}
snmpObsoleteGroup	OG	a collection of obsoleted RFC 1213 groups

OG = Object Group, NG = Notification Group

Table 12.35 SNMPv2 Conformance Group objects

SNMPv2 Architecture

Just as the SNMPv1 architectural model is a collection of network management stations and network elements, so too is the SNMPv2 model.

SNMPv2 managers and agents communicate with each other through the exchange of protocol data units (PDUs). There are seven PDUs defined for use with SNMPv2. SNMPv2 requires all implementations of SNMPv2 to support the seven PDUs, which are: GetRequest PDU, GetNextRequest PDU, Response PDU, SetRequest PDU, Trap PDU, GetBulkRequest PDU, and InformRequest PDU.

All SNMPv2 entities acting as an agent must be able to create the following PDU types: Response PDU and SNMPv2 Trap PDU. Also, these implementations must be able to receive the following PDU types: GetRequest PDU, GetNextRequest PDU, GetBulkRequest PDU, and SetRequest PDU.

All SNMPv2 entities acting as a manager must be able to create the following PDU types: GetRequest PDU, GetNextRequest PDU, GetBulkRequest PDU, SetRequest PDU, InformRequest PDU, and Response PDU. Also, these implementations must be able to receive the following PDU types: Response PDU, SNMPv2 Trap PDU, InformRequest PDU.

SNMPv2 managers and agents exchange information for three primary reasons:

➤ To retrieve or modify management information associated with the managed device.

➤ To notify an SNMPv2 entity acting in a management capacity of management information associated with another SNMPv2 entity, also acting in a management capacity.

▲ To notify an SNMPv2 entity, acting in a management capacity, of exceptional situations which have resulted in changes to management information associated with the managed device.

It is recommended in the RFCs that implementations of SNMPv2 utilize User Datagram Protocol for the SNMPv2 transport service. If UDP is utilized, a transport address consists of an IP address along with a UDP port. Other transport services may be used. If another transport is used, the definition of a transport address is defined by the transport service protocol. SNMPv2 managers and agents receive on UDP port 161 and send on UDP port 162.

The size of an SNMPv2 PDU is determined by the maximum message size the destination SNMPv2 entity can accept and the maximum message size the source SNMPv2 entity can generate. SNMPv2 managers/agents should be able to accept messages at least 484 octets long.

SNMPv2 PDU Processing

An SNMPv2 message is created by a manager/agent according to the following scenario:

1. The manager/agent constructs the appropriate PDU as an ASN.1 object.

2. The manager/agent passes the ASN.1 object along with a community name, its source transport address, and the destination transport address to the service that implements the authentication scheme. The authentication service returns another ASN.1 object.

3. Construct an ASN.1 Message object using the appropriate community name.

4. Serialize the ASN.1 object, then send it via the transport service to the intended destination.

A manager/agent receiving a PDU will process it according to the following scenario:

1. The manager/agent parses the incoming datagram to build an ASN.1 object corresponding to an ASN.1 Message object. If the result is not a valid ASN.1 Message object, the datagram is discarded and no further action is performed.

2. The manager/agent verifies the version number of the SNMPv1 message. If there is a mismatch, the datagram is discarded and no further action is performed.

3. The manager/agent passes the community name and user data in the ASN.1 Message object and the datagram's source and destination transport addresses to the service that implements the desired authentication scheme. The authentication service returns either another ASN.1 object, or it signals an authentication failure. If the authentication attempt failed, the authentication service notes the failure and creates a Trap PDU. The datagram is discarded and no further action is performed.

4. The manager/agent now parses the ASN.1 object returned from the authentication service to build an ASN.1 object corresponding to an ASN.1 PDU object. If the parse fails, the datagram is discarded and no further action is performed. If the parse attempt is successful, the manager/agent uses the named SNMPv1 community, selects the appropriate profile, and processes the PDU.

The GetRequest PDU

A GetRequest PDU is created and transmitted at the request of an SNMPv2 manager/agent. Upon receipt of a GetRequest PDU, the receiving SNMPv2 manager/agent processes each variable binding in the variable-binding list to produce a Response PDU with its request-id field having the same value as in the request unless exceptions are present. The Response PDU is created and transmitted to the originator of the GetRequest PDU.

The GetNextRequest PDU

A GetNextRequest PDU is generated and transmitted at the request of an SNMPv2 manager/agent. Upon receipt of a GetNextRequest PDU, the receiving SNMPv2 manager/agent processes each variable binding in the variable-binding list to produce a Response PDU with its request-id field having the same value as in the request unless exceptions are present. The Response PDU is created and transmitted to the originator of the GetNextRequest PDU.

The Response PDU

The Response PDU is created by an SNMPv2 manager/agent only upon receipt of a GetRequest PDU, GetNextRequest PDU, GetBulkRequest PDU, SetRequest PDU, or InformRequest PDU.

The SetRequest PDU

The form of the SetRequest PDU is identical to that of the GetRequest PDU except for the PDU type. The SetRequest PDU is generated by an SNMPv2 manager/agent only at the request of its SNMPv2 application. Upon receipt of the SetRequest PDU, the receiving application processes the request, then sends to the originator of the SetRequest a GetResponse PDU of identical form except that the error-status field of the generated message is noError and the error-index field is zero.

The Trap PDU

An SNMPv2 Trap PDU is created and transmitted by an SNMPv2 agent when an exceptional situation occurs. The Trap is the SNMPv1 error checking and reporting function of the SNMPv2 for SNMPv2 messages. The Trap PDU is used to notify managers and agents when errors occur. The Trap PDU can report these conditions: coldStart(0), warmStart(1), linkDown(2), linkUp(3), authenticationFailure(4), egpNeighborLoss(5), and enterpriseSpecific(6). The Trap PDU is created by an SNMPv2 manager/agent only at the request of the SNMPv2 application. When the receiving SNMPv2 manager/agent receives the Trap PDU, it presents the PDU contents to its SNMPv2 application node.

The GetBulkRequest PDU

A GetBulkRequest PDU is created and transmitted at the request of an SNMPv2 manager/agent. The purpose of the GetBulkRequest PDU is to request the transfer of a large amount of data. Upon receipt of a GetBulk-Request PDU, the receiving SNMPv2 manager/agent processes each variable binding in the variable-binding list to produce a Response PDU with its request-id field having the same value as in the request. The Response PDU is created and transmitted to the originator of the GetBulkRequest PDU.

The InformRequest PDU

The InformRequest PDU is created and transmitted at the request of an SNMPv2 manager to inform another SNMPv2 manager of information in an MIB view which is remote to the receiving manager. The receiving SNMPv2 manager presents the PDU contents to the appropriate SNMPv2 application, generates an appropriate Response PDU, then transmits the Response PDU to the originator of the InformRequest PDU.

Summary

Two versions of Simple Network Management Protocol now coexist in networks around the world. SNMPv1 is the original network management protocol which was partially replaced by SNMPv2 in 1996. Elements of SNMPv1 are still used by SNMPv2. Simple Network Management Protocol isn't so simple anymore.

Chapter 13

Miscellaneous TCP/IP Issues

Questions answered in this chapter:

What is X?

How does X work?

What is the World Wide Web?

What is the role of Ethernet with TCP/IP?

Introduction

This chapter looks at several TCP/IP-related issues of some interest to TCP/IP users. Such topics as X Windows, the World Wide Web, and Ethernet are discussed in a brief introductory fashion.

A commonly misunderstood part of TCP/IP is X. Even that statement gets misunderstood. X uses TCP/IP as a network protocol and specifically TCP as a transport protocol, but it does not necessarily have to. The focus here is X at work in the garden of TCP/IP. In this chapter, enough information is presented so you can understand X in relation to the other components of TCP/IP.

The World Wide Web, or just Web for short, burst upon the global stage in the mid-1990s. Although the Web is now a familiar household term, most people do not have any real clue what it is. Just exactly what is the Web? And how does the Web relate to TCP/IP? The section on the World Wide Web answers these questions.

When a person gets involved, even in a minimal way, with TCP/IP, Ethernet usually is a topic of interest. What do Ethernet and TCP/IP have to do with each other? The section on Ethernet and TCP/IP gives a brief history of Ethernet and how Ethernet and TCP/IP became interwoven in the fabric of networks.

What is X?

X is not a graphical user interface (GUI), nor is it a window system similar to Microsoft Windows. X is an asynchronous software protocol used to transmit bitmapped data across a network. It can be implemented with a variety of operating systems and hardware operating platforms. X is not a transport level protocol but utilizes TCP as a transport mechanism. Figure 13.1 shows the location of X in relation to other parts of network components.

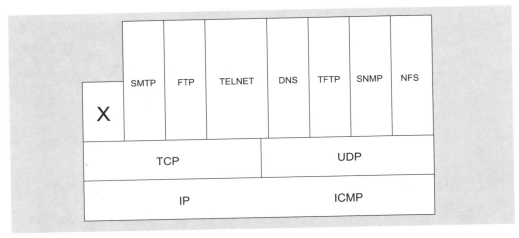

Figure 13.1 X windows and the TCP/IP environment

X divides application software, also known as clients, like TN3270 emulation applications from display software, known as server software. The former is used for a specific purpose such as logging onto an SNA host and performing data translation on the host where the TN3270 application resides. The software application is the client.

On the other hand, software that <u>controls</u> the display is the server. Since display software (known as a server) is separate from application software (known as client software), it can operate locally or on any network host. This works because of the configuration of X software, hosts, and application programs. Collectively, this results in a distributed windowing environment.

The X server program is responsible for two-dimensional drawings on a display. Actually, a server is responsible for everything on the display directly or indirectly. Drawings, however, are the result of "events" generated from a client application, and the server passes messages it receives from a user to the interacting client. Hence, X's event-driven architecture.

In short, X provides components that make a distributed windowing system possible. It is generally called the X window system.

Where Did X Come From?

X is not as old as many think. Its birth can be dated to the early '80s at MIT's computer science laboratory. It emerged out of a group concentrating on programming languages being developed for distributed computing. This development project involved a number of people working on different programs. Those who have programmed in any language understand that "bugs" (errors in the code) are part of any development project. An individual working on this project focusing on distributed computing concluded that a windowing system would be ideal to expedite working through program bugs. This is part of how the idea behind this windowing system began.

As if program bugs were not enough problems, these scientists and researchers were developing programming code for a distributed computing environment (DCE). DCEs were charting new waters at the time, and to complicate matters further they were up against an environment of heterogeneous computers which had fundamental problems with basic communications. Numerous vendors had computers and related devices of all types at MIT. One of the focal points at the time was an intense work group devoted to developing a heterogeneous environment where all computers and devices could communicate with one another in a practically seamless fashion.

Those working on the distributed computing environment project began researching, attempting to determine if anyone (institution, agency, etc.) had explored this concept of a windowing system in a heterogeneous environment before. They discovered work had been done on a windowing system at Stanford. The work at Stanford had been named "W," an abbreviation for windows. This activity took place in approximately 1984.

After working with individuals at Stanford, some at MIT pursued this windows environment and acquired a copy of the "W" software. The copy of windows software from Stanford focused on DEC equipment, but those at MIT were interested in a distributed window environment because of the heterogeneous equipment at MIT. After initial modifications were made to the "W" software from Stanford, MIT's researchers decided to rename it "X."

By 1985, X software had been refined and brought through six versions. By mid-1986, X was at version 9. In 1986, Sun Microsystems announced a product called Network Extended Windowing Systems (NEWS). This announcement added fuel to the fire of X growth because it was so close to X from MIT. In 1987, MIT held an X conference; 11 companies attended and began joint work on X with MIT. The X Consortium (as the 11 companies were dubbed) began taking shape and was formally announced in 1988. X is now at version 11 release 6.

In short order X took the network (and particularly the LAN) marketplace by storm. It was a perfect (close to perfect) match for the UNIX operating system and the TCP/IP protocol suite. It offered a friendly interface for the UNIX operating system and provided distributed windowing support. Combined with UNIX, TCP/IP, and network growth throughout the 1980s, X seemed to meet a much wanted interface and distributed windowing system need. These factors contributed to the proliferation of X.

What are the Components of X?

X itself was created with a layered concept; however, the majority of references to X do not explain it this way. X was intended to have maximum portability, and in order to achieve this a layered approach is required. Table 13.1 depicts X layers, their functions, and associated programs and components.

Layer	X Implementation
5	X user interface
4	X application
3	X toolkit
2	X library
1	X protocol

Table 13.1 X layer functionality

Compare Tables 13.1 and 13.2. Table 13.1 details each X layer functionality. Table 13.2 associates X layers to a function and its associated programs.

Layer	Function	Associated Program/Function
5	user interface	Sun's OPENLOOK OSF's Motif
4	application	window manager olwm mwm
3	toolkit	Xt
2	x library	Xlib
1	x protocol	components of X software

Table 13.2 X layer functions and programs

The topmost layer (what the user interacts with) is the user interface layer. This layer consists of interfaces such as the Common Desktop Environment (CDE) from the Open Software Foundation, OPENLOOK from Sun Microsystems, Motif from the Open Software Foundation (OSF), and NeXT from NeXT Computer, Inc., for example. These interfaces prescribe the look and feel of the interface.

Layer 4 is the X application layer. The window manager operates at this layer. olwm is the acronym for OPENLOOK Window Manager and mwm is the acronym for Motif Window Manager. A window manager in X actually controls the display. It makes multiple, simultaneous "windows" on one display possible. The window manager provides functions such as being able to resize a "window," invoke pop-up menus, etc. Technically, a window manager itself is a client application running against an X server. Because X was designed for maximum flexibility, it can support different window managers as long as they follow X protocol. Hence, different window managers exist, notably from Sun Microsystems, OSF, and NeXT.

Layer 3 represents the X toolkit. Multiple toolkits are possible. A toolkit is a collection of high-level programs (routines) created from lower level programming in the Xlibrary. Frequently, toolkits are referred to as Xt. Toolkits provide programmers with specific functions such as menus, scroll bars, etc. Specific routines in a toolkit are commonly referred to as widgets. The benefit of having toolkits is a programmer does not have to start from nothing when creating an X client application.

Layer 2 is the Xlibrary. The Xlibrary is a collection of C language subroutines. The Xlibrary is frequently referred to as Xlib. These routines are the lowest level programming aid in X. Some Xlibrary subroutines provide functions such as drawing, responding to mouse events, and responding to keyboard events, to name a few. X version 11 Xlibrary is considered the industry standard and is the base for future enhancements.

Layer 1 is the X protocol. This protocol supports asynchronous, event-driven distributed windowing environments across heterogeneous platforms. When used with TCP/IP, X uses TCP as a transport mechanism and resides atop the TCP portion of the transport layer.

What is the Function of X?

X provides windowing capabilities across heterogeneous operating systems, hardware platforms, network protocols, and network implementations (topologies). It appears different because of the versatility in support built into X for user interfaces and window managers. But, at the lower layers (or closer to the core) of X, you find adherence to X protocol and Xlibrary routines.

Seemingly, X's most prevalent implementation is an interface for the UNIX operating environment. Even though X is not as user friendly as many would like, it is somewhat friendlier than UNIX and other environments it operates within.

What Vocabulary is Important?

A point of confusion is the terminology used with X. This section includes some basic terms and their definitions. Many other terms are used, but these will orient you to the world of X.

Access control list—A list of hosts that are allowed access to each server controlling a display is maintained in the /etc/Xn.hosts file. The n here is the number of displays that hosts can access. This list is also called the host access list.

Active window—This is the window where input is directed.

Background—Windows may have a background that consists of a solid color or a pattern of some kind.

Background window—The area that covers the entire screen. This is the area that other windows are displayed against. It is also called the root window.

Client—Also known as an X application program. Examples of client programs include terminal emulation programs, window manager programs, and the clock program. Client programs do not have to run on the same program as the display server.

Display—One or more screens driven by an X server. The DISPLAY environment variable dictates to programs which server to connect to unless this is overridden by the -display command line option.

Event—Something that must happen prior to an action occurring in response.

Font—A specific style of text characters.

Font directory—The default directory where fonts used with X are stored.

Foreground—This term refers to the pixel value used to draw pictures or text.

Geometry—This is an option that can be used to specify the size and placement of a window on the display screen.

Icon—A symbol representing a window, that when selected by a mouse will cause it to take its original form.

Property—A general term used to refer to the properties of a window. The basic purpose of properties is to serve as a communication mechanism between clients. For example, windows have properties such as a name, window type, data format, and data within the window.

Server—Software and hardware that provides display services for X clients. The server accepts input from the keyboard and a mouse.

Window—An area on a display created by a client. For example, the xclock.

Window manager—The window manager is a client program (application). It permits movement, resizing, and other functions to be performed on a display.

How Does X Work?

Put simply, the X server is responsible for managing a display. Programs that interact with the X server, regardless of their function, are X clients. Their particular function is program specific. For example, the xclock is considered a client (program) application.

X works differently from MS Windows because it was architecturally designed differently. X was designed to operate in a distributed environment and with multiple hosts, whereas MS Windows was not. From a practical standpoint, this means those pieces that make an X window environment work can reside physically on different machines. Not so with MS Windows; this windowing environment was designed to operate on one machine at a time. Actually, MS Windows is a shell; it is tied to the operating system. Some call MS Windows a graphical user interface.

Some programs are designed to operate in a windowing environment only. Programs must be designed to operate this way. This is true with both X and MS Windows.

In an X environment, code may reside on one physical machine but not necessarily. With MS Windows, code is physically located on one machine.

Before we explore how X works, some facts need to be presented. For example, the window manager is the major factor in the look and feel of how X works. So if Sun Microsystems' OPENLOOK window manager is used, then the look and feel of the display will take on its characteristics. On the other hand, if the OSF CDE window manager is used, it will have a different look and feel. The window manager is what a user sees on a display.

The X display server is software that keeps up with input from devices like a keyboard and a mouse. In essence, the display server gets messages from an X client, then updates the window on the display to reflect that message. Display servers can operate on the same machine as the X client(s) being used, or they may be located on a different machine, or they can even be stored in ROM on special terminals. Hence the term X terminal.

Another aspect about X to remember is that X itself is about graphics. Its purpose is to support graphics in a distributed window environment and, by default, support text. For years X has been dominant in environments where UNIX is the operating system and TCP/IP has been the network protocol. X is not confined to UNIX and TCP/IP, but it solves a major problem in UNIX environments for many users; that is, a friendlier user interface. Understanding the interaction of X in such an environment is helpful.

X uses TCP as a transport mechanism. TCP is reliable in the sense it retransmits data if some is lost during transmission. TCP is also connection oriented, maintaining a transport layer protocol connection.

From a user viewpoint X boils down to what is seen on the display. This is deceptive because everything is seen on the display; but if the display is analyzed, we can isolate what is coming from where and how it works! Consider Figure 13.2.

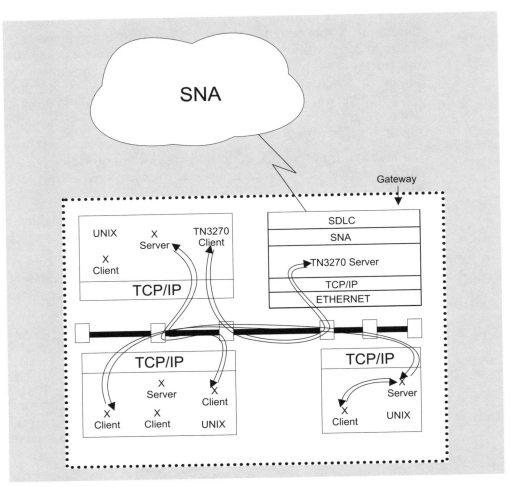

Figure 13.2 The X environment

Notice what can be deduced from the figure:

- The network is TCP/IP based.
- Three hosts are located on the network.
- Each host is implementing X.
- Each host has an X server.
- Each host has X clients.
- A gateway from the TCP/IP to SNA network is present.
- A TN3270 client program operates under X on one machine.
- The TN3270 client provides required terminal emulation between the TCP/IP network and the SNA network.
- The TN3270 client program communicates with the X server as well as the TN server on the gateway between the two networks. The X part of the TN3270 client program communicates with the X server so the X server can perform the necessary functions for the graphical functions. The TN protocol part of the TN3270 application provides the required terminal emulation between the TCP/IP and SNA networks.
- The TN3270 client program can be executed from any of the hosts on the network. The prerequisite is that a network connection be made between the two hosts first. This means a Telnet or rlogin, for example. Once this connection is established, then the TN3270 program can be executed from any host.

In summary, the X environment is complex. It is understandable, but it requires time. I know no shortcuts in this area of technology if your desire is to go beyond just mere button pushing.

How Does X Relate to the Environment?

The environment must be considered! Part of what makes X complex in the UNIX environment is setting environment variables. This is not overly burdensome, but it does require work. One problem encountered with environment variables is they can be changed on the fly, thus affecting variables put in place upon logon. Additionally, some X client programs have certain variables that must be set in order for the program to work properly.

Common problems with environment variables include: First, setting the appropriate variable in the PATH statement in the .profile can be confusing. Second, because of the complexity of some .profiles they become cumbersome. Third, because of the flexibility of the UNIX, variables can be exported on the fly, thus creating additional confusion.

A prudent thing to do if you are working with X and UNIX is to spend time with a knowledgeable system administrator who understands both and has the ability to communicate what you need to understand for your particular environment. Based on my mental bruises working with these areas, I suggest this is the best way to begin.

What is the World Wide Web?

The World Wide Web, or Web for short, is by far the most popular and fastest growing service on the Internet. The Web has opened up a whole new opportunity to deliver rich multimedia content to anyone in the world. In addition, Web content can be viewed on nearly any kind of computer platform, from Macintosh and IBM-compatible PCs to high-end UNIX workstations. Even though the Web is relatively young compared to the rest of the Internet, the variety and number of Web pages is staggering. Each month, the number of new Web servers across the world grows exponentially. Likewise, the number of Web sites being developed continues to grow daily.

So, what exactly is the World Wide Web? Well, the Web is a service that sits on top of TCP/IP intranets and the Internet. Similar to the previous Internet services that we have discussed, the Web consists of two distinct types of machines: servers, sometimes referred to as hosts, and clients. A Web server is simply a machine connected to the network that runs a specific piece of software that allows it to serve special files (called Web pages or home pages) to a machine called a client. A Web client is simply another machine connected to the Internet that runs a piece of software, called a Web browser, that allows it to connect to a Web server and view pages that have been made available for public consumption. These Web pages, or home pages, can contain material as simple as plain text (like a resume or academic vita) or as complex as an interactive multimedia presentation (such as an annual report, complete with narration, musical transitions, video segments, and animated revenue growth charts). The possibilities are endless! Perhaps the most compelling aspect of the Web is how easy it is to navigate from one page to another, or from one Web site to another. With the click of a mouse, you can instantly be transported from one point of the world to another. For example, while reading a Web page describing your local weather, you click on a hyperlink which takes you clear across the world to a Web site describing a beautiful vacation spot along the coast of Thailand.

One important point to remember is that Web servers do not necessarily have to reside on a file server, such as Netware, Windows NT Server, or OS/2 Warp Server. Fundamentally, Web servers deliver Web-related documents specifically to Web browsers. This may seem like an obvious point, but it can get confusing quickly when we consider that the same physical hardware that is running Web server software may be running file and print server software. For example, your Web server software could run on either Windows NT

Workstation or Windows NT Server. If it were running on Windows NT Server, you might also be making use of Windows NT Server's file and print services.

What Makes Up the Web?

In addition to the servers and clients (or browsers) mentioned in the previous section, the Web contains surprisingly few components. Web pages are nothing more than ASCII text documents. In its most fundamental state, there's nothing more to it. Web pages can be thought of as the glue that binds together all of the interesting multimedia elements: the graphics, video segments, 3-D virtual worlds, etc. Although the finer points of Web page construction are not discussed in this book, the following is a basic Web page. Notice its simplicity.

```
<html>
<head>
<title>My First Web Page</title>
</head>
<body>
<h1>Welcome to my Web page!</h1>
Eventually, this will contain information describing my Web page's
purpose in life. At a later time, I might add some colorful graphics.
Take a look at <a href="http://www.microsoft.com/">
Microsoft's home page</a> for information about Windows NT.
</body>
</html>
```

That's all there is to it! Now, there are certainly more things that can be added to this most basic Web page to spice it up a bit (like graphics or a nice blue background), but it has all of the basic elements that make up a typical Web page: a title, a heading, some descriptive text, and a hyperlink to another site on the Web (in this case, the home page for Microsoft). The page also contains some strange elements that are surrounded by "less than" and "greater than" symbols. These are called *markup tags*, or simply *tags*. They tell the browser how to format the text in the page. To illustrate this point more easily, take a look at how this page would look in a Web browser as shown in Figure 13.3 on the following page.

Notice how the line "My First Web Page" appears in the title bar at the top of the Web browser. "Welcome to my Web page!" is displayed as a large heading at the top of the page. The <h1> and </h1> tags tell the Web browser to display the surrounded text as the largest on the page. The paragraph beginning with "Eventually, this will..." appears as normal, plain text. The words that are surrounded by the hyperlink tag, starting with:

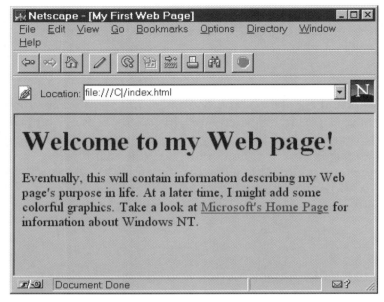

Figure 13.3 Simple Web page

<ahref="http://www.microsoft.com/">, and ending with: </a>, will be blue and underlined. If you click on the enclosed text: "Microsoft Home Page," you will be taken directly to Microsoft's Web site. But what about the rest of the example Web page?

All Web pages must begin with an <html> tag, which stands for Hypertext Markup Language, commonly abbreviated HTML. Unlike a typical word processor, which stores its formatting specifications in a proprietary binary format, HTML is a specification allowing format information to be embedded in an ASCII document. This formatting information is contained within the "less than" and "greater than" signs. The Web browser interprets the tags and displays the page accordingly. However, notice that the tags themselves are not visible in the Web browser window.

There are two parts to a Web page: a head and a body. The head contains basic information about the page, such as the title (which appears in the title bar of the Web browser) and any comments the author includes for future reference (such as revision history information). You may have noticed that some tags are repeated with a slash in front of them. These are referred to as end tags. Most tags, but not all, have a start tag and an end tag. Whatever is in between the start and end tags is formatted accordingly. The <h1> (a "heading one start tag") and </h1> (a "heading one end tag") surround the heading. There are certainly other tags for additional formatting purposes (like bold, italics, etc.), but this gives you a good foundation of knowledge of what is really happening behind the scenes on the World Wide Web.

Where Did the Web Come From?

Since the Internet was established around 1969, it would seem likely that the World Wide Web has been around for quite some time, right? In reality, the Web is extremely young in comparison to the rest of the services on the Internet (FTP, Telnet, e-mail, etc.). Initial development for the Web began in 1989 at a particle physics laboratory called CERN (**http://www.cern.ch/**) in

Geneva, Switzerland. Tim Berners-Lee proposed an information management system that could help alleviate "the problems of loss of information about complex evolving systems" (**http://www.w3.org/pub/WWW/History/1989/proposal.html**). This system was based on a concept called "hypertext," a term coined in the 1950s by Ted Nelson. Hypertext can be defined as "human-readable information linked together in an unconstrained way," as defined on the above Web site. In other words, digital documents can contain hot spots, in the form of text, graphics, or both, that when clicked with a mouse link the reader to another document, which in turn can contain hot spots to yet another document. Berners-Lee's idea was to implement a system that would allow researchers in the European scientific community to create a web of interconnected documents that could evolve over time, changing and growing as the project itself evolved over time. In addition, this web of information would be made available to the scientific community as a whole, to encourage group collaboration while projects were in progress. No more waiting for months to publish or present a ground-breaking idea only to find out that the idea has outlived its usefulness.

Tim Berners-Lee was inspired by some of the early implementations of Ted Nelson's concept of hypertext. He saw the need to make a hypertext system that was both network-centric and platform independent. It couldn't just run on one type of computer, such as a UNIX workstation; it had to be made available to all computer systems currently in existence, as well as those developed in the future. This system has been realized as the Hypertext Transfer Protocol, abbreviated as HTTP. The Hypertext Transfer Protocol is a standardized method of sending data from a Web server to a Web browser over the Internet. In this way, each piece of data (from documents to multimedia elements) has its own unique address called a Uniform Resource Locator, or URL. Literally, every page on the Web could contain a link to any other page on the Web—residing anywhere in the world.

Why Has the Web Grown So Quickly?

Even though the Web is just a few years old, its growth within the last few years is staggering. In 1994 alone, the Web grew an amazing 1000 percent. So, what developments occurred at this time to account for this explosive growth? A group of computer science students, led by Marc Andreessen at the National Center for Supercomputing Applications (**http://www.ncsa.uiuc.edu/**) at the University of Illinois at Urbana-Champaign, developed the first truly cross-platform, graphical Web browser, called Mosaic. The NCSA released a working version of Andreessen's "Mosaic for X" in February 1993. However, the beginning of the Web's phenomenal growth started in September of that same year when the NCSA released working versions of Mosaic for the most common computing platforms: the X Window system, Microsoft

Windows on IBM-compatible PCs, and the Macintosh. Even Andreessen had little idea that the Web would radically redefine not only networks but the fundamental ways that people and companies conduct business with computers.

What Kind of Data Can the Web Deliver?

In March of 1994, Andreessen and a few of his colleagues left the NCSA to join Jim Clark, the founder and former chairman of Silicon Graphics, and form Mosaic Communications Corporation, now called Netscape Communications Corporation. Netscape immediately began work on a new Web browser called Netscape Navigator, nicknamed Mozilla, which continues to be the most dominant figure in the Web browser arena. Netscape's Web browser was one of the first commercially available browsers to incorporate extensions to the original Hypertext Markup Language. Additionally, Netscape encouraged programming teams around the world to write plug-ins for Navigator—add-on programs that extended the capabilities of a simple Web browser. For the first time, plug-ins allowed Web developers to include more than just static text and graphics in their home pages. The first plug-ins provided a way of publishing Web pages that included rich multimedia content. Some of the original plug-ins provided:

- streaming audio (music and narration that can be heard seconds after clicking on a link—prerecorded as well as live segments)

- motion video (short video segments with audio)

- interactive multimedia presentations (complete with animation and responsive buttons)

- three-dimensional virtual worlds (called VRML, short for Virtual Reality Modeling Language)

- portable documents (pages that looked more like their printed counterparts, desktop-publishing style)

Netscape's Navigator was only the first of many popular Web browsers that followed Mosaic. Spyglass, Microsoft, IBM, Sun Microsystems, and others worked furiously to create their own Web browsers, in hopes of becoming the leader in the browser wars. Some of these companies had greater success than others in marketing their browser. Spyglass, for instance, found a niche by providing its Enhanced Mosaic browser to online services and various Internet service providers. Microsoft designed its Web browser, Internet Explorer, as a defensive move against Netscape potentially controlling a significant portion of the Windows interface. Similar to Netscape, Microsoft adopted a strategy of allowing third-party programmers to write plug-in programs that would extend the capabilities of its browser. IBM developed Web Explorer, the first OS/2-based browser, while Sun Microsystems developed

HotJava, the first Java-capable browser. Some companies have since decided to leave the browser market. IBM has partnered with Netscape to identify Navigator as its strategic browser for OS/2, reducing its Web Explorer to maintenance status. Sun Microsystems has decided to leverage its Java technology through licensing it to other browser developers rather than developing a competitive browser itself. Spyglass continues to offer its basic, easy-to-use browser to many different companies as part of their online service package.

Streaming Audio

In the early days of the World Wide Web, users listened to audio by first downloading a digital audio file from a Web server, then using an audio player application to play the downloaded file. While this model worked well for very short audio clips, long audio programs resulted in unacceptably long download times. The download and play model additionally does not provide a mechanism for transmitting live audio across the network. As a result, work began on streaming audio technologies. When working with streaming audio, a streaming helper application or browser plug-in communicates with the audio server. After a brief initial delay to fill a small local buffer with downloaded audio, the client application begins playing the audio. Most such systems stream the outbound audio from the server using the UDP protocol rather than the TCP protocol—TCP's retransmission of lost data packets makes little sense in the context of a real-time audio feed. Progressive Networks was the early leader in streaming audio with its RealAudio server, player, and plug-ins. Netscape has also entered the streaming audio fray with its Netscape Media Server. Conceptually, both products work in the same way. In fact, on a technical level, both adhere to a Real Time Streaming Protocol jointly developed by Progressive Networks and Netscape. In general, users click on an audio link using a Web browser. The Web server identifies the content to the browser as a streaming audio file, causing the browser to invoke the appropriate helper application or plug-in. The streaming audio client then communicates directly with the streaming audio server for the delivery of the audio material.

Streaming Video

The telephone modem connections used by most Internet users severely limit the use of motion video across the Internet. However, a combination of factors has made network video a practical medium when used in moderation and with consideration of bandwidth limitations. First, constantly improving compression algorithms allow better video to be transmitted over a network pipe of a given size. Second, improvements in modem technologies have raised the bar in terms of the minimum bandwidth that a provider can assume to be generally available to users. Finally, as organizations have discovered the potential for delivering network services across high-speed local area networks using Internet protocols, the organizational intranet provides an excellent forum for the delivery of bandwidth-intensive services such as motion video.

There are a number of technologies currently available for the delivery of streaming video. Most such technologies work as plug-ins for Netscape Navigator or Microsoft Internet Explorer. Some technologies are delivered directly from a Web server using the HTTP protocol, while others use a dedicated video server to deliver the video stream.

Quicktime—Apple Computer has modified its Quicktime file format to allow it to be streamed across the network. The Quicktime video system does not require a separate video server. In the Quicktime streaming model, the files are transmitted from a Web server to the client using the HTTP protocol.

VivoActive—VivoActive from Vivo Software is a serverless streaming video product. VivoActive defines its own video file format, the .viv format. The Vivo format uses the H.263 international video and H.723 audio compression standards from the world of low bit rate videoconferencing to achieve its results. There are free VivoActive Players for a variety of browsers and platforms (plug-ins for Netscape Navigator on the Macintosh, Windows 95, Window NT, and Windows 3.1, and an ActiveX control for Microsoft Internet Explorer on Windows 95 or NT) which perform the video and audio decoding on your machine "on the fly." The video is streamed from the Web server via HTTP over TCP. As a result, any user that can access pages from a Web site can access VivoActive video from the site.

VDOLive—The VDOLive system is a server-based video streaming system that streams video from a dedicated video server. The client software consists of a plug-in or helper application for a Web browser, which communicates with the VDOLive server.

RealVideo—The folks at Progressive Networks who brought the world RealAudio have added video to their stable of media types. Based on the same set of underlying protocols as the RealAudio system, RealVideo streams motion video across TCP/IP networks using UDP transport from a dedicated media server. The video can play either through the Real Player, or through a Netscape or Internet Explorer plug-in. Figure 13.4 shows the Real Player.

Figure 13.4 Real Player

What's in Store for the Future?

The leading vendors of desktop operating systems—Microsoft, IBM, and Apple—have each made it clear that their strategy for the future is to integrate Web browsing as a transparent function of the user interface. It remains to be seen how browsers will be further integrated with one's desktop. Likewise, it is difficult to predict which companies will continue to be the leaders in the browser market. Yet, the amount of stiff competition in this arena of software development guarantees that this is only the beginning of exciting developments for the World Wide Web. One thing is for sure: The TCP/IP community won't run out of new technologies to explore any time soon!

What is the Role of Ethernet with TCP/IP?

Ethernet is a term often used in conjunction with TCP/IP. It is a data link level protocol and a broadcast technology. The Ethernet specification does note cable requirements and other specifications. Ethernet is implemented in computer systems and devices by firmware on a network interface card (NIC). The name Ethernet came from a theoretical electromagnetic material named "luminiferous ether" in popular usage in the mid- to late 1800s. This luminiferous ether material was thought to be the fundamental element holding together the universe and its parts! The leap of logic giving us the

Ethernet was that an "Ether"-net could be a link to bind all components connected to the network.

Xerox Corporation started a research facility in Palo Alto, California, in 1970, called Palo Alto Research Center (PARC). Commissioned with the task of charting a course towards what Xerox thought would be an electronic office in the 1990s, PARC devoted time, talent, and teams to envision where Xerox would make its next market since it already had a strong foothold in copying machines, etc.

In 1973 PARC had a team working on networking computers, printers, and other devices. Robert Metcalfe managed a team whose task was to find a way to speed up the link between computers and printers on the network. They created a way to connect computers and printers on a network whereby higher speeds could be achieved than what was used in the past. This is what would become known as Ethernet. Prior to Ethernet, the technology of the day required 15 minutes to transmit and print a page with a resolution of 600 dots per inch. The first implementation of Ethernet cut this 15-minute time period down to seconds; it was a major breakthrough and received a lot of attention. This version of Ethernet was later known as experimental Ethernet and had a data transfer rate of approximately 2.6 megabits per second. Time passed, and in 1982 Digital Equipment Corporation, Intel, and Xerox presented Version 2.0 Ethernet, which specified 10 megabits per second data transfer rate, among other specifications.

Ethernet and TCP/IP are different technologies, but together they create an effective LAN. Ethernet is a transport protocol and operates at layers one and two in a network. TCP/IP is a suite of protocols and operates at network layers three and above. Ethernet has a 48-bit addressing scheme and uses it to communicate with other Ethernet NICs. TCP/IP uses IP's 32-bit addressing to identify networks and hosts. Ethernet and TCP/IP can operate together because of one or more protocols that are part of TCP/IP, namely Address Resolution Protocol (ARP) which maps Ethernet addresses to IP addresses and vice versa.

Although Ethernet and TCP/IP are frequently used in the same sentence, there is no inherent bond between them. IBM's Token Ring network system provides a fine foundation for TCP/IP networks. However, because networks in the academic research environment where much of the TCP/IP protocol was developed ended up being built almost exclusively on a foundation of Ethernet, there is a natural affinity between the Ethernet protocol and TCP/IP.

By the end of the '80s, Ethernet, like TCP/IP, could be bought off the shelf at computer stores. By the late '90s the cost of a generic Ethernet adapter had dropped to $19.95. Ethernet and TCP/IP's maturity as a technology and their inexpensive price make them a good match for a networking solution. These characteristics and others have contributed to the dominance of TCP/IP-based Ethernet LANs.

Ethernet has proved to be a remarkably scalable networking technology. From its beginning as a 10 Megabit shared bandwidth system, it has scaled through multiple incarnations that include:

- Switched 10 Mbs Ethernet
- 100 Mbs Ethernet
- Switched 100 Mbs Ethernet
- Gigabit Ethernet

These advanced Ethernet technologies have found immediate widespread acceptance largely as a result of the incestuous relationship between Ethernet and TCP/IP. Because the high-speed incarnations of Ethernet have maintained the fundamental packet structures for the transmission of data, including TCP/IP data, they have been easier to implement than radical technologies, such as ATM, which relies on techniques for splitting TCP/IP packets across its 53-byte cells that are still not completely defined by internationally accepted standards and as a result are not totally interoperable.

The implementation of Ethernet-based networks using TCP/IP transport services creates a few interesting chores that must be taken care of if the resultant hybrid system is useful. The most significant obstacle to overcome is the addressing incompatibility between Ethernet and TCP/IP. Ethernet uses a 48-bit address field. TCP/IP uses a 32-bit address field. Obviously, the two addressing schemes are not compatible. Ethernet-based networks using TCP/IP services resolve the addressing dilemma by making good use of address cross-reference tables. The information required to generate the address tables is dynamically distributed to hosts periodically. From the information distributed, the hosts easily compile look-up tables to convert an address to and from the appropriate address.

Summary

X provides the means whereby a graphical interface can be achieved. Typical applications used with X are emulators permitting access to SNA environments along with other popular graphical-oriented programs. X is not intuitively obvious to learn. It is not like MS Windows, nor was it designed to be. Setup and customization of X and the UNIX operating system requires knowledgeable individuals who understand both environments. Remember, just because a system administrator may understand UNIX does not make him or her an X guru. They are large disciplines to understand. Implemented correctly with adequately trained users, X can report user performance and provide an indication of user satisfaction.

From its inauspicious beginnings as an academic experiment to make the exchange of scholarly scientific data more timely, the World Wide Web has come to be one of the major driving forces behind the growth of the Internet. Not only has the Web revolutionized the ways in which people access information across networks, it is reshaping the definition of client-server computing and redefining the ways in which people do business. The graphical user interface provides the functionality to make network computing resources accessible to millions. The cross-platform nature of both the clients and servers provides freedom from the domination of any single computer hardware or operating systems vendor. Just when some thought that all the computing questions had been settled and that we would declare one company the "winner," along came the Web and changed all the rules.

Ethernet and TCP/IP sort of grew up together in the same (networking) neighborhood. As each technology passed through childhood and on into adulthood, their combined ability to provide an effective networking solution was instrumental in the explosive growth of company-based networks in the late 1980s. Now, with low-priced Ethernet cards and computers, the world will see an explosion of home-networked computers, if for no other reason than the appeal of playing multiplayer games with the family.

Chapter 14

Administering a TCP/IP Network

Introduction

What is network administration? Network administration involves every aspect of network evolution, from acquiring the network pieces (hardware and software) and installing the pieces to setting up the initial user accounts and maintaining the network over its life cycle.

Who administers a TCP/IP network? Well, there are those usually, but not always, nerdy-looking individuals seen constantly peering into the phosphorus monitor miasma, mumbling sometimes incoherent profanities to an uncaring and unloving piece of machinery, who go by the very official and important-sounding name of Network Administrator. And sometimes, there are just the everyday plain ol' folks who look like you and me who go about their daily work routine with only a fraction of their recommended daily dose of frustration expended in the salt mines of network administration. Anyone who sets up and maintains a network is administering to the network, regardless of the size and amount of time required. Some companies have such large networks that network administration is a full-time job for one or more employees. Other companies' network resources may be such that only a small portion of a person's time is required to administer the network. But regardless of the toil involved, network administration involves certain key elements that are described in the following sections.

One of the key tasks of network administrators is the creation and/or the upkeep of certain local host files. These files are native to the UNIX environment. Generally TCP/IP is considered in a UNIX working environment. The association of TCP/IP and UNIX is the result of both platforms evolving through the joint efforts of government and academia at the same time. Because of the close relationship between UNIX and TCP/IP, the following discussion centers around the UNIX implementation of TCP/IP. Other operating platforms, to ensure compatibility with the TCP/IP standards, will have very similar TCP/IP implementations.

The various software applications associated with TCP/IP must have certain information about the user system, user environment, and user preferences. Such information is maintained in various files in the system home directory and the */etc/* directory. The following sections describe the files and gives some useful information concerning the file structures.

Hosts File

The */etc/hosts* file maintains the names of all the nodes in the network. This file provides the ability to translate node names to Internet addresses. Any node named in the file can be sent TCP/IP messages. The structure of an /etc/hosts/ file is shown in Table 14.1.

Internet Address	Host Name	Host Alias	Host Alias	Host Alias
168.115.24.100	local host			
168.115.24.101	host 1 (Node 1)	host 1 alias 1	host 1 alias 2	host 1 alias 3
168.115.24.102	host 2 (Node 2)	host 2 alias 1	host 2 alias 2	host 2 alias 3
168.115.24.103	host 3 (Node 3)	host 3 alias 1	host 3 alias 2	host 3 alias 3
168.115.24.104	host 4 (Node 4)	host 4 alias 1	host 4 alias 2	host 4 alias 3

Table 14.1 /etc/hosts file

As shown in the table, a host can be known by more than one name. The /etc/hosts file does not have to list all possible names of the other hosts. Node names and addresses that are not listed in the /etc/hosts file can still be located if their Internet address is known or if a name server is running on the network.

We can use the author's e-mail address to illustrate the idea of a node/host name and an Internet address. The e-mail address is mbusby@airmail.net. The *airmail.net* portion of the address is a node/host alias. The airmail.net is resolved by name servers as 204.178.72.1, which is the physical Internet address of the Internet service provider airmail.net.

For other interesting Internet facets, visit **http://rs.internic.net/sitemap .html**.

WhoIs is found at the Internic Web site at **http://rs.internic.net/cgi-bin/ whois/**.

Domain name registration is at **http://rs.internic.net/cgi-bin/domain**. Internic will bill you for $70 and give you several months to pay.

The following is an example of a domain name found using WhoIs. I searched the domain name of my ISP (airmail.net). The (public) information I found follows. Using WhoIs gives you much more information about a domain name than the typical Yahoo search inquiry.

WhoIs results for airmail.net:

> Registrant:
> Internet America AIRMAIL2-DOM
> 350 North Saint Paul, Ste #200
> Dallas, TX 75201
> US
>
> Domain Name: AIRMAIL.NET
>
> Administrative Contact:
> Davis, Doug DD344 cto@AIRMAIL.NET
> 214.979.9009
> Technical Contact, Zone Contact:
> NOC, IA IN167 noc@AIRMAIL.NET
> 214.861.2577
> Billing Contact:
> Chaney, Jim JC12164 cfo@AIRMAIL.NET
> 214.861.2553 (FAX) 214.861.2663
>
> Record last updated on 02-Mar-98.
> Record created on 02-Mar-95.
> Database last updated on 24-Sep-98 04:54:35 EDT.
>
> Domain servers in listed order:
>
> NS1-ETHER.IADFW.NET   204.178.72.1
> NS2.IADFW.NET   204.178.72.30
> NS3.IADFW.NET   206.138.224.150

A name server will convert the alias to the proper Internet address before the message is forwarded on to the correct, we hope, host. Say, is there a dead letter post office for incorrectly addressed e-mail?

Equivalent Hosts File

The */etc/hosts.equiv* lists those hosts that are allowed to run, or execute, remote commands without supplying a password. The names of the equivalent hosts must also be listed in the /etc/hosts file for the equivalent, or remote, host to command the local host to execute some command. The commands that can be remotely executed include rcp, rlogin, rsh, tftp, and mount. When a remote host telnets a local host and requests services, the lpd server, rlogin server, and the rshd server verify the remote host's authorization to utilize that service by comparing the remote host's transmitted name to the names stored in the /etc/hosts.equiv file.

Host Name
host name 1
host name 2
host name 3

Table 14.2 /etc/hosts.equiv file

The format of the file is simple. One name per line is listed and there is no limitation on the number of names that the file can have.

Rhosts File

The *.rhosts* file lists the names of the remote users who are not required to supply a password whenever they use the rcp, rlogin, and rsh commands when remotely logged onto a local host. The .rhosts file is located in the home directory of the local host. The local user must own the file and the file permissions must restrict access to the local user only. This file allows remote access to the files on the host and therefore is very important to the security of the host. An example is the "anonymous ftp" utilized to transfer documents to/from Web sites. To use such service, one is not required to supply a password. The "anonymous" serves as the remote user name that the local host recognizes. Of course, the remote user has access to only those files whose permissions are set accordingly.

Remote Host Name	Remote User Name
host *a*	michael
host *b*	lizzy
host *c*	tommy
host *d*	harry
host *e*	anonymous

Table 14.3 .rhosts file

In the example .rhosts file shown in Table 14.3 the italicized letters in the Remote Host Name column represent any numerical value. For example, host a could be host 3 and host b could be host 3, or host 4, or host 5, etc. So, there can be more than one remote user name for any given host. Each remote user name is listed on a single line. As in the /etc/hosts.equiv file, there is no limitation on the number of hosts and remote users.

Netrc File

The *.netrc* file is located in the local users home directory on the local host as specified in the /etc/passwd/ file or the $HOME environment variable. The .netrc file allows remote access to a local host without a password when the ftp and rexec commands are executed by the remote host. Of course the file ownership with appropriate permissions must belong to the remote user.

Key Word	Host Name	Key Word	User Name	Key Word	Password
machine	host *a*	login	michael	password	archangel
machine	host *b*	login	lizzy	password	borden
machine	host *c*	login	tommy	password	gun
machine	host *d*	login	harry	password	armpit
machine	host *e*	login	johnny	password	redwalker

Table 14.4 .netrc file

In Table 14.4, when lizzy logs on to the host, the password "borden" is automatically supplied by the .netrc file, relieving lizzy from the tedious duty of entering the password herself.

Password File

Each host has a */etc/passwd* file that lists all the users names and passwords that are authorized to use the host. Attempts to log on to the host are usually blocked if the user cannot provide the correct password associated with a particular name. Of course, the name and password do not have to actually be the person's who is attempting to log on.

The /etc/passwd file format consists of multiple single-line entries with the following format: user name:password:user ID:group ID:user information:home directory:shell name. Each line or entry is composed of multiple fields separated by a colon (":"). The definition of each field is given in Table 14.5. There is no limitation on the number of single line entries an /etc/passwd file may have.

Field	Definition
user name	name of user
password	either an "!" if password is kept elsewhere or the user encrypted password
user ID	unique identification tag, such as the user's name, attached to files; used to associate files with the user
group ID	unique identification tag for the group the user is part of
user informaion	some character string about user
home directory	directory path locating user files
shell name	shell program that is executed when user logs in

Table 14.5

An example of a single line entry in the /etc/passwd file is: **mbusby:lickem:Michael Busby:authors:writer:/users/mbusby/: /bin/rsh**. In this example the user name = **mbusby**, the password is **lickem**, the user ID is **Michael Busby**, the group ID is **authors**, the user information is **writer**, the home directory is **/users/authors/mbusby/**, and the shell name is **rsh** in the **/bin** directory. How useful can this be? Perhaps, the example /etc/passwd file could be located on the computer of an editor, which could then give me the ability to transmit over TCP/IP my finished manuscripts. This is a hypothetical example. I know of no publishers that are this wired for the 21st century. However, there are many other corporations around the globe with this ability.

A short discussion of network security seems appropriate right now. User name and password protection are serious security issues for major corporations, which are somewhat adverse to divulging proprietary corporate information. Both industrial espionage and casual hacking are anthema to a corporation's best interests. So, the Fortune 500 will have you changing your password periodically, which is somehow supposed to reduce the likelihood of an unauthorized person gaining entry to the corporate virtual netherworlds or at least shorten the lifetime of that unauthorized visitation. Anyone with enough savvy to crack the Internet firewall once, can easily do it again and again and....

Shell Games

In the /etc/passwd file the term *shell* came up. While not strictly a TCP/IP implementation, shells are typically used to provide an interactive user interface to the operating system that is running TCP/IP. Some shells provide a menu-oriented interface, while others are just a command line interpreter.

Shells provide the ability to customize the UNIX session, provide a programming environment, and provide for interactive sessions. Of course, those using Windows or Windows-type environments have as the shell the window itself. Interactive sessions are characterized by the machine waiting until the user types a command on the command line (at the system prompt). Customizing a UNIX session involves defining variables, which are stored in the appropriate files, to control the UNIX working session. An example is specifying the user's home directory. UNIX shells provide a set of programming commands useful for creating shell scripts. Shell scripts are similar to MS-DOS batch files in that a series of individual UNIX commands can be specifed and executed in the order specified. The scripts can be executed conditionally and/or repeatedly using high-level constructs such as if-then or repeat-until.

There are various UNIX shells available for use. Among the more well known are the Bourne shell, the Korn shell, the C shell, and the SCO shell. The entries in the /etc/passwd file for the named scripts are:

/bin/sh	Bourne shell
/bin/rsh	Restricted Bourne shell
/bin/ksh	Korn shell
/bin/rksh	Restricted Korn shell
/bin/csh	C shell

When a remote user logs in to a local host, the host will place the user in the home directory that is identified in the /etc/passwd file. Depending upon directory and file permissions, the user may or may not have access to other parts of the system. When the logon occurs, the user's host will load whatever shell program is specified in the /etc/passwd shell name field.

Of course, MS-DOS does the user interface somewhat different from the UNIX user interface. But, regardless of the presentation to the user, underneath the ugly/pretty user interface is the basic functionality of TCP/IP. It is just a question of aesthetics for anyone who is not rabid about one operating system versus another.

Services File

/etc/services provides information to help network managers determine where a packet originated and where it is going to. The /etc/services file lists the port number and protocol of each particular application the host uses. Each host "listens" at these ports for requests for the particular service from users. A port is nothing more than a software convention that identifies which of many services are available on a server. In other words, the "port" is not a

physical entity such as a printer "port" or a monitor "port" but a numerical value that is passed to the host as a variable parameter in a software routine.

The /etc/services/ file lists each service offered by the host, the port number used by the service followed by a "/" and the associated transport protocol (TCP or UDP), and any aliases used by the service. Table 14.6 illustrates some of the contents of the /etc/services file. As an example, telnet uses port 23 and either TCP or UDP transport protocol.

Service	Port #	Alias
qotd	17/tcp	Quote of the Day
qotd	17/udp	Quote of the Day
chargen	19/tcp	Character Generator
chargen	19/udp	Character Generator
ftp-data	20/tcp	File Transfer [Default Data]
ftp-data	20/udp	File Transfer [Default Data]
ftp	21/tcp	File Transfer [Control]
ftp	21/udp	File Transfer [Control]
telnet	23/tcp	Telnet
telnet	23/udp	Telnet
smtp	25/tcp	Simple Mail Transfer
smtp	25/udp	Simple Mail Transfer
time	37/tcp	Time
time	37/udp	Time
nameserver	42/tcp	Host Name Server
nameserver	42/udp	Host Name Server
nicname	43/tcp	Who Is
nicname	43/udp	Who Is
login	49/tcp	Login Host Protocol
login	49/udp	Login Host Protocol
domain	53/tcp	Domain Name Server
domain	53/udp	Domain Name Server
tftp	69/tcp	Trivial File Transfer
tftp	69/udp	Trivial File Transfer
gopher	70/tcp	Gopher
gopher	70/udp	Gopher
www-http	80/tcp	World Wide Web HTTP
www-http	80/udp	World Wide Web HTTP
pop2	109/tcp	Post Office Protocol - Version 2

Service	Port #	Alias
pop2	109/udp	Post Office Protocol - Version 2
pop3	110/tcp	Post Office Protocol - Version 3
pop3	110/udp	Post Office Protocol - Version 3

Table 14.6 Port number assignments

The port numbers 0-1,023 are called the well-known port numbers. These port number assignments are made by IANA and are not to be used for any other purpose. With the port number standardized for the well-known services and some not-so-well-known services, otherwise known as "registered port numbers," users know what port numbers to use to communicate with remote servers for the services they wish to use.

When an application written by a user utilizes TCP services, the port number assignments the application uses must be listed in the /etc/services file to ensure there is no mix-up between the server and any remote users. Of course, the port numbers, both well known and registered, already assigned for other purposes should not be used for user-written applications.

Ping for a Pong

TCP/IP utilizes a support protocol called Internet Control Message Group (ICMG) to determine if a host is physically connected to another host. This network management tool is very valuable in determining if the local host (your computer) is connected to anyone else on the network. It is an invaluable troubleshooting aid. The ICMG command used to indicate whether a remote host can be reached is ping. Some writers claim ping is an acronym for Packet Internet Groper. Actually, ping comes to us from early (1960s) military applications of networks. A rather mundane exercise to verify whether slave nodes were still listening to the master control node—the transmission of a control signal by the master node and subsequent reception of an acknowledgment from a slave node—was referred to as a "ping-pong" exercise, largely due to the fact that the frequencies used and the speed of transmission reminded one of the sound of ping-pong balls hitting the paddles in a lively match.

When ping is executed on the local host, the message ECHO_RESPONSE is sent out to a specific host. When the intended host receives the ECHO_RESPONSE message, it will send an acknowledgment back to the originating host. The ICMG routine will then determine the time for the ECHO_RESPONSE and acknowledgment to transit the Internet. Besides verifying the physical connection of remote hosts, the use of the ping command can be useful for determining how long to set the time-to-live parameter of TCP packets.

What happens if the remote host is either not connected to the network or does not respond with the acknowledgment? Well, not much. Usually, the sending host will wait, and wait, and wait for the acknowledgment for whatever period of time specified by the network administrator in the setup of ping variables.

TCP/IP User Commands

These commands are considered "user" commands because they are the suite of commands a typical user will use.

biff	Notify when mail arrives
finger	Look up user information
ftp	Start/stop file transfer program
ping	Test for remote host connection
rcp	Copy files to/from remote host
rlogin	Login to remote host
snmp	Start/stop SNMP
talk	Send interactive text message to remote user
telnet	Connect to another host

TCP/IP Administration Commands

These commands are considered "administration" commands because they are the suite of commands a typical network administrator will use to set up the network and the individual network interfaces. There is some commonality with user commands.

biff	Notify when mail arrives
dig	Query the DNS name service
finger	Look up user information
ftp	Start/stop file transfer program
ifconfig	Configure network interface parameters
mkhosts	Make node name commands
netstat	Display network status
netconfig	Configure network devices
netutil	Administer network
nslookup	Query the DNS name service
ping	Test for remote host connection
rcp	Copy files to/from remote host
rdate	Notify time server of date change

snmp	Start/stop SNMP
talk	Send interactive text message to remote user
telnet	Connect to another host

Network Reports

Networking reporting is crucial for maintaining healthy and efficient network links.

Network reports provide such information about the health of a network as number of dropped packets, number of transmitted packets, number of received packets, port speeds (especially IP over ATM), packets received damaged, etc. Various reports are available depending upon the application software used and its capabilities. Also, third-party vendors now offer network reporting online with reports updated every 15 minutes using the previous 30-minute window. So, at best every report is already 45 minutes out of date, but a 45-minute-old report is still much better than getting reports a day or a week old. The savvy network manager will attempt to acquire the most timely reports possible.

Summary

Network administration is the art of "administering," or getting the most bang for the buck out of, a TCP/IP-based network. We have only scratched the surface of network administration in this chapter. The art of administering a network well comes with much reading, studying, and practical experience. However, this introduction to the topic may whet your appetite for more information.

A note concerning usage: In the previous discussions, the term "host" was used often. "Host" can mean computer, machine, terminal, and, generically, any computing device that is capable of understanding and performing TCP/IP commands.

Networks are as diverse as computing devices. The two most commonly found operating systems for running TCP/IP are MS-DOS and UNIX. Virtually all commercial TCP/IP implementations are found on UNIX-based machines. For those individuals born in the Age of Gates who have led a sheltered life as the children of MS-DOS, UNIX can seem archaic, weird, complex, stupid, and just plain scary. It is a good mix of all those descriptive adjectives. Just persevere and persistence will (sometimes) win the day.

Appendix A

Conventions

Octets and Bytes

A **byte** is a binary representation of some quantity using eight digits. An **octet** is just another word for byte. As an example, take the decimal number 3. The binary representation of 3, using byte or octet notation is: 00000011. The leading zeroes in the binary representation are just placeholders and are not numerically meaningful, except to inform the reader that the grouping of the bits is byte size. There are two reasons for representing numbers as bytes. First, it is easier to discern the value of large binary numbers when the bits comprising the number are grouped in bytes. And some machine functions operate on byte size quantities.

But what is a bit, you ask? A **bit** is a single electronic signal that assumes one of two possible values: a 1 (typically 2 to 5 volts) or a 0 (0 to 1.5 volts). Bits are the most fundamental unit of digital electronic signals.

Data Notation

Numbers are expressed in "big endian" order. The most significant octet is called the "big endian" and the least significant octet is called the "little endian." Data fields are listed left to right with the most significant octet on the left and the least significant octet on the right. Also, the most significant bit is on the left and the least significant bit is on the right. The order in which the octets, and bits, are transmitted is also left to right.

	big endian	little endian
Octet	1st Octet	2nd Octet
bit	7 6 5 4 3 2 1 0	7 6 5 4 3 2 1 0
binary value	0 0 0 0 0 0 1 1	1 0 0 0 0 0 1 1
decimal value	512 256 64	1 1
	decimal = 512 + 256 + 64 + 2 + 1 = 835	

Figure A.1 Bit and byte order

Appendix B

Acronyms

ACB	Access Control Block
ACF	Advanced Communication Function
ACK	Acknowledgment
ANSI	American National Standards Institute
API	Application programming interface
APPL	Application
ARP	Address Resolution Protocol
ARPA	Advanced Research Projects Agency
ASCII	American Standard Code for Information Interchange
ASN.1	Abstract Syntax Notation One
BER	Basic Encoding Rules
BISDN	Broadband ISDN
BGP	Border Gateway Protocol
BOOTP	Bootstrap Protocol
BP	Bootstrap Protocol
BSD	Berkeley Software Distribution
CCITT	Consultative Committee for International Telegraph and Telephone
CDE	Common Desktop Environment
CMIP	Common Management Information Protocol
CMIS	Common Management Information Services
CMOT	Common Management Information Services and Protocol over TCP/IP
CRC	Cyclic redundancy check
CSLIP	Compressed Serial Line Internet Protocol
CSMA/CD	Carrier Sense Multiple Access with Collision Detection
DAP	Directory Access Protocol
DARPA	Defense Advanced Research Projects Agency
DCA	Defence Communications Agency
DCE	Distributed Computing Environment
DDN	Defense Data Network
DEC	Digital Equipment Corporation
DEV	Deviation
DFS	Distributed File Service
DHCP	Dynamic Host Configuration Protocol

DISA	Defense Information Systems Agency
DIX	Digital, Intel, and Xerox Ethernet protocol
DME	Distributed Management Environment
DNS	Domain Name System
DSA	Directory System Agent
DSAP	Destination Service Access Point
DTE	Data Terminal Equipment
DUA	Directory User Agent
DVMRP	Distance Vector Multicast Routing Protocol
EBCDIC	Extended Binary Coded Decimal Interchange Code
EGP	Exterior Gateway Protocol
EOF	End-of-file
EOR	End-of-record
FCS	Frame Check Sequence
FDDI	Fiber Distributed Data Interface
FTAM	File-Transfer Access and Management
FTP	File Transfer Protocol
FYI	For your information
GGP	Gateway to Gateway Protocol
GOSIP	Government Open Systems Interconnection Profile
GTF	Generalized Trace Facility
GUI	Graphical user interface
HDLC	High-level Data Link Control protocol
HTTP	Hypertext Transfer Protocol
IAB	Internet Architecture Board (also known as Internet Activities Board)
IAC	Interpret as command
IANA	Internet Assigned Numbers Authority
IBM	International Business Machines
ICMP	Internet Control Message Protocol
ID	Identifier
IEEE	Institute of Electrical and Electronic Engineers
IESG	Internet Engineering Steering Group
IETF	Internet Engineering Task Force
IGMP	Internet Group Management Protocol
IGP	Interior Gateway Protocol
IGRP	Interior Gateway Routing Protocol
IP	Internet Protocol
IRTF	Internet Research Task Force
ISDN	Integrated Services Digital Network
ISO	International Organization for Standardization
ISODE	ISO Development Environment
ISP	Internet Service Provider

ITU-T	International Telecommunications Union-Telecommunicator
LAN	Local area network
LAPB	Link Access Procedures Balanced
LAPD	Link Access Procedures on the D-channel
LLC	Logical Link Control
LLD	Low-level Driver
LDAP	Lightweight Directory Access Protocol
login	Log-in
LPP	Lightweight Presentation Protocol
lpr	Line printer
MAC	Media Access Control
MAN	Metropolitan area network
MIB	Management Information Base
MIME	Multipurpose Internet Mail Extensions
MS	Millisecond
MTA	Message Transfer Agent
MTU	Message Transfer Unit
ND	Network disk
NetBIOS	Network Basic Input/Output System
NFS	Network File System
NIC	Network interface card
NIS	Network Information Service
NLM	Network Lock Manager
NREN	National Research and Education Network
NSAP	Network Service Access Point
NSFNET	National Science Foundation Network
NTF	Network File Transfer
NTP	Network Time Protocol
NVT	Network Virtual Terminal
OSF	Open Software Foundation
OSI	Open Systems Interconnection
OSPF	Open Shortest Path First
PC	Personal computer
PDU	Protocol Data Unit
PI	Protocol Interpreter
PING	Packet Internet Groper
PLP	Packet Level Protocol
PMAP	Port mapper
POP	Post Office Protocol or Point of Presence
PPP	Point-to-Point Protocol
PSTN	Public switched telephone network
RARP	Reverse Address Resolution Protocol

rcp	Remote Copy
rexec	Remote Execution
RDA	Remote Data Access
RFA	Remote File Access
RFC	Request for Comments
RIP	Routing Information Protocol
rlogin	Remote Log-in
RMON	Remote Network Monitor
RPC	Remote procedure call
RPC	Remote process communications
rsh	Remote shell
RST	Reset
RSVP	Resource Reservation Setup Protocol
SDLC	Synchronous Data Link Control
SLIP	Serial Line Internet Protocol
SMI	Structure and Indentification of Management Information
SMTP	Simple Mail Transfer Protocol
SNA	Systems Network Architecture
SNMP	Simple Network Management Protocol
SONET	Synchronous Optical Network
SPF	Shortest Path First
SSAP	Source Service Access Point
SSCP	System Services Control Point
SYN	Synchronizing segment
TCB	Transmission control block
TCP	Transmission Control Protocol
TDM	Time division multiplexing
TELNET	Terminal Networking
TFTP	Trivial File Transfer Protocol
TLI	Transport Layer Interface
TTL	Time-to-live
UA	User agent
UDP	User Datagram Protocol
ULP	Upper Layer Protocol
VT	Virtual terminal
WAN	Wide area network
WWW	World Wide Web
X	Window system
XDR	External data representation
XNS	Xerox Network Systems

Appendix C

RFC Listing

RFC 2153   PPP Vendor Extensions — This is an information document and does not specify any level of standard.

RFC 2152   UTF-7 — This is an information document and does not specify any level of standard.

RFC 2151   Not yet issued.

RFC 2150   Not yet issued.

RFC 2149   Multicast Server Architectures for MARS-based ATM multicasting — This is an information document and does not specify any level of standard.

RFC 2148   Not yet issued.

RFC 2147   TCP and UDP over IPv6 Jumbograms — A Proposed Standard protocol.

RFC 2146   U.S. Government Internet Domain Names — This is an information document and does not specify any level of standard.

RFC 2145   Use and Interpretation of HTTP Version Numbers — This is an information document and does not specify any level of standard.

RFC 2144   The CAST-128 Encryption Algorithm — This is an information document and does not specify any level of standard.

RFC 2143   Encapsulating IP with the Small Computer System Interface — An Experimental protocol.

RFC 2142   Mailbox Names for Common Services, Roles and Functions — A Proposed Standard protocol.

RFC 2141   URN Syntax — A Proposed Standard protocol.

RFC 2140   TCP Control Block Interdependence — This is an information document and does not specify any level of standard.

RFC 2139   RADIUS Accounting — This is an information document and does not specify any level of standard.

RFC 2138   Remote Authentication Dial In User Service (RADIUS) — A Proposed Standard protocol.

RFC 2137   Secure Domain Name System Dynamic Update — A Proposed Standard protocol.

RFC 2136   Dynamic Updates in the Domain Name System (DNS UPDATE) — A Proposed Standard protocol.

RFC 2135   Internet Society By-Laws — This is an information document and does not specify any level of standard.

RFC 2134   Articles of Incorporation of Internet Society — This is an information document and does not specify any level of standard.

RFC 2133   Basic Socket Interface Extensions for IPv6 — This is an information document and does not specify any level of standard.

RFC 2132   DHCP Options and BOOTP Vendor Extensions — A Draft Standard protocol.

RFC 2131   Dynamic Host Configuration Protocol — A Draft Standard protocol.

RFC 2130   The Report of the IAB Character Set Workshop held 29 February - 1 March, 1996 — This is an information document and does not specify any level of standard.

RFC 2129   Toshiba's Flow Attribute Notification Protocol (FANP) Specification — This is an information document and does not specify any level of standard.

RFC 2128	Dial Control Management Information Base using SMIv2 — A Proposed Standard protocol.
RFC 2127	ISDN Management Information Base using SMIv2 — A Proposed Standard protocol.
RFC 2126	ISO Transport Service on top of TCP (ITOT) — A Proposed Standard protocol.
RFC 2125	The PPP Bandwidth Allocation Protocol (BAP), The PPP Bandwidth Allocation Control Protocol (BACP) — A Proposed Standard protocol.
RFC 2124	Cabletron's Light-weight Flow Admission Protocol Specification — This is an information document and does not specify any level of standard.
RFC 2123	Traffic Flow Measurement: Experiences with NeTraMet — This is an information document and does not specify any level of standard.
RFC 2122	VEMMI URL Specification — A Proposed Standard protocol.
RFC 2121	Issues affecting MARS Cluster Size — This is an information document and does not specify any level of standard.
RFC 2120	Managing the X.500 Root Naming Context — An Experimental protocol.
RFC 2119	Key words for use in RFCs to Indicate Requirement Level — This is a Best Current Practices document and does not specify any level of standard.
RFC 2118	Microsoft Point-To-Point Compression (MPPC) Protocol — This is an information document and does not specify any level of standard.
RFC 2117	Not yet issued.
RFC 2116	X.500 Implementations Catalog-96 — This is an information document and does not specify any level of standard.
RFC 2115	Not yet issued.
RFC 2114	Data Link Switching Client Access Protocol — This is an information document and does not specify any level of standard.
RFC 2113	IP Router Alert Option — A Proposed Standard protocol.
RFC 2112	The MIME Multipart/Related Content-type — A Proposed Standard protocol.
RFC 2111	Content-ID and Message-ID Uniform Resource Locators — A Proposed Standard protocol.
RFC 2110	MIME E-mail Encapsulation of Aggregate Documents, such as HTML (MHTML) — A Proposed Standard protocol.
RFC 2100	The Naming of Hosts — This is an information document and does not specify any level of standard.
RFC 2099	Request for Comments Summary - RFC Numbers 2000-2099 — This is an information document and does not specify any level of standard.
RFC 2094	Not yet issued.
RFC 2093	Not yet issued.
RFC 2076	Common Internet Message Headers — This is an information document and does not specify any level of standard.
RFC 1886	DNS Extensions to support IP version 6. December 1995
RFC 1752	The Recommendation for the IP Next Generation Protocol. January 1995
RFC 1671	IPng White Paper on Transition and Other Considerations. August 1994
RFC 1563	The text/enriched MIME Content-type. January 1994
RFC 1542	Clarifications and Extensions for the Bootstrap Protocol — Elevated to Draft Standard.
RFC 1534	Interoperation Between DHCP and BOOTP — Elevated to Draft Standard
RFC 1531	Dynamic Host Configuration Protocol. October 1993
RFC 1341	MIME (Multipurpose Internet Mail Extensions) Mechanisms for Specifying and Describing the Format of Internet Message Bodies. June 1992
RFC 1340	Assigned numbers. July 1992
RFC 1271	Remote network monitoring Management Information Base. November 1991
RFC 1267	A Border Gateway Protocol 3 (BGP-3). October 1991
RFC 1254	Gateway congestion control survey. August 1991
RFC 1253	OSPF version 2: Management Information Base. August 1991
RFC 1250	IAB official protocol standards. August 1991

RFC 1247	OSPF version 2. July 1991
RFC 1246	Experience with the OSPF protocol. July 1991
RFC 1245	OSPF protocol analysis. July 1991
RFC 1244	Site Security Handbook. July 1991
RFC 1243	AppleTalk Management Information Base. July 1991
RFC 1241	Scheme for an Internet encapsulation protocol: Version 1. July 1991
RFC 1240	OSI connectionless transport services on top of UDP: Version 1. June 1991
RFC 1239	Reassignment of experimental MIBs to standard MIBs. June 1991
RFC 1238	CLNS MIB for use with Connectionless Network Protocol (ISO 8473) and End System to Intermediate System (ISO 9542). June 1991
RFC 1237	Guidelines for OSI NSAP allocation in the Internet. July 1991
RFC 1236	IP to X.121 address mapping for DDN. June 1991
RFC 1233	Definitions of managed objects for the DS3 Interface type. May 1991
RFC 1232	Definitions of managed objects for the DS1 Interface type. May 1991
RFC 1231	IEEE 802.5 Token Ring MIB. May 1991
RFC 1230	IEEE 802.4 Token Bus MIB. May 1991
RFC 1229	Extensions to the generic interface MIB. May 1991
RFC 1228	SNMP-DPI: Simple Network Management Protocol Distributed Program Interface. May 1991
RFC 1227	SNMP MUX protocol and MIB. May 1991
RFC 1224	Techniques for managing asynchronously generated alerts. May 1991
RFC 1222	Advancing the NSFNET routing architecture. May 1991
RFC 1220	Point-to-Point Protocol extensions for bridging. April 1991
RFC 1219	On the assignment of subnet numbers. April 1991
RFC 1215	Convention for defining traps for use with the SNMP. March 1991
RFC 1214	OSI Internet management: Management Information Base. April 1991
RFC 1213	Management Information Base for network management of TCP/IP-based internets: MIB-II. March 1991
RFC 1212	Concise MIB definitions. March 1991
RFC 1209	Transmission of IP datagrams over the SMDS Service. March 1991
RFC 1208	Glossary of networking terms. March 1991
RFC 1207	FYI on Questions and Answers: Answers to commonly asked "experienced Internet user" questions. February 1991
RFC 1206	FYI on Questions and Answers: Answers to commonly asked "new Internet user" questions. February 1991
RFC 1205	Telnet 5250 interface. February 1991
RFC 1201	Transmitting IP traffic over ARCNET networks. February 1991
RFC 1198	FYI on the X window system. January 1991
RFC 1196	Finger User Information Protocol. December 1990
RFC 1195	Use of OSI IS-IS for routing in TCP/IP and dual environments. December 1990
RFC 1188	Proposed standard for the transmission of IP datagrams over FDDI networks.. October 1990
RFC 1187	Bulk table retrieval with the SNMP. October 1990
RFC 1086	ISO-TP0 bridge between TCP and X.25. December 1988
RFC 1085	ISO presentation services on top of TCP/IP networks. December 1988
RFC 1184	Telnet Linemode option. October 1990
RFC 1180	TCP/IP tutorial. January 1991
RFC 1179	Line printer daemon protocol. August 1990
RFC 1178	Choosing a name for your computer. August 1990
RFC 1175	FYI on where to start: A bibliography of internetworking information. August 1990
RFC 1172	Point-to-Point Protocol (PPP) initial configuration options. July 1990

RFC 1171	Point-to-Point Protocol for the transmission of multiprotocol datagrams over Point-to-Point links. July 1990
RFC 1173	Responsibilities of host and network managers: A summary of the "oral tradition" of the Internet. August 1990
RFC 1169	Explaining the role of GOSIP. August 1990
RFC 1166	Internet numbers. July 1990
RFC 1164	Application of the Border Gateway Protocol in the Internet. June 1990
RFC 1163	Border Gateway Protocol (BGP). June 1990
RFC 1157	Simple Network Management Protocol (SNMP). May 1990
RFC 1156	Management Information Base for network management of TCP/IP-based internets. May 1990
RFC 1155	Structure and identification of management information for TCP/IP-based internets. May 1990
RFC 1251	Who's who in the Internet: Biographies of IAB, IESG, and IRSG members. August 1991
RFC 1149	Standard for the transmission of IP datagrams on avian carriers. April 1990
RFC 1148	Mapping between X.400(1988) / ISO 10021 and RFC 822. March 1990
RFC 1147	FYI on a network management tool catalog: Tools for monitoring and debugging TCP/IP internets and interconnected devices. May 1990
RFC 1143	Q method of implementing Telnet option negotiation. February 1990
RFC 1142	OSI IS-IS Intra-domain Routing Protocol. February 1990
RFC 1136	Administrative Domains and Routing Domains: A model for routing in the Internet. December 1989
RFC 1234	Tunneling IPX traffic through IP networks. June 1991
RFC 1129	Internet time synchronization: The Network Time Protocol. October 1989
RFC 1127	Perspective on the Host Requirements RFCs. October 1989
RFC 1125	Policy requirements for Inter-Administrative Domain routing. November 1989
RFC 1124	Policy issues in interconnecting networks. September 1989
RFC 1123	Requirements for Internet hosts application and support. October 1989
RFC 1122	Requirements for Internet hosts communication layers. October 1989
RFC 1119	Network Time Protocol (version 2) specification and implementation. September 1989
RFC 1118	Hitchhikers guide to the Internet. September 1989
RFC 1115	Privacy enhancement for Internet electronic mail: Part III August 1989
RFC 1114	Privacy enhancement for Internet electronic mail: Part II August 1989
RFC 1113	Privacy enhancement for Internet electronic mail: Part I August 1989
RFC 1112	Host extensions for IP multicasting. August 1989
RFC 1108	Security Options for the Internet Protocol. November 1991
RFC 1104	Models of policy based routing. June 1989
RFC 1102	Policy routing in Internet protocols. May 1989
RFC 1101	DNS encoding of network names and other types. April 1989
RFC 1097	TELNET SUBLIMINAL-MESSAGE Option. April 1989
RFC 1094	NFS: Network File System Protocol specification. March 1989
RFC 1091	Telnet terminal type option. February 1989
RFC 1090	SMTP on X.25. February 1989
RFC 1089	SNMP over Ethernet. February 1989
RFC 1088	Standard for the transmission of IP datagrams over NetBIOS networks. February 1989
RFC 1084	BOOTP vendor information extensions. December 1988
RFC 1080	Telnet remote flow control option. November 1988
RFC 1079	Telnet terminal speed option. December 1988
RFC 1074	NSFNET backbone SPF based Interior Gateway Protocol. October 1988
RFC 1073	Telnet window size option. October 1988
RFC 1072	TCP extensions for long-delay paths. October 1988

RFC 1070   Use of the Internet as a subnetwork for experimentation with the OSI network layer. February 1989

RFC 1069   Guidelines for the use of Internet-IP addresses in the ISO Connectionless-Mode Network Protocol. February 1989

RFC 1068   Background File Transfer Program (BFTP). August 1988

RFC 1058   Routing Information Protocol. June 1988

RFC 1057   RPC: Remote Procedure Call Protocol specification: Version 2. July 1988

RFC 1056   PCMAIL: A distributed mail system for personal computer. June 1988

RFC 1055   Nonstandard for transmission of IP datagrams over serial lines: SLIP. June 1988

RFC 1053   Telnet X.3 PAD option. April 1988

RFC 1044   Internet Protocol on Network System's HYPERchannel; Protocol specification. February 1988

RFC 1043   Telnet Data Entry Terminal option: DODIIS implementation. February 1988

RFC 1042   Standard for the transmission of IP datagrams over IEEE 802 networks. February 1988

RFC 1041   Telnet 3270 option. January 1988

RFC 1035   Domain names—implementation and specification. November 1987

RFC 1034   Domain names concepts and facilities. November 1987

RFC 1033   Domain administrators operations guide. November 1987

RFC 1032   Domain administrators guide. November 1987

RFC 1027   Using ARP to implement transparent subnet gateways. October 1987

RFC 1014   XDR: External Data Representation standard. June 1987

RFC 1013   X Window System Protocol, version 11: Alpha update. June 1987

RFC 1011   Official Internet protocols. May 1987

RFC 1009   Requirements for Internet gateways. June 1987

RFC 1008   Implementation guide for the ISO Transport Protocol. June 1987

RFC 1006   ISO transport services on top of the TCP: Version 3. May 1987

RFC 1002   Protocol standard for a NetBIOS service on a TCP/UDP transport. March 1987

RFC 1001   Protocol standard for a NetBIOS service on a TCP/UDP transport. March 1987

RFC 995   ISO End System to Intermediate System Routing Exchange Protocol for use in conjunction with ISO 8473. April 1986

RFC 994   ISO Final text of DIS 8473, Protocol for Providing the Connectionless-mode Network service. March 1986

RFC 982   Guidelines for the specification of the structure of the Domain Specific Part (DSP) of the ISO standard NSAP address. April 1986

RFC 980   Protocol document order information. March 1986

RFC 974   Mail routing and the domain system. January 1986

RFC 959   File Transfer Protocol. October 1985

RFC 954   NICNAME/WHOIS. October 1985

RFC 951   Bootstrap Protocol. September 1985

RFC 950   Internet standard subnetting procedure. August 1985

RFC 949   FTP unique named store command. July 1985

RFC 946   Telnet terminal location number option. May 1985

RFC 941   International Organization for Standardization. ISO Addendum to the network service definition covering network layer addressing. April 1985

RFC 933   Output marking Telnet option. January 1985

RFC 932   Subnetwork addressing scheme. January 1985

RFC 922   Broadcasting Internet datagrams in the presence of subnets. October 1984

RFC 920   Domain requirements. October 1984

RFC 919   Broadcasting Internet datagrams. October 1984

RFC 911   EGP Gateway under Berkeley UNIX 4.2. August 1984

RFC 906   Bootstrap loading using TFTP. June 1984

RFC 905   ISO Transport Protocol specification ISO DP 8073. April 1984
RFC 904   Exterior Gateway Protocol formal specification. April 1984
RFC 903   Reverse Address Resolution Protocol. June 1984
RFC 896   Congestion control in IP/TCP internetworks. January 1984
RFC 895   Standard for the transmission of IP datagrams over experimental Ethernet networks.
             April 1984
RFC 894   Standard for the transmission of IP datagrams over Ethernet networks. April 1984
RFC 893   Trailer encapsulations. April 1984
RFC 888   "STUB Exterior Gateway Protocol." January 1984
RFC 886   Proposed standard for message header munging. December 1983
RFC 885   Telnet end of record option. December 1983
RFC 879   TCP maximum segment size and related topics. November 1983
RFC 877   Standard for the transmission of IP datagrams over public data networks. September 1983
RFC 868   Time Protocol. May 1983
RFC 867   Daytime Protocol. May 1983
RFC 866   Active users. May 1983
RFC 865   Quote of the Day Protocol. May 1983
RFC 864   Character Generator Protocol. May 1983
RFC 863   Discard Protocol. May 1983
RFC 862   Echo Protocol. May 1983
RFC 861   Telnet extended options: List option. May 1983
RFC 860   Telnet timing mark option. May 1983
RFC 859   Telnet status option. May 1983
RFC 858   Telnet Suppress Go Ahead option. May 1983
RFC 857   Telnet echo option. May 1983
RFC 856   Telnet binary transmission. May 1983
RFC 855   Telnet option specifications. May 1983
RFC 854   Telnet Protocol specification. May 1983
RFC 827   Exterior Gateway Protocol (EGP). October 1982
RFC 823   DARPA Internet gateway. September 1982
RFC 822   Standard for the format of ARPA Internet Text messages. August 1982
RFC 821   Simple Mail Transfer Protocol. August 1982
RFC 815   IP datagram reassembly algorithms. July 1982
RFC 814   Name, addresses, ports, and routes. July 1982
RFC 813   Window and acknowledgment strategy in TCP. July 1982
RFC 799   Internet name domains. September 1981
RFC 792   Internet Control Message Protocol. September 1981
RFC 793   Transmission Control Protocol. September 1981
RFC 791   Internet Protocol. September 1981
RFC 783   TFTP Protocol (revision 2). June 1981
RFC 781   Specification of the Internet Protocol (IP) timestamp option. May 1981
RFC 779   Telnet send location option. April 1981
RFC 768   User Datagram Protocol. August 1980
RFC 775   Directory oriented FTP commands. December 1980
RFC 749   Telnet SUPDUP Output option. September 1978
RFC 736   Telnet SUPDUP option. October 1977
RFC 732   Telnet Data Entry Terminal option. September 1977
RFC 727   Telnet logout option. April 1977
RFC 726   Remote Controlled Transmission and echoing Telnet option. March 1977
RFC 698   Telnet extended ASCII option. July 1975

Index

About the CD

The CD distributed with this book contains Request for Comments (RFC) text files. RFCs define the original computer internetworking protocols, such as TCP/IP and SNMP. Everyone seeking to understand today's networking protocols and systems will benefit from combing through the RFCs. Every protocol and system is descended in some manner from these original, and still used, protocols.

The RFC files are in plain MS-DOS text. All that is needed is a word editor/processor to read the files from the CD. I suggest you start with RFC 1118, titled "The Hitchhiker's Guide to the Internet," by E. Krol. Another good starting place is RFC 2200, "Internet Official Protocol Standards," which lists the RFCs and their title/subject.

 **Notice:** Opening the CD package makes this book nonreturnable.